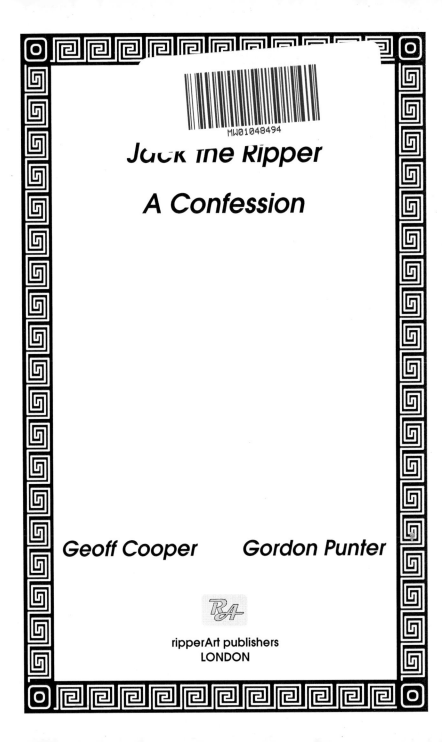

Jack The Ripper

A Confession

Geoff Cooper　　　**Gordon Punter**

ripperArt publishers
LONDON

Published in the United Kingdom by:

ripperArt
ripperArt.com

Content copyright © Geoff Cooper and Gordon Punter 2005

All rights reserved. No portion of this book, including text, maps, or
its front or back cover photograph, may be reproduced, stored in
a retrieval system or transmitted at any time or by any means
mechanical, electronic, photocopying, recording or otherwise,
without the prior written permission of the publisher

The right of Geoff Cooper and Gordon Punter to be identified as
the authors of this work has been asserted by them in accordance
with the Copyright, Designs and Patents act 1988

ISBN 0-9546603-3-1

First printed August 2005
by alphagraphics Ltd, Al-Khobar
Kingdom of Saudi Arabia

To our wives, Janice and Cindy, whose
unwavering support continues to inspire us.

CONTENTS

MAPS

INTRODUCTION

Imagine, if you will, that towards the end of 2003, a classified British Home Office file, circa 1888, was discovered by Margaret Stoughton, Great Grand Niece of the late Evelyn Ruggles-Brise who was, at the time of the Whitechapel Murders, Private Secretary to the then Home Secretary, Henry Matthews. Contained within the tatty boxed file, along with Home Office and London Metropolitan Police memos, was found a confession, consisting of 141 pages, hand-written in black ink, and secured in a stiff brown leather binder. Margaret Stoughton was, and still is, mystified as to how a confidential government file could have found its way into her Great Grand Uncle's private library. Although somewhat embarrassed by the fact that Evelyn Ruggles-Brise may have ultimately abused his position as Private Secretary and spirited the file away, the present British Home Secretary has wisely not demanded its return, honouring the recent Freedom of Information Act and the Home Office 100 year rule which, in principle, decrees that most historical government files can be periodically released for public scrutiny.

Who was Jack the Ripper and what made him commit such nightmarish murders? A recurring question that has continually eluded an answer. That is - until now. The previously classified confession has now been reproduced in its entirety, grammatical errors and all. Supported by historical memos from The Home Office, London Metropolitan Police and newspaper articles of the time, it graphically reveals the terrible motive that may have driven a sexually obsessed young man to slaughter six women.

Geoff Cooper
Gordon Punter
2005

The year is 1888. Queen Victoria, Empress of India, sits on the throne of Great Britain and has done so for nearly fifty years. She reigns over the greatest Empire the world has ever known, stretching across two thirds of the globe. Although the sun does not set on the British Empire, in the East End of London the opposite can be said to be true. In the district of Whitechapel, amid its narrow cobblestone streets and squalid alleyways, the sun refuses to shine, reluctant to illuminate the appalling existence of the populace.

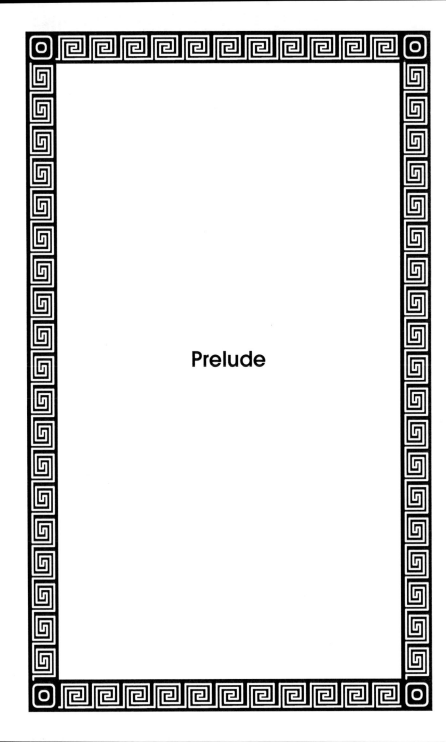

Prelude

Prelude

HOME OFFICE 3 DEC. 88 RECEIVED and METROPOLITAN POLICE
RECEIVED 29. NOV. 88 CRIMINAL INVESTIGATION DEPT.) A49301/191
                          METROPOLITAN POLICE.
                  CRIMINAL INVESTIGATION DEPARTMENT,
                              SCOTLAND YARD
                       4th day of December 1888
SUBJECT Anonymous Confession
Com. Home Office
Re a Whitechapel resident
Whom writer thinks is the
Murderer.

Reference the attached anonymous confession, forwarded to
the Criminal Investigation Department by the Home Office. I beg
to report that the police feel justified in making further enquiries to
identify the Writer of the confession. Writer may have indeed
spoken with the Whitechapel murderer.

                                    Donald S Swanson
                                    ChInspr.
                                            J.Shore Supt.

Home Office A49301/191 retained for C.I.D files.

5185/14   6 DEC. 88
Pressing A49301/191   WHITEHALL
                                       5 December 1888
Sir,
    With reference to previous correspondence. I am directed by
the Secretary of State to signify the utmost urgency in identifying
the Writer of the anonymous confession. Mr. Secretary Matthews is
of the opinion that the Writer had indeed spoken with the
Whitechapel murderer.

                                    I am,
                                      Sir,
                                    Your obedient Servant
                                       E. Ruggles-Brise.

The Commissioner
of the Metropolitan Police.

HOME OFFICE   12 DEC. 88 RECEIVED and METROPOLITAN POLICE
RECEIVED 7. DEC. 88 CRIMINAL INVESTIGATION DEPT.) A49301/191
METROPOLITAN POLICE
CRIMINAL INVESTIGATION DEPARTMENT
SCOTLAND YARD
10th day of December 1888
SUBJECT Anonymous Confession
Com. Home Office
Re <u>Pressing</u> investigation.

With reference to previous correspondence, I beg to report that Insp. Abberline has been charged with locating the surgery referred to in the anonymous confession. Further enquiries will also be made by Insp. Abberline to establish the identity of the Writer.

I am
Sir,
Your most obedient Servant
J. Monro

The Under Secretary
of State
Home Office.

Home Office A49301/191 received by Home Office 3rd Dec. 1888

A
CONFESSION

I wish you misery and shame,
Shame will be your torture.
Torture will be your life,
I wish you a long life.

Anon

I had immediately become fascinated with the East End of London when I first visited my cousin's surgery in the Minories. The extreme poverty, the filth, the utter hopelessness of its inhabitants had stroked my morbid curiosity. Here at last I had found a modern Babylon, were I could throw aside my stifling etiquette and wallow in the company of young boys whom, for the price of a bowl of hot skilly, fervently engaged in sodomy. Colleagues of mine, had they known of my association with the abyss, would have called it 'slumming'. I called it freedom.

My licentious weekends had included the pleasures offered by the degenerate opium dens of Limehouse. It was during one such exotic visit, whilst under the blissful influence of the oriental narcotic substance, that a titillating thought had taken hold of me. Might I find the flesh of a woman also enjoyable? I had decided to test the hypothesis and advance my physical prowess.

The very centre of this festering district was Whitechapel, Spitalfields to be precise. Here a gin-sodden whore could be bought for a few pennies and then discarded as one might discard cigar ash. I had made my way along Commercial Street and entered the Ten Bells public house. I drank avariciously. I had felt exhilarated. Not through the intake of cheap alcohol but by the presence of those vile night creatures whom some called women. They were shameless sirens. Luring men into darkened alleyways to earn the price of a doss-house bed for the night. They had squandered their womanhood long ago and fornication for them had now become a mechanical act. I had felt empathy for them. They had been heartless. And so had I.

She had spoken with an Irish accent, telling me her name was Mary. She had been a little younger than I. Twenty-five, perhaps. Compared to her compatriots, she had been quite attractive, but I had known that would rapidly recede like the eclipse of the sun. She had said that for a shilling she would give me a special. Of course, the idea of something special had immediately intrigued me. I had quickly given her a shilling and we had staggered from that den of iniquity into the street. She led me past Hawksmoor's Christ Church and into a squalid courtyard off Fashion Street. My heart had quickened noticeably. The moment had arrived. I was about to be baptised.

Behind a small cart and beneath a flickering gas lamp, she had slowly knelt, sensually taking my organ in her mouth. I had never before encountered a shilling special and for a fleeting moment I had felt delight with her inventive technique. She had tried to stiffen me but I had remained limp. I had tried to imagine that she was a boy but the grave reality of her kneeling before me had demolished such a thought. She had scornfully spat me out and pushed me away. I had provoked a Gorgon. I became instantly paralysed.

Leaning forward, she had contemptuously shook my manhood with her hand, "Arthur no dick, eh? The ale has sent him to sleep, ain't it?" Sniggering, she had stood, raised her skirt, revealing her womanhood, "Come on, dearie, prove you're a man." The vile spectacle had struck me like a thunderbolt and shaken me from my paralytic posture.

I had quickly turned away, retching, but she continued to mock me. I had dropped to my knees and vomited. Something damp had hit my exposed buttocks. It was animal dung. She threw another piece but missed. My forehead throbbed, my body shook with rage. I was a volcano about to erupt. She leeringly stood over me. "That's the trouble with you bleedin' toffs, all candle and no wick, ain't you?" She spat at me. Spittle had trickled down into my ear.

I had risen unsteadily to my feet, desiring to strike her down, but she had gone. I stood alone, trembling. Then the sheer horror of the incident had struck me. I had been utterly humiliated. I had lost my dignity. It had been taken from me. Nay, stolen from me. Stolen by a 'shilling' whore.

> If all the Harm that women have done
> Were put in a bundle and rolled into one,
> Earth would not hold it,
> The sky could not enfold it,
> It could not be lighted nor warmed by the sun;
> Such masses of evil
> Would puzzle the devil
> And keep him in fuel while Time's wheels run.

> James K. Stephen
> (1859 – 1892)

I had retreated to the banality of my own class, desperate to regain my composure, determined to stay away from Spitalfields. The very thought that I might inadvertently meet that loathsome woman again filled me with such dread as to wish her dead. For what seemed like an eternity, I had suffered persistent nightmares, *reliving the horrid incident over and over again. I avoided sleep and became dependent on prescribed medication to relax my weary body. But no sooner had I closed my eyes and slipped blissfully into the void then she would be there, scorning me with her laughter. I would awake and curse her. I cursed the day she had been born. I cursed the day I had been born.*

My mundane birth into the English privileged class had occurred during a troublesome year. Abroad, the Indian mutiny had just flared into being. Trained by the British East India Company, Indian soldiers, sepoys, had adamantly refused to use the new Enfield rifle, which involved them biting off one end of a greased cartridge and pouring its contents down the barrel to load the rifle. Rumours had abounded that the grease used for these cartridges was derived from either beef drippings or pork fat. To the devoutly religious Hindu and Muslim sepoys these were the fats of forbidden animals. When pressed by their British officers to use the new cartridges, tens of hundreds mutinied and began an orgy of killing.

May God in his mercy preserve me from ever witnessing again such a sight as I have seen this day. The house they were kept in was close to the hotel – opposite the theatre – it was a native house – with a court in the middle, and an open room with pillars opposite the principal entrance. The whole of the court and this room was literally soaked with blood and strewn with bonnets and those large hats now worn by ladies – and there were long tresses of hair glued with clotted blood to the ground – all the bodies were thrown into a dry well and on looking down – a map of naked arms, legs and gashed trunks was visible. My nerves are so deadened with horror that I write this quite calmly. It is better you should know the worst – I am going this very moment to fill the well up and crown its mouth with a mount. Let us mention the subject no more – silence and prayer alone seem fitting.

J. W. Sherer
Magistrate
Kanpur
1857

British retribution had been swift. Many standing mutineers were lashed to the mouth of cannons and blown apart with grapeshot.

On one occasion, a cannon was so zealously overcharged that it literally blew the mutineer to smithereens, showering English female spectators with blood and fragments of flesh. Oh, if only I could have disposed of that odious bitch the same way.

My father had been a distinguished surgeon and a staunch advocate of the Christian way of life. An evangelist with a knife. A reassuring quality that must have calmed his patients before he cut into their flesh. My mother, like so many other reticent women of the age, had listlessly whiled away her time, seemingly unaware that she was supposed to be alive.

I know there is an obscure feeling, a feeling which is ashamed to express itself openly – as if a woman had no right to care about anything, except how they may be the most useful servants of some men. This claim to confiscate the whole existence of one half of the species for the supposed convenience of the other appears to me, independently of its injustice, particularly repulsive.

John Stuart Mill
(1806 – 1873)

As a child I never had a childhood. My parents had deemed it unnecessary. In their eyes, I had not been a child at all, but a small adult. Thus, the early part of my education had been conducted in private or, to be more precise, in near isolation. My ability to learn quickly, however, was only exceeded by my capacity to fantasise. I read everything I could about ancient Rome and, much to the displeasure of our gardener, had often acted out Julius Caesar's rout of the Gauls by charging the privet hedges and mercilessly slashing at them with his garden shears.

Who loves war for war's own sake
Is fool, or crazed or worse;

Alfred, Lord Tennyson
(1809 – 1892)

One morning my father had given me a copy of the Bible and then proceeded to lecture me for the rest of the day on its redeeming spiritual qualities. By the time he had dismissed me for the night I had felt so angered by his pious sermon that I could have wiped out the entire Christian civilisation single-handed. However, what he had failed to realise during his sanctimonious ravings was that his rhetoric had inadvertently introduced me to the iniquities of the damned.

> The laws of God, the laws of man,
> He may keep that will and can;
> Not I: let God and man decree
> Laws for themselves and not for me,

> A.E. Houseman
> (1859 – 1936)

I had become captivated by the decadent history of Sodom and Gomorrah and its depraved citizens. Ancient Babylon, a symbol of power, greed and cruelty, enthralled me. I soon realised that past empires had been dominated by males as ours is today. Indeed, throughout the history of man, the muscular qualities of the male physique had been sexually worshipped while women were merely looked upon as vassals for procreation. The Emperor Claudius had been an oddity among the great Caesars for he retained an unusual taste for women. All the others had preferred not only men, but also boys. The same could be said for the empires of Alexander the Great or the Ottomans. Men had sought sensual pleasure with men rather than women.

Slowly a thought had occurred to me. My parents had surely been cast from the same mould. True, my father was hardly a Caesar, partaking in sodomy, but he was a devoted worshipper of a deity, and my mother was undoubtedly a vassal for procreation. And I? I was the result of their union. But had I been desired? And now that I existed, was I cherished? I decided to approach my mother, intent on hearing an answer.

> She is older than the rocks among which she sits:
> Like the Vampire,
> She has been dead many times,
> And learned the secrets of the grave.

> Walter Pater
> (1839 – 1894)

7

I had sat in the garden with my mother and gazed into her pale blue eyes. They appeared to be entirely without life or expression, as if I was staring into the eyes of a corpse. Though her eyes did not suggest one ounce of intellectualism, her face had a magnetic charm about it that appeared quite irresistible. I had broached the question of my birth. She had looked at me with a pained expression. I felt an odd sensation, as if she had seized my heart and turned it to ice. Time seemed to stand still. She mournfully stared at me and then turned away. My heart had instantly thawed and thumped with anger. I knew then that I despised her. I had sought an affiliation with her; instead she had chosen to reject me. I hurried away, but as I had glanced back over my shoulder, I had experienced a brief moment of compassion, the irregular movements of her bowed head had told me that she was secretly weeping.

God did not intend all mothers to be accompanied by doctors, but He meant all children to be cared for by mothers.

Florence Nightingale
(1820 – 1910)

Enraged by my mother's rejection, I had sought revenge. Within the hour, I had throttled Athena. She was my mother's Siamese cat. I had found her in the garden and squeezed the life from her whilst I watched her face contort. I had then thrown her to the ground and stomped on her again and again until her intestines burst from her body. Still not satisfied, I had kicked the carcass across the lawn where, beneath some hedges, it had slid to a rest. No sooner had I finished, I became acutely aware of a sense of inner calmness, a feeling of serenity that I had not experienced before. I felt a surge of confidence, a feeling of being all powerful. The beast within me had been pacified. I had rid myself of both anger and torment. I had felt wonderful. Nay, I had felt elated.

Let it be borne in mind how infinitely complex and close fitting are the mutual relations of all organic beings to each other and to their physical conditions of life.

Charles Darwin
(1809 – 1882)

That night I had lain awake in bed, reliving the entire incident. Athena may have been the Greek goddess of wisdom, but I had not been. I was somewhat perplexed that I still retained a sense of euphoria after committing a seemingly indefensible act. But had not Charles Darwin himself recognised that life had evolved from the survival of the fittest? The weak will not inherit the earth, I had thought. Slowly, I had grasped the significance of those words. My heart had begun to race. I quickly sat upright in bed. I alone was accountable for my life and I alone would decide what was right or wrong, not the archaic laws of our country ruled by a monarch in perpetual mourning. If necessary, I would personify Caligula and smite down all of those who might stand against me. I slowly laid my head upon my pillow and, for the first time in my life, had slept splendidly.

Deliverance! My period of parental imposed isolation had finally ended. I entered prep-school and joined the rest of humanity.

The sand of the desert is sodden red,
Red with the wreck of a square that broke;
The Gatling's jammed and the Colonel dead,
And the regiment blind with dust and smoke.
The river of death has brimmed his banks,
And England's far, and Honour a name,
But the voice of a schoolboy rallies the ranks:
'Play up! Play up! And play the game!'

Henry Newbolt
(1862 – 1938)

My sense of liberation had immediately faded. Upon the first day, to be exact. A regime of near fossilised teachers, all clutching the Book of the Common Prayer in one hand and a ceaseless swishing cane in the other, taught Christian tolerance and meted out physical punishment with such regularity as to suggest that their patron saint must have been none other than the Marquis de Sade. That night, as I had tried to sit on my flogged buttocks, I wondered whose cat I would have to throttle next.

I had decided to persist with their heartless teaching methods, having determined that if I was going to be regularly thrashed in such a manner then my compensation would certainly have to be

9

a college scholarship. It was then that I had begun to notice a peculiar persistent trait about one particular teacher, Mr. H. After he had handed out a thrashing, and he always gave six of the best, he would swoon slightly. His bellicose attitude was instantly replaced by an unfamiliar benign personality. Similar, I thought, to how I must have appeared after I had dispatched Athena.

It was not to be long before I suffered his wrath firsthand. A trivial matter of foolishly raising my hand in class before he had invited me to do so had been enough to have me hauled from my desk and thrown across his bench for righteous punishment. He had cut the air above my head with his cane numerous times. I had resolved not to flinch when struck. But more importantly, I had been eager to know why, when having just thrashed a boy, his personality altered.

He struck me the first blow, then the second and then the third, but I had felt nothing at the time. It was as if my curiosity of him had numbed the pain. Or was it that I had not cared that it hurt? I heard him softly moan after he had delivered the fourth blow, but had not turned to investigate. The fifth and sixth blows were delivered, again with no sensation of pain. Survival of the fittest, I had thought. I turned my head and glanced over my shoulder at him. He towered above me, holding his cane limply at his side. He had swooned briefly and his eyes had rolled back. I saw a bulge in his trousers, and it was only much later that I had realised what had happened. Flogging boys had become an erotic pastime for him. He had spent in his trousers whilst thrashing me. Thus his seemingly benign change of personality was due to the physical fatigue he immediately experienced after each and every episode.

And, mark me, flogging, used with sound judgement, is the only fundamental principle upon which our schools can be properly conducted. I am all the better for it and am, therefore, one who has been well swished.

Algernon C. Swinburne
(1837 – 1909)

I had quickly learnt that Mr. H. favoured only virginal backsides. Thus, I began to take advantage of my bestowed immunity by frequently raising my impatient hand during his lectures without fear of bodily reprisals. On one occasion, however, he became so furious with my interruptions that he physically threw me out of the classroom. The following day, he had died suddenly from a burst heart. Flogging another boy, no doubt.

I ultimately obtained a scholarship for my endurance and entered one of England's leading private colleges. It had been the year of the Franco-Prussian conflict. Yet again, another arrogant Bonaparte, Napoleon III, had declared war on Prussia, vowing to protect the Papacy. Though I had favoured neither country, I had expected Prussia to defeat France, as England and Prussia had previously done under Wellington and Blücher at Waterloo. But none of this had really concerned me. I had been upon the threshold of life and earnestly wanted to study for my university scholarship. And then tragedy had struck. My mother had tried to commit suicide by taking an overdose of laudanum.

She peeped over the edge of the mushroom, and her eyes immediately met those of a large blue caterpillar, that was sitting on the yop, with its arms folded, quietly smoking a long hookah, and taking not the smallest notice of her or of anything else.

Alice's Adventures in Wonderland
Lewis Carroll
(1832 – 1898)

Laudanum had been, and still is, a popular opium-based drug approved by doctors for the cure of anything from headaches to consumption. The drug had been prescribed by my father for my mother in the hope that it would ease her melancholy disposition. As I was to learn much later, my grandmother and aunt had been plagued by a similar malady and had eventually taken their own lives. Of course, at the time, I had not been privy to such sinister information, but later, when I was, it was to cause me much consternation. My father appointed a private nurse, whose sole duty was to care for and watch over mother. And then, when not cutting into his patients, he once again turned to the Almighty for solace and salvation.

I had put the whole shameful affair behind me and had thrown myself into my studies. I became heavily involved with the college intellectual society, eagerly debating political issues of the day. Though Benjamin Disraeli was Prime Minister, Gladstone led the opposition, increasing his already acclaimed reputation as a formidable orator. Thus, I had begun to emulate his method and gradually gained distinction as an eloquent speaker myself. I was invited to join the college cricket team after I pitched a cricket ball over ninety-two yards in an enrolment contest. The average length of a cricket pitch was, and still is, twenty-two yards.

There were, of course, the inevitable floggings but by now I had begun to enjoy the administered pain. So much so that I had begun to consider what it would be like to thrash a boy myself. Would the pleasure be the same as being flogged, or would it sensually arouse me like it had the late Mr. H?

It had been autumn when we met. I had been seventeen. He sixteen. I had spotted him during one of my daily walks through the College Cloisters. He had not been a particularly attractive young man, but had possessed a roguish quality about him that I had found amiable. I had formally introduced myself to him and then, to my complete surprise, he had agreed to meet me the following Sunday in an orchard just behind the Pilgrims' School. I had approached the day, and the orchard, with a sense of trepidation. What exactly had I wanted from this furtive meeting? I knew then what I desired, but that was not the entire answer. Nevertheless, I entered the orchard and found him leaning against the trunk of a tree. We talked for a while and then he had gently slipped his hand between my legs, caressing my manhood. I had felt my member stir and begin to stiffen. I nervously reciprocated and unbuttoned his trousers. Oh, what a delight it had been to hold his organ in my hand as it grew larger. He unbuttoned my trousers and stroked me vigorously. I had never before felt such a sense of bodily excitement. Now I knew the answer to my question. The door of my cloistered life had at last been thrown open. I could now begin to evolve sensually, develop at will. Oh, ecstasy! I had felt so damn good. We had continued to stroke each other and then spent almost simultaneously.

We had triumphantly lain upon the grass, looking up at the clouds. I asked him how frequently he had given himself to other boys. He smiled, saying I had been the first. The irony had amused me so much that I had laughed loudly. I never met him again. I had not wanted to. I began to cast my net wider, slowly catching sprats, but continuously looking out for bigger, more prestigious fish.

I once more obtained a scholarship and entered university. It had become the period of one's life where you were supposed to adopt the etiquette of a gentleman, become an Englishman, so to speak. Indeed I had, at least for the first year. I studied classical languages, literature and history. I made the jovial acquaintance of other graduates, but graciously kept them at arms length. I continued to excel at cricket, becoming a member of the county cricket club. And I had consciously refrained from any involvement with another boy. That was, until my second year.

Meanwhile, the physical health of my mother had remained somewhat stable, but I must confess that I thought she had already departed this world and was spiritually lingering in the hereafter, waiting for her body to join her. My father had by now added spiritualism to his holy armoury, probably in the hope that it would allow him to communicate with my mother. The household servants had become deeply troubled by the gloomy situation, daring to hope that a death or two in the house would release them from their miserable employment and allow them to seek happier pastures elsewhere.

He had first loaned me a book written by the Marquis de Sade, entitled 120 Days of Sodom. It had been primitively translated into English from the original French version which, at the time of its publication, had been banned by Napoleon Bonaparte.

> Either kill me or take me as I am,
> because I'll be damned if I'll
> ever change.
>
> Marquis de Sade
> (1740 – 1814)

Like myself, my honourable friend had been a member of the county cricket club. The eldest son of an Earl, his dignified face had accentuated his aristocratic upbringing. Of slender build, he had been able to strike a cricket ball as confidently as I could pitch one. I enthusiastically read the book, appreciating its prose and explicit descriptions of depravity. After I had finished reading it, I courteously returned the book to him, having decided that I would exploit its theme to further bond our friendship.

Our cricket club had never won a major tournament, but through persistent enthusiasm and dogged determination we had reached the county final. Both him and I agreed that our team had to win the championship, even if it meant shooting the entire opposition to obtain the trophy. He had played magnificently, gaining a run for every ball he had struck. Our final score had been well above the seasonal average, leaving the opposing team a difficult mountain to climb. I had been determined that they would never reach that summit. I had bowled with such energy, force and accuracy that their final score culminated in a humiliating defeat for them and a resounding victory for us. Afterwards, our entire team had been inundated with congratulations from local visiting dignitaries, especially him and I.

That evening, his parents had given a lavish dinner in our honour, toasting our victory as both cricketers and Englishmen. His charming mother enquired after my own parents and I, being somewhat ashamed of their existence, evaded the question. Mr. V., a widely respected headmaster of a private boy's school, had declared that if I could teach as well as I could bowl a cricket ball then he would offer me a teaching post once I had graduated. It had been a wonderful dizzy affair. We had drunk champagne, port and brandy, and I had been thankful that the weekend had been upon us, over which I had ultimately recovered.

He had come to my room the following Sunday afternoon at around six o'clock. After informal preliminaries, I had broached the subject of the book he had lent me. His response had been quite passionate, informing me that descriptive, eloquent words were not enough, but that pleasurable deeds counted most of all. I had, of course, feigned deliberation for a moment and then had posed him a rhetorical question. Had he ever considered being birched as described in the book? He had raised a jovial eyebrow, saying that my question was deliciously wicked, which it was. With a mischievous smile, he had added that he would certainly give the proposal serious thought and, if agreed upon, then the utmost discretion would obviously be required. He had stood, graciously tipped his head and departed for the night, leaving me eagerly awaiting his decision.

14

The right honourable gentleman said flogging was degrading, yet that was the punishment inflicted on our soldiers and sailors, and when attempts had been made to substitute some other punishment, they were always told that discipline could not be maintained without it. He knew nothing so likely to stop the committal of these offences as flogging the offenders.

Mr. W. Williams MP
House of Commons
March 12, 1856

We had gone horse riding across his father's estate. Halting at a disused barn, he had said that such an isolated spot offered seclusion and that we would not be disturbed. He had capitulated to my proposal, insisting that I behave as a gentleman and that he be afforded all the dignities befitting his hereditary title. What he had meant, of course, was that I should not flog him senseless.

He had stripped naked and, throwing aside a piece of soiled canvas, revealed a birch. I reciprocated, removed my clothes, picked up the birch and threw him down prone over a bale of hay. I struck him forcibly across the buttocks with the birch and heard him moan with delight. I struck him again, again and again. And as I did, his organ hardened significantly with each strike. I slowly began to draw blood. Intoxicated by the sight, I started to harden myself. He moaned incessantly and began to quickly stroke his organ, begging me to strike him yet again. I obliged and struck once again, drawing more blood. He cried out in ecstasy, straightened his body and spent over the hay. I had become delirious. Dropping the birch to the ground, I had stepped forward and, against his will, sodomised him.

To some men, the shriek of torture is the essence of their delight, and they would not silence by a single note, the cry of agony over which they gloat.

William T. Stead
(1849 – 1912)

After I had spent, he had angrily pushed me away, arrogantly stating that it was beneath his dignity to be soiled by a commoner unless he had so desired it. I became incensed. Stepping forward, I had struck him across the face and knocked him to the ground. I wanted to pierce him with a nearby pitchfork, but thought better of it. I quickly dressed, mounted my horse and rode away. I had learnt an invaluable lesson. In order to survive and prosper, one had to remain within one's own class. Since time immemorial, the aristocracy had governed England and, unless they desired it otherwise, they would continue to look upon all other classes with contempt. I never saw him again, even at county cricket matches. I heard that he had graduated and entered a military academy, which I had found most peculiar. Aristocrats tended to purchase their commissions, thus evading military training and remaining utterly incompetent to command. Thus, the Crimean War of 1854 has forever remained notorious as a prime example of aristocratic ineptitude.

Talk to me of the aristocracy of England! Why, look to that glorious charge of the cavalry at Balaclava – look to that charge, where the noblest and wealthiest of the land rode foremost, followed by heroic men from the lowest classes of the community, each rivalling the other in bravery, neither the peer who led nor the trooper who followed being distinguished the one from the other.

Lord Palmerston
(1784 – 1865)

In fact, that infamous charge had decimated the finest brigade of light cavalry that had ever left the shores of England.

Forward, the Light Brigade!
Was there a man dismay'd?
Not tho' the soldier knew
Some one had blunder'd.
Theirs not to make reply,
Theirs not to reason why,
Theirs but to do and die,
Into the valley of Death
Rode the six hundred.

Alfred Lord Tennyson
(1809 – 1892)

I had once more thrown myself into my studies and resumed the debating of relevant social issues, again attracting the attention and praise of Mr. V. It appeared that my recent aristocratic clash had not diminished my academic standing in his eyes. It had been about this time that I had first begun to experience mild bouts of weariness, a sense of melancholy. At times, I would become bored with all and sundry. Even my beloved game of cricket had suffered immensely when the malady struck me. I had sought the advice of my doctor who prescribed medication, which revived my bodily functions, but had done nothing to banish the cobwebs of my mind.

Contagious disease sufferers are the social lepers of the 19th century.

Anon

My anxiety had further increased when my elder brother had divulged to me the mental histories of my grandmother, aunt and mother. On this, one of his rare visits to see me at university, he had also censured me, saying that my unconventional peculiarities had reached the ears of our family and that I should either be very discreet or cease such abnormalities all together. Although I had been taken aback, I feigned obedience which, of course, I had no intention of honouring. His hypocritical outburst also prompted me to think more about the absurdities of some of our laws.

When Queen Victoria had ascended to the throne in 1837, she had issued a proclamation to encourage piety, virtue, and the punishment of immorality. Twenty-one years later, in 1858, Prime Minister Gladstone had righteously declared that nudity had not been tolerated by either the ancient Greeks or Romans, or by any other civilised country similar to Great Britain. However, in the same year it had become legal in England, but not Ireland, to permit men and women to divorce through a special court, at a cost of £100. The existence of this new law had unwittingly admitted that men and women did indeed commit adultery, thus the law could no longer simply define individuals as property owners, but had to now recognise them as sensual beings.

But six years later, in an effort to combat venereal diseases, the law had taken a step backwards. The Contagious Disease Act of 1864 had been an abysmal attempt to regulate prostitution in *military garrison towns, in order to control the deadly disease, syphilis. An earlier law had previously reasoned that for men to use the services of prostitutes was 'natural' even though such women were morally corrupt. However, the new 1864 law had decreed that any woman found within a certain radius of all garrison towns could be arrested, which many were, along with innocent mothers and daughters. Those arrested had their rights suspended and were imprisoned indefinitely if they refused a medical examination.*

By this law, a crime has been created in order that it be severely punished, but observe, that has been ruled to be a crime in women, which is not to be a crime in men.

Josephine Butler
(1828 – 1906)

Male liberties were also curtailed in 1885, when Queen Victoria had been asked to sign the new Criminal Law Amendment Act, which included penalties for homosexual and lesbian conduct. Unable to believe that any woman could conduct herself in such a disgraceful manner, Victoria crossed out all references to female homosexuality, thereby endorsing a law that would eventually single out men for future criminal punishment.

After two notable years at university, I had obtained a second class degree. I entered my third university year just as the British invaded Zululand, thereby initiating another colonial war. But this time, the British had bitten off more than they could chew.

Did I ever tell Mr. Shepstone I would not kill? I do kill!

Zulu King Cetewayo
(d. 1884)

In January of that year, the Zulus, in overwhelming numbers, had launched a disciplined attack on the slopes of Isandhlwana, successfully annihilating a British force of thirteen hundred men. Immediately afterwards, another four thousand Zulus, led by Prince kaMpande, had attacked the small mission station at Rorke's Drift, defended by only one hundred and thirty-nine men, mostly from the 2nd Battalion, 24th Regiment of Foot. The vastly outnumbered British soldiers had stood their ground, inflicting heavy casualties on the Zulus, who withdrew a day later, leaving behind six hundred of their dead. The absurd disparity between aristocratic leadership, or complete lack of it, and the ordinary British soldier had been vividly highlighted in the opening phase of the conflict. Having entered enemy territory, the British Commander-in-Chief, Lord Chelmsford, had left behind thirteen hundred men at Isandhlwana and had then proceeded to scout the terrain, looking for a Zulu impi, whose size had been completely unknown. The slaughter of British troops at Isandhlwana had fundamentally occurred because gentlemen officers had made no preparations to defend their position against an enemy attack. When the attack had occurred, the British force, strung out across the slopes of Isandhlwana, had been unable to defend itself against a superior force of twenty thousand Zulus. At Rorke's Drift, where an excellent defensive position had been adopted, the discipline and raw courage of the ordinary British soldier had prevailed, repelling a Zulu force of four thousand warriors. Eleven of the defenders at Rorke's Drift were ultimately awarded the Victoria Cross, totalling the highest number of awards for valour ever won in a single British military engagement.

A very remarkable people the Zulus. They defeat our generals; they convert our bishops; they have settled the fate of a great European dynasty.

Benjamin Disraeli
(1804 – 1881)

My cousin, whom I have always held in high esteem, had paid me a surprise visit at university, informing me that he was about to open a surgery in the Minories. He had explained that the Minories was an important street location because it did, in fact, border both the City of London and the East End of London. His plan was to offer wealthy businessmen a private surgical service and, in turn, a free but limited service for the poor people of Whitechapel.

The people live in squalid dens, where there can be no health and no hope, but dogged discontent at their own lot, and futile discontent at the wealth which they see possessed by others.

Thorold Rogers
(1823 – 1890)

He had also suggested that I might like to follow in my father's footsteps and pursue a medical career once I had graduated.

Up the close and down the stair,
In the house with Burke and Hare.
Burke's the butcher, Hare's the thief,
Dr. Knox's the boy who buys the beef.

19th Century Sing-song Rhyme

If I should opt for such a profession, he had offered, on my behalf, to ask his medical colleagues to assist me and remarked that there would be a very good possibility that I might find future employment at his surgery. I had expressed my gratitude and politely declined his generous offer, saying that I would have to defer any decision to a later date. I wished him every success with his new enterprise and had cheerfully bade him farewell.

It had been July and all the newspapers had unanimously proclaimed victory. Having totally defeated the Zulus at the battle of Ulundi, Lord Chelmsford had by now redeemed himself in the eyes of both the British government and the populace. Zulu King Cetewayo had yet to be captured and exiled to Cape Town, but that the war had been fought to a victorious conclusion had been all that mattered to anyone. His Lordship had been the hero of the day and the Empire had once more heaved a huge sigh of relief.

A few weeks later, my elder brother had paid me another visit at university and, much to my surprise, congenially suggested that I might wish to consider a legal career once I had graduated. Unlike his previous self-righteous visit, he had praised my oratory skills, saying that my knowledge of related social issues would be a distinct advantage in handling civil disputes. Although the cost of legal studies would be beyond my financial capabilities, he had offered to speak to our father and ask him that I might borrow a sum against any arranged inheritance. It had been heartening to know that such support from my brother existed. I assured him that I would give his proposal serious thought and, as I had previously done with my cousin, had cheerfully bade him farewell.

Oh, what delight! I had no longer felt that I had to cling to life. In fact, life seemed to be clinging to me.

Turmoil

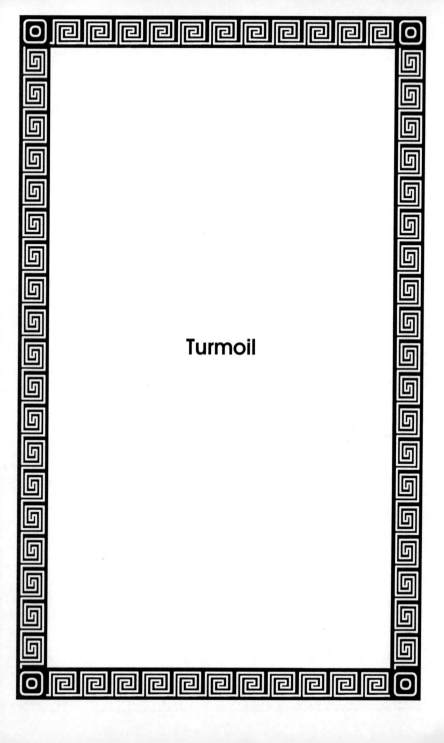

Turmoil

Oh, will time not allow me to forget when our eyes had first met?

It had been a pleasant summer's afternoon and my innings in the county cricket match had been a resounding performance. In fact, I had scored the highest runs credited to any team member so far. On that glorious day I had reached a half-century and had not been bowled, caught or run out. I felt confident, even without divine intervention, that I could go on to score a century. During the match interval, I had retired to the county club pavilion for light refreshments and was about to resume my batting position on the playing field when I had seen him, standing amid other spectators. His youthful face and exquisite beauty had been utterly beguiling. Although not a mythical being, I had instantly likened his face to that of Venus, which I had seen portrayed in several historical paintings. Similar to her face, his had been captivating. It was then that our eyes had met. It had been a moment of sheer absorption.

His eyes were a wonderful mixture of green and blue. Delightful pools of turquoise. I had wanted to savour the moment, but other team members were edging me back to play. And then he had tenderly smiled at me. I had instantly been overwhelmed, struck by a sense of warmth that had engulfed my entire body. His voice permeated my mind, softly asking me to strike every ball for him. Resolute, I had returned to the playing field, taken up my batting position and struck the first ball for a six. Thereafter, I had felt that an ethereal being had been consistently guiding the bat to strike the ball, not me. I attained my century and had been rapturously congratulated by team members and spectators alike. I should have felt elated, but I only had thoughts of him. Those irresistible eyes, that beautiful smile. I had searched the crowd, but alas he had vanished. Then a thought had struck me, which had caused my entire body to shiver. Perhaps he had never existed at all. Perhaps I had imagined him. And if that be true, then I must be going mad, or worse still, I was already mad.

That night, I had lain in bed unable to sleep. The thought that I might have inherited a family malady had troubled me immensely. Why had my grandmother and aunt taken their own lives and how on earth could I possibly take my own life after experiencing such a breathtaking moment? My mind had been besieged with such illogical thoughts that I had wanted to split my skull apart and cast my brain asunder. The entire night became a mental ordeal, with daybreak offering no respite from the torment. I had spent the next week trying to harness my thoughts, to rationalise the irrational. Then in a moment of inspiration I had set myself free and escaped the gloom. What I had seen and felt that summer's afternoon should not have caused me consternation later. In fact, I had experienced something truly divine, something to be treasured. If indeed he had only existed in my mind, then what a beautiful image I had created. There was also the question of the century I had attained. Although I had felt another hand guiding my bat, it had been my own mind that had created the illusion, thus ensuring that I had won the day. Therefore, what my moment of inspiration had later told me was that, if I was indeed going mad, then this was going to be an immensely pleasurable journey.

Due to this bewildering yet heartening episode, my studies had somewhat suffered. I had been determined to regain lost ground. So without delay I had thrown myself back into the task at hand. A late afternoon found me seated at a reading table in the university library, quite alone. I had just turned the page of a manuscript when I had experienced the unusual sensation of being watched. I had looked up and although I had seen no one, I could not rid myself of the feeling that someone had been there, gazing at me. I had risen from my chair and called out but had heard nothing, except that of my own echo. I had been about to resume my work when a figure had calmly stepped out from the shadows. Regally illuminated by a shaft of light falling from a nearby window, he had moved towards me. I could hardly move. I could scarcely breathe. His exquisite face had once more transfixed me to the spot.

He had courteously extended his hand and apologised for the intrusion. His tone of voice had been disarmingly lyrical. I politely shook his hand, thankful to know at last that he was most definitely of this world and not a figment of my imagination. He had praised me for scoring such a remarkable century and again apologised that his praise had been somewhat belated. It did not matter. I had attained the score because of him. But being aware that such a disclosure might embarrass him had prevented me from saying so. He could have said that the earth was flat when I knew it was most certainly round. It would not have mattered. To be standing before him, in his presence, was utterly magical. He had honoured me by seeking me out. The very least I could do was to invite him to dinner, which he had graciously accepted.

Six months younger than I, he had informed me that he came from a middle-class family and that his widowed mother lived in a modest terraced house in South London. Politically minded, he had thought that the new labour movements, whose source of membership was the underprivileged, would ultimately challenge Disraeli's and Gladstone's government policies, which continually favoured the rich. Though not a revolutionary himself, he had believed that Lev Nikolayevich Tolstoy, Emile Zola and Karl Marx were right to advocate revolution if repressive governments failed to reform. I had been enthralled. Not merely by his intellectualism, but by his eloquence of speech. He had been a kindred spirit and, as such, was to soon warrant my undivided loyalty.

When not studying, we were inseparable. We spent a delightful holiday in Venice, absorbing the architectural and artistic wonders of the Grand Canal, along with the gastronomical delights and tragic operas of its numerous restaurants and theatres.

On our return to England, he had introduced me to his mother, who had been a pleasant woman with a satirical sense of wit. When given the opportunity, she would frequently entertain us, humorously ridiculing Queen Victoria for ceaselessly mourning her late husband, Prince Albert. He had asked to meet my parents, insisting that whatever their social standing, it would not alter his opinion of me. At first, I had been hesitant but, encouraged by his thoughtful affection, I had relented. My father, whose health had been gradually deteriorating, had found him instantly agreeable; my mother's eyes had even begun to show signs of life during his congenial presence.

We returned to university, where I would spend the happiest few months of my life. As passionately as I had loved him, and still do, this love had not inclined to sensual pleasures, even in my dreams of him. Many were the days and nights I had spent by his side in conversation, only once to taint our companionship when I had foolishly implied such an exchange. Our love had been entirely emotional. Nay, spiritual. I had yielded to its eminence, which had released such a profound profusion of emotions within me that, given enough time, I would have gladly imparted all to him. Alas, fate had interfered, determining that it had not meant to be.

Christmas had come and gone, and with it, so had he.

Life is never fair. And perhaps it is a good thing for most of us that it is not.

An Ideal Husband
Oscar Wilde
(1854 – 1900)

Cholera had been a waterborne disease. It would be at least another three years before the German doctor, Robert Koch, would isolate and successfully identify the microbe.

Leading from a cesspool, a privy drain had burst and flooded the kitchen of his home in South London. Two days later, his mother had collapsed with choleric diarrhoea. I had wanted to be there, die with him, if need be, but he had warned me away. He had nursed his mother for three entire days, until she finally expired peacefully. Having already succumbed to the disease himself, he had collapsed and crawled to his bed. Disregarding his previous warning, I had immediately rushed to the house and found him there, dying.

I had held him in my arms, gazing upon his pallid face. Oh, I can still see those eyes now. Delightful pools of turquoise. He had raised his head and gently kissed me upon my lips. My eyes had glazed over. And then he had smiled and died. I cannot remember what I had felt, if indeed I had felt anything at all. I could not truly grasp the significance of what had happened. He was there, in my arms, but he had gone. How could this be? I had been devoid of any rational thought. I had been utterly devastated.

Looking hard and harder I knew what it meant.
The sudden shine sent from the livid east scene;
It meant the west mirrored by the coffin of my friend there,
Turning to the road from his green.

To take his last journey forth, he who in his prime,
Trudged so many a time from the gate athwart the land!
Thus a farewell to me he signalled on his grave-way,
As with a wave of his hand.

Thomas Hardy
(1840 – 1928)

I had attended his funeral and watched as his coffin had been lowered into the grave. Then the terrible inescapable truth of what had happened had struck me like a thunderbolt. Death was so utterly final. A day later, two churchyard workers had found me still sitting beside his grave. Although motionless, the fact that I was still breathing had convinced them that I was alive. They had taken me away to my doctor, who had instantly confined me to bed.

For days, perhaps weeks, my mind had lingered somewhere between the here and the hereafter. I had been fed hot broth, which had sustained my body but did nothing to soothe my grief. Slowly, very slowly, I had recovered and regained my reason. I had resumed my studies, determined that when I graduated it would be to solely honour him. I became a man obsessed with my work and befriended no one. I began to despise the mortal world, which had permitted a terrible disease to take him away from me. I had become convinced that when he had departed, my spirit had departed with him. Now all that remained of me was the flesh, which could easily be serviced.

The more one analyses people, the more all reasons for analysis disappear. Sooner or later one comes to that dreadful universal thing called nature.

The Decay of Living
Oscar Wilde
(1854 – 1900)

I had increasingly recovered my licentious appetite and sought out other students for nourishment. I entertained only those who would accept sodomy as standard practice, or those who would submit to bodily pain. After such activities, I would feel invigorated. But the feeling would soon subside, leaving me utterly miserable. During such bouts of melancholy, I would think of him and feel that I had thoroughly betrayed our union. I had felt ashamed. However, I eventually reasoned, that in order to resolve this dilemma, I would have to separate my desires of the physical world from my spiritual thoughts of him. Gradually, I began to achieve just that. But to this day, and given the opportunity, I would kneel before him and beg his forgiveness that I had.

I had obtained a third class degree and prepared for graduation.

Although only my elder brother and my cousin had attended my graduation, it nonetheless turned out to be an auspicious occasion for me. No sooner had I been presented with my diploma, than Mr. V. had been at my side, offering me a post as a resident master at his private boy's school. Requiring somewhere to live immediately, I had promptly accepted his offer and terms, informing my cousin that I had deliberated upon his suggestion of a medical career, but had decided to pursue a legal one instead. Much to my brother's delight, I had then asked him to approach our father to secure the necessary funds required for my studies.

I had been somewhat glad to put those university years behind me. Except for one brief moment of magical happiness and my beloved cricket, the rest of the time had been a rather laborious experience. I was, I thought, ready to face the world. The boy's boarding school had been, and still is, situated at the edge of a village, bordering a heath from which the district had acquired its name. Originally a Georgian residence, the four storey house had been enlarged over the past twenty-five years to include, of all such things, a swimming pool. In fact, this educational edifice was just one of nine boys schools to be found in this illustrious area.

Partially below ground, the dining hall was a long, dimly lit room with a passage running its entire length. Above the dining hall and passage stood the schoolroom, connected to a somewhat smaller classroom. Over these two rooms was the long-room and above this, the dormitories, which could only be reached by climbing a narrow staircase. Beside the teachers, the school employed ten domestic staff, including a matron, Mrs. S. If I had known that this despicable woman was to ultimately contribute to my downfall, I would have immediately dispatched her as I had Athena.

An unusual feature of the dormitory area was that the beds were partitioned off, so that each boy slept in his own private compartment. This I had considered very liberal, given our social obsession with adolescent self-abuse. Beside Mr. V. and myself, there had been only one other resident master, Mr. M., who had originated from Guernsey. His private room was on the other side of the common room at the end of the corridor, whilst mine had auspiciously adjoined the dormitories.

Mr. V. had regarded me as an ascending star, whilst Mrs. S. had regarded me as poison. Maybe it was a woman's intuition that had told her that I was somewhat different. A bit queer, perhaps?

My task at the boarding school had been to help prepare boys for admission to public schools, universities, the professions and the army. It had been only eleven years since I first entered college; I now found myself in the enviable position whereby, if I so desired, I could inflict the same sort of punishment on pupils that I, myself, had endured. It was an authority that I intended to wield with the utmost discretion. After all, I hardly needed to initiate a disciplinary act that might expose my somewhat unsociable peculiarities. To further remove the chance of any possible scandal, I had decided not to involve myself with any boy belonging to the school. At least for the time being.

My agreed terms of employment with Mr. V. had granted me the right to apply to the City of London's Inns of Court for training as a barrister. Should my admittance application prove successful, I would still be able to retain my position as night housemaster at his school, leaving most of my days free to concentrate on legal studies. At my brother's request, my father had agreed to grant me a loan of £500 to cover the admittance fee and future exam costs.

Attempting to alleviate the frustration of self-imposed celibacy, I had joined both the local cricket and hockey clubs. Whilst hockey was a much more energetic game than cricket, it still required the same type of ball, but painted white. I was again stricken by bouts of melancholy, with each spell increasing in duration. Whatever medication was prescribed, none had any effect, except to make me feel very nauseous. I had begun to suspect that these lethargic moods were somehow induced by my lack of sensual activities. Private self-abuse seemed to ease the malady, but once again, only the flesh had proved to be the ultimate cure.

My admittance to the City of London's Inner Temple had finally been approved. Although I had been quite elated, I knew that an arduous three years of legal studies lay ahead. I would leave the school each morning and take the train to London, returning late every afternoon to continue my duties as housemaster for the remainder of the evening. Though the return journeys proved to be rather tiresome, once the boys were asleep I had ample time to relax and prepare my papers for the following day. One particular afternoon, having both the time to spare and the evening off, I had decided to visit my cousin at his surgery in the Minories. It turned out to be an auspicious afternoon. I had been introduced to Whitechapel.

My numerous nocturnal and weekend visits to Whitechapel ultimately increased my knowledge of the district, enabling me to gain a comprehensive picture of the entire area. Leaving the Inner Temple and travelling along Leadenhall Street into Aldgate, the Minories was found just off to the right where Aldgate High Street begun. Further along Aldgate High Street, Whitechapel High Street started, whereupon at the junction with Osborn Street, it became Whitechapel Road.

The first dominant landmark of Whitechapel Road was the Church of St. Mary Matfellon, with its unique exterior pulpit and inner White Chapel. Thus, when the area had initially required a name, it had been christened Whitechapel. On the same side, but further along the road, was The London Hospital, where my cousin had often lent his support, treating the hospital's excess of casual patients at his surgery. Returning to Whitechapel High Street and turning right into Commercial Street, Spitalfields was reached.

Nowhere in the East End of London had abject poverty been more evident than in Spitalfields. Except for its Hawksmoor Church and fruit and vegetable market, the entire squalid neighbourhood was infested with foul, filthy doss-houses, noisy smoke-filled pubs and a multitude of cackling degenerate whores. Its grimy streets were constantly plagued by a wretched race of people, short on good manners, who persistently squabbled and fought with each other. Unlike death, food was continually in short supply. I had seen a cluster of shoeless infants thrust their arms into a discarded pile of putrefying fruit and draw forth rotten morsels, which they quickly devoured, whilst hungrily probing for more. Throughout the entire district, it was an accepted fact that many of these infants would be dead before they reached the age of five.

Due to the severe shortage of essential shelter, famished people were regularly forced to live in the streets. A chill, raw wind had blown that night as I had stepped into the neglected graveyard beside Christ Church. Huddled on benches on both sides of a narrow pathway had sat the saddest collection of human beings

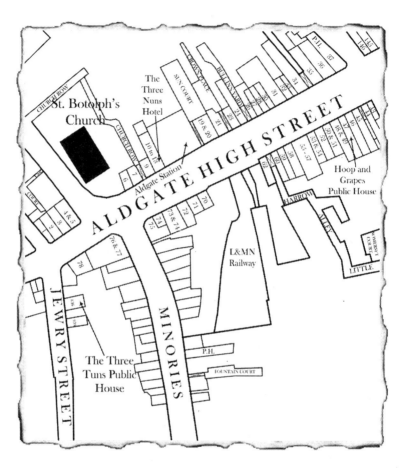

Aldgate High-street
&
Minories
1888

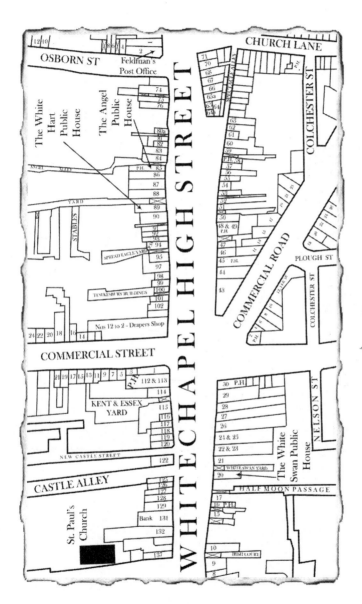

Whitechapel High-street & Commercial-street 1888

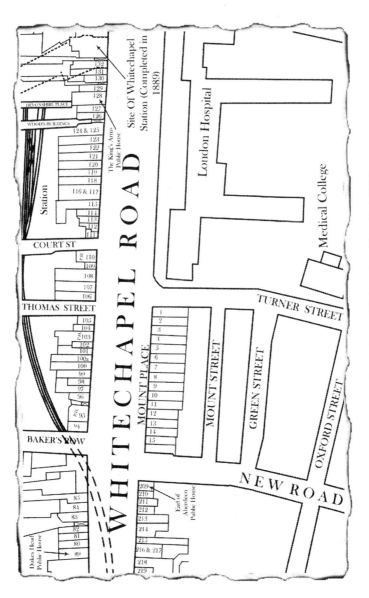

Whitechapel-road & London Hospital 1888

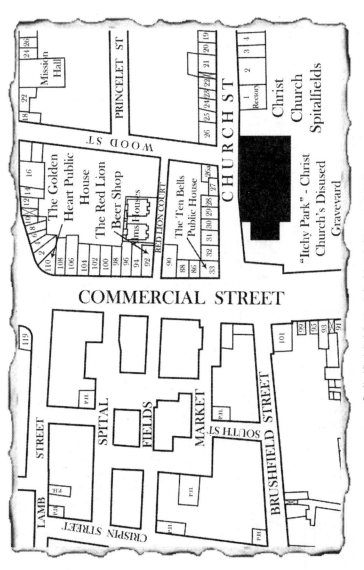

Spitalfields Market & Christ Church 1888

that I had ever seen in my life. A dozen women, aged between twenty and seventy years, had sat in their rags, sleeping, or trying to sleep. A baby, ten months old, lay beside one woman, pale and motionless. It had appeared dead. Further along, six men, their clothes caked with mud, were propped upright, leaning against one another as they slept. Beside them, an old man lay asleep, his head in the lap of a young girl, whose dirty face had remained tilted towards the night sky as she had murmured in her sleep. It had been somewhat difficult for me to accept that such extreme poverty could exist at the very heart of the greatest, wealthiest, and most powerful empire the world has ever known.

Anyone or anything could be bought in Spitalfields, particularly sinful pleasures. With a plethora of syphilitic whores, whom soldiers and merchant sailors eagerly paid for a quick thrill and an everlasting disease, the entire impoverished area was actually one large pulsating brothel. In dimly lit courtyards, houses of ill repute catered for the gentry, offering the services of foreign ladies skilled in the ways of fornication that their English compatriots were not. For those with unusual tastes, child brothels afforded protection from police arrest, where children gladly ate the food they were given, seemingly unaware of their unnatural bondage.

I had slowly gravitated to a boy's brothel, paying mere pennies for a pound of flesh. Here I had been able to indulge myself, thus avoiding the risk of igniting a scandal at either the boarding school or the Inner Temple. Whenever a bout of melancholy had struck me, I would merely idle the weekend away, whilst two, nay three brothel boys would vulgarly bicker amongst themselves for my attention. It had been a splendid cure indeed. Nay, it had been utopia. So much so that I had once more extended my physical prowess, becoming a member of another cricket club. Mr. V. had continued to praise my sporting achievements, informing the entire school that I was a sportsman to be admired. Mind you, if Mrs. S. had known of my Spitalfields escapades, I am sure she would have instantly hauled me to the village green and hanged me from the nearest tree. At the time, I had remained forever hopeful that one day I might find her dead, having swallowed her own venom.

It had been my second year as both housemaster and law student. Whilst I had relaxed, enjoying a pleasant English summer, a natural force had unleashed an awesome power.

A fearful explosion. A frightful sound. I am writing this blind in pitch darkness. We are under a continual rain of pumice stone and dust. So violent are the explosions that the eardrums of over half my crew have been shattered. My last thoughts are for my dear wife. I am convinced that the Day of Judgement has come.

> Captain Sampson
> 'Norham Castle'
> 1883

Seven thousand miles from England, off the western tip of Java, a gigantic volcanic eruption had blown the island of Krakatoa into oblivion. The death throes of the volcano had lasted twenty-one hours, culminating in the most violent explosion ever experienced by modern man. Similar to being blasted from a gigantic cannon, white-hot pumice had been hurled many miles into the air. Tidal waves, washing away the Telok Betong lighthouse, had swept over the shores of Java and Sumatra, killing forty thousand people and depositing the Dutch gunship 'Berouw' a quarter of a mile inland.

In essence, Krakotoa had disappeared; six cubic miles of rock had been blasted out of existence. Billions of dust particles entered the atmosphere and drifted around the earth, forming immense clouds that blocked out the sun, turning day into night. In stark contrast, London witnessed brilliant sunsets and unusual afterglows. William Ashcroft, who had been fortunate enough to live beside the River Thames, painted images of these. Aware that he was witnessing a unique occurrence, he produced five hundred and thirty-three watercolours over a period of four months.

Try as I might, I had not been able to shed the ominous feeling that the destruction of Krakatoa had been an omen for something else. A human deed, perhaps? Something just as shocking. But by whom, when and where?

As I entered my third year of studies at the Inner Temple, I had begun to question if, indeed, I wanted to become a barrister. Yes, of course, I could wear the celebrated wig and gown of office, and have exclusive rights to address my peers in any court of law, including the House of Lords, but the failure rate of a fledgling barrister was extremely high. Assuming I did take this route, I would have to rent chambers, employ a clerk and acquire briefs all at the same time. And in the interim period, how would I afford my pleasures of life? How would I be able to continue with my sport activities? My beloved cricket?

A practising solicitor himself, my elder brother had kindly offered me a solution. I was to continue with my legal studies and finally graduate from the bar as a barrister. To avoid the initial costs incurred by young barristers, I would serve two probationary years under him, working as a 'special pleader'. To ensure that I had a secondary income and a place to live, I could retain my position at the boarding school. This had been a splendid solution to my dilemma, for which I had thanked my brother whole-heartedly.

It had been the anniversary of his death. I had visited his grave, as I had done every year since he died. Though the grief of losing him was sadly resurrected, I nonetheless had valued the solitary hour or two, reflecting on how our lives might have been had he lived. I would certainly have behaved more benevolently, more compassionately towards my fellow man than I had at present. In fact, I very much doubted that he could find it in his heart to love me once again if he knew of my disgraceful behaviour now. It had been beside his grave that I had frequently heard his gentle voice advising me not to be so incessantly despicable. In my defence, I had informed him that one could not entirely banish evil from the world because evil was necessary to define goodness. Indeed, my deplorable conduct had truly demonstrated that other men were intrinsically good. How else could they have known otherwise?

Afterwards, I had to confess that my rationalisation had seemed quite preposterous. Evil could never be justified. In fact, I would have found it extremely difficult to defend my own dishonourable behaviour. However, none of this mattered, as long as one did not cause a scandal, which was considered by every gentleman of the land to be the most heinous crime of all.

It had been an ominous start to the year. In the Sudanese city of Khartoum, its citizens, presided over by General Charles Gordon, had been besieged for months by a large army of Dervishes led by Mohammed Ahmed, otherwise known as the Mahdi. Attempting to relieve the beleagued city, a British column, led by Sir Herbert Stewart, had clashed with the Dervishes, who had utterly routed *the column, slaughtering many soldiers and mortally wounding Stewart himself.*

Several days later, under the leadership of a warrior named Shahin, hordes of Dervishes had stormed Khartoum and cornered Gordon, standing at the top of some stairs. Although he wore his sword and held a revolver, he had made no attempt to use either. Shahin threw his spear, striking Gordon in the chest. As he reeled from the impact, another spear struck him in the back. Fatally wounded and falling to the ground, Gordon had been pounced upon by other attacking Dervishes and instantly hacked to pieces.

Of course, here in England, the death of General Gordon had been seen as Christian martyrdom. Prime Minister Gladstone had steadfastly refused to accept any responsibility for the debacle, although initially his Cabinet had dithered about whether to send a relief force to Khartoum or not. This, along with the ramifications of the Irish Home Rule Bill, would soon drive Gladstone from office.

It had been spring and I was called to the bar. Deemed a fit and proper person, I had become a barrister. I was twenty-eight and could now put my educational trials and tribulations behind me. I had felt liberated, freed from bondage. I experienced both jubilation and relief. Mr. V. once again praised me and had given a lavish dinner in my honour, attended by both my elder brother and my cousin. It was during the course of this celebratory evening that I had the first inkling that my brother might try to determine my personal life.

A slip of his tongue had revealed that he thought my trips to the East End of London, for whatever reasons, were foolhardy and unwise. He had warned that to visit such a scandalous district was tantamount to insanity and, if continued, could bring the good name of our family and his practice into disrepute. Troubled that a future rift between the two us might disrupt my two probationary years under him, I had immediately retained chambers at the Inner Temple for a nominal rent, secure in the knowledge that if the need arose I could resume my role as a barrister.

In due course, spring had become summer. During the hottest month of the year, the Criminal Law Amendment Act had been introduced. For those people of a puritanical mind, a legalised witch-hunt could now begin, where pious bigots of the land could charge, prosecute and imprison gentlemen, such as myself, for participating in homosexual activities. It was a troublesome law. Therefore, I reluctantly decided that discretion would indeed be the better part of valour.

We are each our own devil, and we make this world our hell.

The Duchess of Padua
Oscar Wilde
(1854 – 1900)

The following month my father had suddenly died of a burst heart, aged sixty-five. His funeral had been a mournful spectacle, befitting his position in life. The hearse, a glass coach bedecked with flowers, was pulled by six horses with black plumes, preceded by a group of solemn gentlemen dressed in long coats and tall silk hats. Seated in carriages, family mourners and guests had followed behind. Unlike a colourful day at the Ascot races, these affluent people now wore black. The crawling cortège eventually reached the church and, after a monotonous service, the coffin had been ceremoniously interned in the family vault. Throughout the entire service, the noticeable ill health of my mother had suggested that, at any given moment, she could have accompanied my father to the hereafter as well.

For what had seemed like an eternity, the entire family, myself included, dutifully mourned my father's fateful departure. In due course, the whole insincere nonsense had abated and we finally gathered to hear the reading of his will. It was to be an occasion that completely astounded everyone, particularly me. Along with substantial property, my father had left a monetary estate of £16, 579. My three younger sisters each inherited a significant amount, providing they did not marry before the age of twenty-one. My two younger brothers each received £500 and my elder brother an entire farm, plus responsibility to care for our mother. I had been awarded £600 less the £500 I had borrowed for my legal studies, leaving me with a mere inheritance of £100. I was stunned.

That night, bewildered, I had wandered the squalid streets of Spitalfields, trying to make sense of it all. It seemed that in death my father had abandoned me as my mother had in life. The more I had thought of their rejection of me, the angrier I had become. My meandering had brought me to a darkened narrow street lit by a single overhead gas lamp. Halfway along the unpleasant street, I had partially stumbled over what looked like a pile of rags lying across my path. The pile had stirred and extended a pleading hand to me. The hand belonged to an old toothless hag who had apparently fallen to the ground as a result of being quite drunk. She had muttered something inaudible, revealing her filthy face, which was covered in open sores and bruises. In a frantic appeal for assistance, she had grabbed at my ankle. I had stepped back and then scornfully driven the front of my boot into her chest. She had inhaled hoarsely. I furiously kicked her again and again. She wheezed and then her eyes had rolled back. Stepping over her, I had hurried to the end of the street.

I had paused and regained my composure, instantly feeling the same sense of serenity that I had experienced after I had slain Athena. Looking back over my shoulder, I had seen no movement from the old hag. Was she dead? Had I killed her? If so, who really cared? The obnoxious, scavangerous people of Spitalfields did indeed permeate beyond the major thoroughfares of Whitechapel in search of cheap thrills, but scarcely a stones throw away, within a labyrinth of putrid streets, alleyways and courtyards, an old hag may have been murdered and not one of the populace had been present to see it happen. It had been as if the wretched people, like scurrying rats, had bolted from a sinking ship.

Somewhere above me a window had been drawn down. I had stepped back into a darkened doorway, intrigued to see if anyone might stumble upon the old hag. I had waited and waited. I had heard distant footsteps but saw no one. How could this be? Where were the patrolling police constables? Perhaps they were fearful of the gloomy streets? Perhaps they were determined to avoid the unruly residents. But why? There was no one about. I then heard a female cackle. It had grown increasingly louder. A gin-sodden, unkempt woman lurched around the corner, towing along a drunken man. They had staggered past me and paused beside the pile of rags. My heart had quickened. The woman wavered momentarily, nudged the old hag with the tip of her boot and had then thrown back her head and laughed mockingly. Uninterested, the man had jerked the woman away and, pushing her towards a darkened, dingy alleyway, had begun to unbutton his trousers. I was astonished. If I had indeed been the unseen murderer of the old hag, I had just seen two loathsome creatures stumble upon her dead body and then wantonly disregard her in favour of carnal pleasures. What depths of callousness had these people sunk to? This incident had clearly shown me that any person, hell bent on murder, could undoubtedly elude detection in Whitechapel. I had been excited by the experience and decided to celebrate. I had visited my boys brothel, where I had wallowed in the delights of their warm bodies, whilst thinking of the old hag lying cold in the streets. Dead, perhaps.

When Sir Robert Peel had established the London Metropolitan Police Force in 1829 to curb rampant crime, he must have had districts like Whitechapel in mind. Similar to Spitalfields, vast areas of London were inhabited by criminals. Murder and burglary were commonplace; a citizen's only defence being a cudgel or a pair of pistols.

The primary object of an efficient police is the prevention of crime. The next is that of detection and punishment of offenders if crime is committed. To these ends all the efforts of the police must be directed.

Sir Richard Mayne
(1796 – 1869)

From its headquarters in Whitehall Place and consisting of twenty local uniformed divisions, the authority of the London Metropolitan Police had primarily extended over a radius of seven miles. Several attempts had been made by the larger Metropolitan Police to absorb the smaller City of London Police Force but it had always met with failure, leaving the latter independent. The Criminal Investigation Department, C.I.D, had been created in 1844, whilst another police division, J Division, Bethnal Green, had been added in 1886. At the time, there were just over thirteen hundred police constables on the streets of London to supervise a city population of five million. That had been one police constable for about every three thousand, eight hundred people. In a military engagement those odds would had been completely unacceptable. Now I had known why I had not seen a police constable that night. There were not enough of them to go around.

My elder brother's legal practice had been situated on the south coast of England, in the county where we had both been born, and where I had attended college. Almost opposite the coastal town, across a narrow strip of sea, was the island where the dear departed husband of our sombre queen had finally been laid to rest. Returning to the region where I had been raised and first educated had not been a happy experience for me. I had found it tedious to work with antiquated colleagues whose beliefs were consistent with those of our archaic monarch. Although I had retained my position at the boy's boarding school, thereby earning another income, I had nonetheless missed the genial company of my cousin and, of course, the shameless delights of Spitalfields. A fact that would have immensely displeased my brother had he known. Under his administrative wing, my insufferable daily duties had hardly extended beyond those of an office clerk. I became so inundated with legal documents that one could have been forgiven for thinking that the entire population of the country had been attending court at precisely the same time.

I had sometimes accompanied my brother to court only to endure his monotone tongue when he had presented a case. I had found his court presentations pretentious and dull. At times, his deliberate, ponderous pauses between lines of speech would be so long that court officials thought he had suffered a lapse of memory. The skill of persuasion in court had always been to start slowly, build methodically, strike a crescendo and then go for the jugular, so to speak. Not to bore magistrates and court officials to death as my brother consistently had. Why he had previously praised my oratory skills and then persisted with his own wretched performance mystified me then as it still does today. However, a change of government had loomed upon the horizon. A change for the worst, unfortunately.

A committed Anglican, Prime Minister Gladstone had tried to convince his party and Parliament to accept Irish Home Rule. The proposal spilt his party and Parliament soon rejected the measure. Defeated in the ensuing general election, Gladstone had resigned to be succeeded by the Marquis of Salisbury, who had appointed the conservative leader of the House of Commons, Lord Randolph Churchill, as Chancellor of the Exchequer and Mr. Henry Matthews as Home Secretary. Married to the beautiful American, Jennie Jerome, Lord Randolph Churchill, a gifted, skilful orator, had been perceived by his party as a future prime minister. Alas, this was not to be. In a dispute over military expenditure, he had resigned at the end of the year, thereby committing political suicide. Mr. Henry Matthews, whose authority commanded the newly appointed London Metropolitan Police Commissioner Sir Charles Warren, was able to enjoy a somewhat more fortuitous career.

Equally fortuitous for me had been my second probationary year under my brother. Due to my resolute persistence, he had ultimately conceded that the major role of a 'special pleader' was not to simply prepare lengthy documents, but was to submit legal rulings on any criminal or civil statements presented to him by the courts. As a result, my brother had begrudgingly released me from my clerical bondage, granting me the mantle of 'special pleader', which allowed me to alternate between the three Assizes on the Western Circuit. Although I had been rather flattered to be asked my opinion on the legal ambiguities involving numerous civil cases, I had nonetheless frequently wondered what the cut and thrust atmosphere of the New Law Courts of London must have been like compared to the repetitive rituals of county courts.

After much deliberation, I had decided that upon completing my second probationary year, I would throw all caution to the wind and return to the Inner Temple in an attempt to pursue a career as a barrister. I had spoken with Mr. V. who whole-heartedly supported my decision, unlike my brother who stubbornly opposed it. His opinions had no longer mattered to me. The die had been cast. I had longed for excitement. I needed my beloved cricket and, of course, the sensual delights offered by Spitalfields.

One month before her Golden Jubilee, our illustrious monarch had visited the East End of London, complaining afterwards to Prime Minister Salisbury that she had heard a horrid noise, quite new to her ears, in fact. Lining the squalid streets, jobless and starving people had jeered and booed her. Much grieved to hear her complaint, Salisbury had explained that the booing almost certainly came from either the socialists or the Irish. Men who would stop at nothing to express their anger. What Salisbury had chosen to ignore was that the majority of the protesters who had voiced their grievances had been destitute women and children. He had also failed to recognise that the entire East End of London was a smouldering tinderbox waiting to explode.

Four months later, after almost continuous daily demonstrations, ten thousand ragged men and women had marched out of the East End of London, intent on holding a protest in Trafalgar Square against British brutality in Ireland. Salisbury had earlier ordered the Commissioner of the Metropolitan Police, Sir Charles Warren, to disperse the protestors with the maximum vigour, using all available forces at his disposal.

A former military man, Warren had deliberately allowed the peaceful protesters to enter Trafalgar Square, whereupon they had immediately found themselves penned in by railings which had been erected some weeks earlier. From that point onwards, the marchers had been doomed. Supported by two squadrons of Life Guards with drawn swords, two thousand police, wielding their truncheons, had charged the protestors, striking indiscriminately in all directions. Struck about the face and head, men and women had fallen to the ground, blood flowing freely from their wounds. Many were so badly beaten they had required hospital treatment. Impatient to protect the empire, an intolerant government had bludgeoned its own people into submission. Two of the organisers, Johns Burns and Robert Cunninghame-Graham, had been quickly arrested and unjustly imprisoned for six weeks. Later referred to as 'Bloody Sunday', the populace of the East End and the radical newspapers repeatedly held Warren responsible for the casualties. A public hounding that would not abate until his resignation a year later.

I had begun the New Year with a celebratory visit to Spitalfields, only to meet that 'shilling whore' and endure the scornful disgrace, which drove me from the district. Shortly afterwards, my bouts of melancholy had severely increased, prompting the thought of suicide. I had known that the only reason for such a notion had been the intense awareness of the existence of that loathsome woman. Oh, if I had only found the courage myself. I would have returned to Spitalfields, sought her out and flayed her alive. I would have heartily punished her for punishing me.

It had been during such a moment of anguish that I had foolishly broken my own cardinal rule. I had previously noticed him but had retained a discreet distance so as not to invite any undue attention, especially with Mrs. S. continually lurking throughout the boarding school, ready to pounce on any indiscretion. Plagued by *persistent nightmares of that 'shilling whore', I had invited him to my room on the pretext of additional tuition. Although his pleasant company had to some extent calmed my anxieties, I had at first refrained from bodily contact, dreading rejection. But within a short time I had soon overcome that fear.*

As I concluded my two years probationary period under my brother, the Royal Society's Krakatoa Committee had published its five-year study on the aftermath of that historic explosion. In addition to four hundred and ninety-four pages of text, the final report had included countless drawings, graphs and exquisite coloured prints. The entire report had been a masterpiece of determined study, elegantly composed and splendidly collated.

In an unrelated incident, but nevertheless just as historic, a heated exchange had occurred between my brother and myself. Unable to dissuade me from returning to the Inner Temple, he had arrogantly dismissed my decision, saying that I was irrepressible, reckless and addicted to life. Whilst I had not admitted so, his uncanny appraisal of me had indeed been correct. Without his consent or approval, I had returned to the Inner Temple, knowing that if I could somehow regain my former courage, the licentious delights of Spitalfields were now within easy reach.

It had begun as it always begins. Standing before me and looking into my eyes, he had, at first, nervously stroked my hand. I had responded by slipping my hand between his legs and gently caressing his manhood. His member began to stir and harden. The pleasure that he had felt did not, however, entirely conquer his reticence. Thus, I had led his hand to mine and he had begun to stroke me vigorously. Embracing and kissing, we had undressed and slipped between the sheets of my bed. He had suddenly climaxed early, spending between the two of us. I had turned him over and, thrusting forward, entered him. He moaned, stiffened and then relaxed. I continued to thrust back and forth until I had finally spent over his buttocks. Although he was only thirteen, he dutifully responded to my bodily necessities, regularly visiting my room when requested. Yes, the flesh had found nourishment. But had my mind?

Now aged thirty and, putting aside my sporting activities, I had but only one other dominant interest in life. The pursuit of deviant pleasures. Love? Yes, I had most certainly experienced that emotion. And it had distressed me enormously to know that since his tragic death I had been utterly alone without him. All and sundry had rejected me and I had now become a solitary gentleman, content only when I could inflict bodily pain on others and enjoy their suffering. I had by now recognised the terrible inescapable truth. I had been gradually losing my mind. I was possibly going mad.

Unlike my ignominious flight from Spitalfieds, my mother had once more shown a modicum of suicidal courage, attempting to join my father in the hereafter by swallowing laudanum. Drawing upon two other opinions, our family doctor had diagnosed acute melancholy and delusional tendencies as the cause of her mental disorder. Deemed to be a danger to herself, our doctor had no alternative but to certify her as insane.

It had been a glorious English summer's day, but an extremely forlorn one for me. Although I had been somewhat out of favour with my brother, I had nonetheless accompanied him, escorting our mother to an insane asylum in the East End of London. I now consider it rather ironic that she should have been incarcerated near the very district that I yearned to visit and which would also feature notably in my eventual demise.

Grim Reaper

Grim Reaper

Around the same time that my mother had been incarcerated in the insane asylum, a group of East London women had fought their employers for better working conditions and had won.

In order to increase production of its successful Lucifer match, Bryant & May had added an additional storey to its factory, thereby significantly reducing the ventilation inside the building. Phosphorus fumes pervaded the premises and many of the female workers developed a bone deformity known as 'phossy jaw'. As it had been compulsory to consume all meals on the premises, phosphorus had also been ingested. In an attempt to evade adverse publicity, the proprietors had the rotting teeth of any worker extracted by the duty foreman, who immediately pressed them back to work, despite blood seeping from their mouths. The hours had been intolerable and the wages abysmal.

Supported by the socialist activist, Annie Besant, the women of Bryant & May had formed a potent matchmakers union and had withdrawn its membership of fourteen hundred workers from the factory. Within three weeks the proprietors had conceded to most of their demands: shorter hours, better wages and improved working conditions. It had been a major triumph for the deprived women. A fact that must have caused Prime Minister Salisbury some anxiety and perhaps had prompted him to wonder how else might these exasperated people demonstrate their anger?

Punch Magazine – 5 August 1888

GHOULISH PERFORMANCE

Thomas Russell Sullivan's theatrical adaptation of Robert Louis Stevenson's Strange Case of Dr. Jekyll and Mr. Hyde premiered last night at the Lyceum-theatre in the Strand. I must defer my criticism of this strange story until I have quite recovered from the awful jumpy, creepy, crawly effect produced on me by Mr. Richard Mansfield's extraordinary performance as both the misguided Dr. Henry Jekyll and the brutish Mr. Edward Hyde. It is a ghastly extravaganza, with a marvellous 'transformation scene'.

In the company of my cousin, I had sat through the first night of this theatrical melodrama. I had been utterly spellbound by the portrayal of the physical duality of Dr. Jekyll, which to some degree had reflected my own sinful character. Similar to the staid Henry Jekyll, I had been looked upon as a gentleman, whilst in truth I had behaved more like the immoral Edward Hyde. I had indeed been disappointed that Jekyll, having once swallowed his mixed potion and freed the dormant Hyde, had finally sought to suppress such a vicarious individual. At some stage during the performance an intoxicating thought had taken hold of me. Might a person murder another but remember nothing of the crime? Just as Henry Jekyll had been unable to do so, after he had committed murder as Edward Hyde. Two entirely different minds dwelling within a single brain, so to speak. Unaware of each other's existence, one would not present a threat to the other. In fact, their entire ignorance of one another would be the ultimate protection against detection. Perhaps in the future our medical fraternity might acknowledge such a cerebral possibility and grant it a clinical expression.

The goal of all life is death.

Sigmund Freud
(1856 – 1939)

Later that night, in a dream, I had returned to Spitalfields. In the squalid darkened narrow street, lit by a single overhead gas lamp, I had risen from the body of the old toothless hag, bloodied knife in my hand. The essence of life seeped from her slashed throat, whilst her intestines slowly oozed from her slit stomach. I had gazed down at my ghastly handiwork, knowing that, similar to Edward Hyde, I had embraced the loneliness of evil. I was Lucifer, the angel cast out of Heaven. I had become Death.

From behind me, I had heard a cackle. I had spun on my heel and had once more looked upon the scoffing face of that 'shilling whore'. She had sneered at me, raised her skirt and exposed her womanhood, "Come on, dearie, prove you're a man." Exploding with rage, I had instantly sprung forward, pushing her back through a gloomy archway and throwing her to the ground. I leapt upon her, straddled her, raised my knife and stabbed her repeatedly, but to no avail. Her taunting laughter had persisted, abating only when I had suddenly awoke. Was there to be no escape from this loathsome bitch? Was I eternally damned? And if so, what might be my salvation? My own death, perhaps? I had shuddered at the thought and, for the first time in my life, I had openly wept.

Star Newspaper – 7 August 1888

A WHITECHAPEL HORROR

A woman, now lying unidentified at the mortuary in Whitechapel, was ferociously murdered, between two and four o'clock this morning, on the landing of a stone staircase in George-yard buildings, George-yard, Whitechapel.

George-yard buildings are tenements occupied by the poor labouring class. A lodger says the body was not on the stone landing when he returned home about two o'clock. Another lodger going early to his work found the body. The woman had been stabbed in 39 places. No weapon was found near her, and her murderer has left no trace. She is of middle age and height, has black hair and a large round face, and apparently belonged to the 'unfortunate' class.

My heart had skipped a beat when I had read the newspaper article. I had barely been able to breathe. Might the dead woman have been that same creature who had incessantly haunted me? Had another person done what I had been unable to do in a dream? The article had said that the slain woman had belonged to the 'unfortunate' class. A prudish euphemism for 'whore', which at least had been an honest description of the 'shilling bitch' I had desired to see dead. Maybe the harsher realities of life were too much for the delicate sensibilities of our society, which required palatable words in order to discuss unsavoury issues. I have since hoped that the next generation will not distort words as we have done, which utterly corrupts language and mollycoddles the truth, however unpleasant the subject might be.

I had soon learnt that palatable words could not hide the fact that, since the second month of this year, brutal attacks on East London women had progressively increased, culminating with the George Yard murder. Annie Millwood had been the first victim. A resident of a lodging house at 8 White's Row, Spitalfields, she had been viciously attacked by an unknown man, who had inflicted several knife wounds to her lower torso and legs. Although she had recovered from her injuries, she had collapsed five weeks later, dying apparently of natural causes.

The next victim had been Ada Wilson, 19 Maidman's Street, Mile End. About to retire for the night, she had opened the front door of

White's-row, Spitalfields 1888

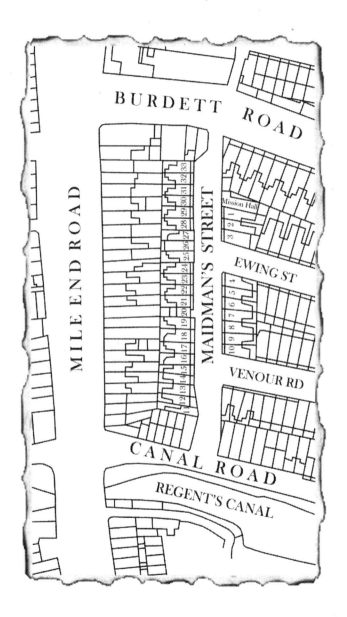

Maidman's-street, Mile-end 1888

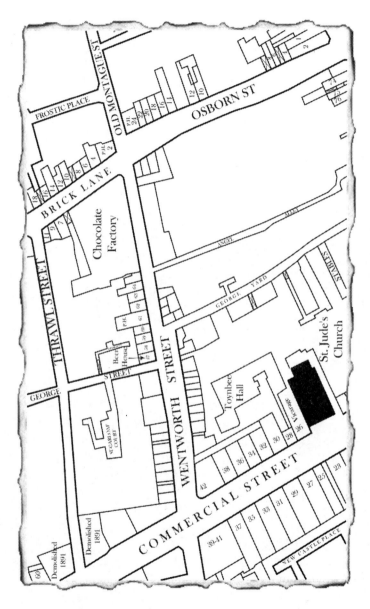

Brick-lane & Wentworth-street, Spitalfields 1888

her house to an unfamiliar man and had been stabbed twice in the throat. Given little or no chance of survival, Ada Wilson had nonetheless made a full recovery and had been released from hospital five weeks later.

The same could not be said of the third victim, Emma Smith. She had lodged at 18 George Street, Spitalfields, and had been cruelly attacked by three men directly outside the chocolate factory at the corner of Brick Lane and Wentworth Street, Spitalfields. Taken to the London Hospital, where it had been discovered that a blunt object had been thrust into her womanhood, she had died from peritonitis the next day.

I had been disappointed to learn a few days later that the woman found murdered in George Yard Buildings had not been the bitch I had so desperately wanted dead, but merely another whore named Martha Turner or Tabram. Having parted company with her friend, Mary Ann Connolly, outside the White Hart public house, Whitechapel High Street, Martha had taken a soldier along George Yard to George Yard Buildings whilst Mary had led another into Angel Alley, running parallel with George Yard. The northerly direction taken by both women had indicated that they may well have intended to meet again in Wentworth Street, which could easily be reached from both George Yard and Angel Alley.

Having entered George Yard Buildings with John Reeves, the dockside labourer who had first stumbled across Martha's body, Police Constable Thomas Barrett had noticed that her skirt had been suitably raised to suggest that intimacy had been intended or had taken place at about the time she was murdered. Upon his arrival, Dr. Timothy Killeen had pronounced life extinct, concluding that a right-handed person, wielding a dagger or a bayonet, had ferociously stabbed Martha thirty-nine times. Most of the wounds had been inflicted to the chest with one to the abdominal region. There had been no apparent signs of a struggle.

Since Martha had last been seen in the company of a soldier, and because Constable Barrett had happened upon another one loitering in Wentworth Street some thirty minutes before she had actually been murdered, the police had assumed the killer to be a soldier. Therefore, arrangements were made for Constable Barrett and Mary Ann Connolly to independently visit the Tower of London

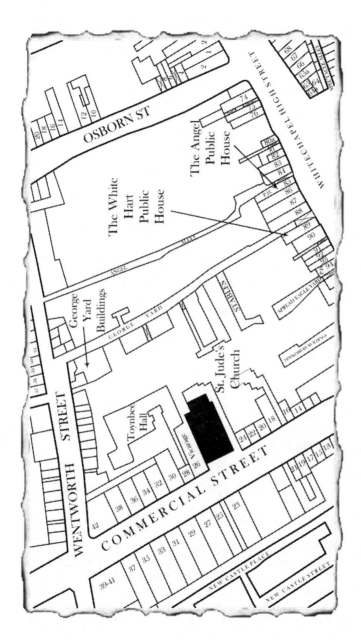

George-yard buildings, George-yard, Spitalfields 1888

in the hope that they could identify the soldiers. Constable Barrett had picked out one soldier, admitted a mistake, and then had chosen another, Private John Leary. When a fellow soldier, Private Law, had provided Leary with an alibi, the police had immediately eliminated Leary from their inquiries.

Having failed to appear at the first identification parade held at the Tower of London, Mary Ann Connolly had been hauled before another parade, but had failed to pick out anyone. She had then revealed that the two suspect soldiers sought by the police had been Coldstream Guards and not Grenadier Guards that had been paraded before her. The police had then promptly arranged another parade, this time at the Wellington Barracks, home of the Coldstream Guards.

On the day of my thirty-first birthday, Mary Ann Connolly had attended the second parade and picked out two soldiers, stating that one had been the corporal who had accompanied her along Angel Alley and the other being the private who had gone into George Yard with Martha. Protesting his innocence, Corporal George had been able to prove that he had been at home with his wife on the night of the murder, whilst Private Skipper, also protesting his innocence, had actually never left the barracks that evening. Entirely discouraged by the incompetence of Mary Ann Connolly, the police had discarded her statement and relegated Martha Tabram's death to a lengthening list of unsolved crimes.

It had been quite apparent to me, if not to the police, that the spiritual embodiment of Edward Hyde was loose in Spitalfields and had now begun to attack and murder women, particularly whores. I had prayed that whosoever he might be, he might inadvertently rid me of the vile creature that continually haunted me. Daring to hope that fate may have furnished a person that could deliver me from damnation, I had dined with my cousin that evening.

Although I had no desire to celebrate my thirty-first birthday, the congenial company of my cousin had at least eased the misery of the past few months. However, during the course of our meal, he had remarked upon my pallid appearance and that my hands had shook whilst I ate. Although I had been sorely tempted to lay before him my entire shameful life and recent suffering, I had explained away my poor health, informing him that since resuming my role as a barrister I had found it difficult to acquire legal briefs and feared that I might be destined for failure. He had empathised with me, saying that he was considering emigrating to Australia to improve his lot and that if my life was not to be fulfilled in England then I might like to think about joining him abroad. His words had shone through my gloom like a beacon. But alas I had not been able to contemplate his offer. My mind had not entirely been my own. It had been dominated by a solitary thought. Eternal release from that 'shilling whore'.

Whilst my boarding school boy had offered sensual distraction from mental torment, I had however become increasingly irritated by him. His physical stimulus had proven to be negligible and he had recently shown an abnormal tendency to submissively swoon over me whenever we met. In fact, he had gradually become infatuated with me. Why he, or anyone else, should interpret a simple bodily function as a sublime act of love had been an irrational emotion that I had not encountered before. Retreating to my beloved cricket, I had foolishly shrunk from the problem, not knowing how or when I might remedy his obsession.

TELEGRAPHIC ADDRESS, "WINTERINE", LONDON, TELEPHONE No. 536
L.&P. WALTER & SON
Manufacturers of
CLOTHING FOR   11,12, & 13 Church-street
EXPORTATION   Spitalfields
                                               LONDON 31/ Aug
                                                         1888

The Secty of State for
        The Home Dpt

Sir/
    We beg to enclose a newspaper report of this most recent fearful murder & to say that such is the state of affairs in this district that we are put to the necessity of having a night watchman to protect our premises. The only way in our humble opinion to tackle this matter is to offer at once a reward.

                                          Yours Very obediently,
                                          L &P Walter & Son.

Star newspaper report enclosed.

The Star Newspaper – 31 August 1888

HORRIBLE MURDER IN
WHITECHAPEL

Scarcely has the horror and sensation caused by the murder of Martha Tabram had time to abate, than another discovery is made, which; for sheer brutality, is even more shocking, and will no doubt create a greater sensation in the district than its predecessor. The affair, up to the present, is shrouded in mystery, and the police have procured no evidence from which to trace the perpetrator of the horrible deed.

The facts are that as Police Constable John Neil was walking down Buck's-row, Whitechapel, about a quarter to four this morning, he found a woman, between thirty-five and forty years of age, lying at the side of the street with her throat cut open from ear to ear. The wound was about two inches wide and blood was flowing profusely. In fact, she was lying in a pool of her own blood.

The body was immediately conveyed to the Whitechapel Workhouse Infirmary Mortuary, where it was found that, besides the wound in the throat, the lower part of her person had been completely ripped open. The wound extended nearly to her breasts, and must have been effected with a dagger or a long sharp knife.

The corpse of the woman presents a ghastly sight. The victim is 5ft. 2in. in height. The hands are bruised and show evidence of having engaged in a severe struggle. There is the impression of a ring having been worn on one finger, but nothing to indicate that it had been wrenched from her. Some of her front teeth have been knocked out and her face is bruised on both cheeks and very much discoloured.

The deceased had worn a rough brown ulster with large buttons in the front. Her clothes had been torn and cut up in several places, leaving evidence of the ferocity with which the murder was committed. She has yet to be identified.

My entire body had trembled with excitement as I had read the newspaper article. I had instantly thought of the unusual sensation that I had experienced after the destruction of Krakatoa. Yes, that huge, explosive eruption had indeed been an ominous forecast for something equally as shocking. I now knew what and where. The

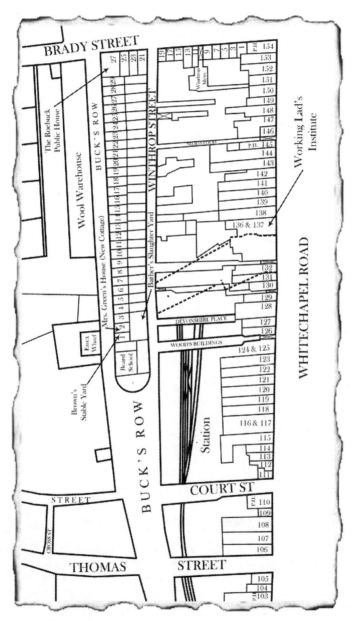

Buck's-row, Whitechapel 1888

audacity of the murderer had to be applauded. But had he rid me of that odious bitch?

The Times Newspaper – 3 September 1888

THE
WHITECHAPEL
MURDERS

Up until last night the police had obtained no clue to the perpetrator of the two murders which have recently taken place in Whitechapel. There is, it must be acknowledged, no ground for blaming the officers in charge, should they fail to solve the mystery surrounding the crimes.

The murder of Mary Ann Nichols in Buck's-row is so similar to the murder of Martha Tabram that the police are now forced to admit that the two crimes are probably the work of the same individual, especially since both murders were committed within a short distance of each other. Both women were of the 'unfortunate' class, each so desperately poor, that robbery has been eliminated as a possible motive for the murders.

It is now understood that the police investigation into the George-yard mystery will now proceed hand-in-hand with that of the Buck's-row murder.

On Saturday afternoon, Mr. Wynne E. Baxter, a coroner for the South-Eastern Division of Middlesex, opened his enquiry at the Working Lad's Institute, Whitechapel-road, into the death of Mary Ann Nichols. Inspectors Abberline, Helson, and Sergeants Enright and Godley attended on behalf of the Criminal Investigation Department.

Of course, when I had read the second newspaper article I had realised that, although the murdered woman's name had been Mary, she had, in fact, been much older than the bitch I yearned to see dead. I had not, as I might have recently done, slipped into despair. On the contrary, I had been somewhat heartened by this second murder. I had inexplicably sensed that, given time, I would ultimately obtain freedom from my accursed nightmares.

The inquest held at The Working Lad's Institute, Whitechapel Road, had revealed that Police Constable John Neil had not been the first person to stumble across the mutilated body of Mary Ann

Nichols. At about 3. 40 a. m. that morning, a carman, Charles Cross, had been walking to work along the northern side of Buck's Row, when he had noticed what he thought was a tarpaulin lying in front of the darkened gateway to Brown's Stable Yard. Crossing the cobbled street to take a closer look, he had found a woman sprawled upon the ground. Hearing footsteps approaching from behind, Cross had quickly turned around and had met another carman, Robert Paul, also on his way to work. Quite relieved by the arrival of Paul, Cross had showed Paul the body.

The woman had lain on her back, her head towards Brady Street from where both men had come. Her legs were slightly apart and her skirt had been raised. The two men had crouched, touched her hands and face, agreeing that she felt cold. Neither of them detected breathing. Concerned that they might be late for work, they decided to leave the body and report its location to the first policeman that they might encounter. To preserve the modesty of the woman, Cross had pulled down her skirt and walked off with Paul towards White's Row. At the junction of Baker's Row, Hanbury Street and Old Montague Street, Paul and Cross had met and reported their find to Police Constable Jonas Mizen, who, allowing both men to continue their journey to work, had hurriedly strode off towards Buck's Row.

Some twenty-five minutes before Charles Cross had found the body in Buck's Row, Police Constable John Neil had walked along the dingy street, seeing nothing suspicious. At 3. 45 a. m., seconds after Cross and Paul had left to find a policeman, Neil had again entered Buck's Row from Brady Street and had discovered the woman himself. Illuminating the body with his lantern, he saw that the throat of the woman had been cut and that blood still flowed from the wound. Rapidly flashing his lantern, Neil had attracted the attention of Police Constable John Thain, who was immediately dispatched by Neil to fetch a police doctor. A few minutes later, Constable Mizen arrived and, in a similar fashion to Thain, was dispatched by Neil to seek assistance from Bethnal Green Police Station and to return with a handcart ambulance.

Once more alone, Neil had gingerly sought for any clues that may have indicated what had actually taken place. The gates to Brown's Stable Yard were closed and firmly locked. He examined the darkened cobbled street for cartwheel indentations, finding nothing. Directly opposite from where the body lay, Neil had rung the doorbell of Essex Wharf. Popping his head out of a first-floor window, the manager, Walter Purkiss, had told Neil that he and his wife had not seen or heard anything. In fact, they had found it an unusually quiet night.

Alerted to the murder, Police Sergeant Kirby arrived to assist Neil and had immediately knocked on the door of New Cottage, 2 Buck's Row, the first terraced house adjoining Brown's Stable Yard. The occupant of the house, Mrs Emma Green, had informed Kirby that she and her family of two daughters and a son had heard nothing, even though the body lay to the side of her ground-floor street window. At 4 a. m., having been awaken by Constable Thain, Dr. Rees Llewellyn arrived. He made a quick examination of the woman, pronounced life extinct, placing the earliest time of her death at about 3. 30 a. m. Thus the murderer had struck fifteen minutes after Constable Neil had seen nothing suspicious in the gloomy street and ten minutes before Charles Cross had stumbled upon the body. An interval of twenty-five minutes. Plenty of time to murder a drunken whore, I had thought.

Behind Brown's Stable Yard had stood Barber's Slaughter Yard in Winthrop Street. Having been immediately informed of the murder by Constable Thain on his way to fetch Dr. Llewellyn, slaughtermen Henry Tomkins, James Mumford and Charles Britton had strolled around the corner into Buck's Row, joining a group of morbid onlookers, staring at the body. Although Thain would later deny having told the three men of the murder, the slaughtermen were to be painstakingly questioned by the police but in due course cleared of any involvement in the crime.

Further along Winthrop Street, past Barber's Slaughter Yard and behind the Working Lad's Institute, a watchman, Patrick Mulshaw, had been on night duty, guarding some sewage works. Although he had earlier noticed Constable Neil and another constable on patrol, he had not seen anyone else until an unknown man had hurriedly walked past him, telling him that somebody had been murdered down the street. Mulshaw had quickly left the sewage works, dashed along Winthrop Street, past Barber's Slaughter Yard and joined the small group of onlookers in Buck's Row. Later, Mulshaw would be unable to recall the identity of the mysterious man who had informed him of the murder.

Assisted by Constable Mizen, Constable Thain had lifted the dead woman onto the handcart ambulance, discovering that the back of her clothes were soaked, having absorbed most of her blood. This had explained why Dr. Llewellyn had detected only a little blood on the ground. Enough to fill two wineglasses, or half a pint at the most. Leaving Thain on guard in Buck's Row and pushing the handcart ambulance, Neil, Mizen and Kirby had taken the body to the Workhouse Infirmary Mortuary, Eagle Place, Old Montague Street. Finding the mortuary locked, the three officers had parked the ambulance in the yard and had then inexplicably departed, leaving the body alone. Perhaps they went in search of the key, or to locate the mortuary keeper, or both?

Meanwhile, having hurried from Hackney Road, Inspector John Spratling had arrived at Buck's Row whilst the body was still being conveyed to the mortuary. Shown by Constable Thain the spot where the body had lain, Spratling saw that Mrs Green's son had washed most of the blood away, although traces still remained between the cobble stones. Aware that he could accomplish no more in Buck's Row, Spratling strode off to the mortuary, taking Constable Thain with him. Upon his arrival at the mortuary yard he had found the mortuary still locked and, to his complete horror, the ambulance containing the body unattended. He had immediately dispatched Thain to find the mortuary keeper and begun writing down a description of dead woman as she lay in the ambulance.

At about 5. 15 a. m., Constable Thain returned with the mortuary keeper, Robert Mann, and together they had lifted the body from the ambulance and carried it into the mortuary, placing it upon a table. Continuing with his notes, Spratling had raised the skirt of the dead woman and instantly recoiled, having discovered that her abdomen had been ripped open, exposing her intestines. Thain had once again been hurriedly dispatched to fetch Dr. Llewellyn and escort him back to the mortuary.

Hastily arriving at the mortuary, Dr. Llewellyn began his second examination of the body, later remarking that he had seen many terrible cases but never such a brutal affair as this.

On the right side side of the face was a recent and strongly marked bruise, which was scarcely perceptible when I fist saw the body. It might have been caused either by a blow from a fist or by pressure of the thumb. On the left side of the face was a circular bruise, which might have been produced in the same way. A small bruise was on the left side of the neck, and abrasion on the right. All must have been done at the same time. There were two cuts in the throat, one four inches long and the other eight, and both reaching to the vertebrae, which had also been penetrated. The wounds must have been inflicted with a strong-bladed knife, moderately sharp, and used with great violence. It appeared to have been held in the left hand of the person who had used it. There were no injuries about the body until just about the lower part of the abdomen. Two or three inches from the left side was a wound running in a jagged manner. The wound was a very deep one, and the tissues were cut through. There were several incisions running across the abdomen. There were also three or four similar cuts, running downwards, on the right side, all of which had been caused by a knife which had been used violently and downwards. The wounds were sufficient to cause instant death. No part of the viscera was missing. The body was fairly nourished, and there was no smell of alcohol in the stomach. Although no blood was found on the front of the woman's clothes, the back of them was saturated with blood. The murder might have occupied four or five minutes. It could have been committed by one man so far as the wounds are concerned

At 6. 30 a. m. and despite police instructions to the contrary, Robert Mann and James Hatfield had indifferently stripped the body, cutting and tearing away the clothes. After washing the body, both men had unceremoniously dumped the clothes in the mortuary yard. Returning to the mortuary, Inspector Sprartling had petulantly examined the discarded clothes and noticed that the petticoats bore the stencil stamp of the Lambeth Workhouse.

News of the crime had started to spread quickly throughout Whitechapel, resulting in women coming forward to identify the body. It soon transpired that a woman, resembling the deceased, had been living in a common lodging house at 18 Thrawl Street. The police had promptly called upon the house and subsequently escorted an occupant, Mrs. Ellen Holland, to the mortuary, who mournfully identified the body as a woman known to her as 'Polly'.

Although earlier, the matron of the Lambeth Workhouse had failed to recognise the body, it had been an inmate of the workhouse, Mary Ann Monk, who had ultimately identified the deceased as Mary Ann Nichols at 7. 30 p. m. that evening.

Undoubtedly coincidental, it had been nonetheless bizarre that Mary Ann Connolly, Mary Ann Monk and Mary Ann Nichols had possessed the same Christian names. It seemed to me that Mary was indeed a common name in Whitechapel. Influenced by the name of our Virgin Mary, no doubt?

Apart from the murderer, Ellen Holland had been the last person to see Mary Ann Nichols alive. At about 2. 30 a. m. that morning, Mrs. Holland had bumped into her at the corner of Osborn Street and Whitechapel Road and was told by Mary that she had drunk all her pennies at the Frying Pan public house and was now out and about, endeavouring to earn her doss-house bed money. A kindly soul, Ellen had implored Mary to return home with her, but Mary had snubbed her good-willed gesture. Confident that she would raise her bed money, Mary had drunkenly lurched off along the Whitechapel Road in the direction of Buck's Row. Just over an hour later her dead and mutilated body had been found. It was barely the fifth day after her forty-third birthday.

I could scarcely believe the inept performance of our police, the medical inconsistencies offered by seemingly astute doctors and the fabrications reported as facts by the press. Mary Ann Nichols had not been found laying in a pool of her own blood, nor had her clothes been savagely torn and cut up in several places, leaving evidence of the ferocity with which the murder had been committed. She had, in fact, succumbed to death quietly, without a struggle. Her clothes had absorbed most of her blood and the various inflicted cuts had been made to her throat and abdomen only.

Dr. Killeen had believed that a right-handed person had killed Martha Tabram, whilst Dr. Llewellyn had thought that a left-handed man had murdered Mary Ann Nichols. It was, however, utterly conceivable that two entirely different men had committed two separate murders. One left-handed, the other right-handed. But perhaps the doctors had been right. Maybe the murderer was ambidextrous? There was, of course, another startling and chilling possibility. Perhaps two men, working in unison, one right-handed, the other left-handed, had killed both women? Or perhaps one of the doctors had indeed been wrong, meaning that one man may have murdered both women.

Mary Ann Nichols had been drinking heavily that night and was undeniably drunk when Mrs. Ellen Holland last saw her alive. When swallowed, any liquid, including alcohol, goes straight to the stomach, where it is digested. However, alcohol releases an odour that does linger for a considerable length of time, especially in a confined space such as the stomach. Unless the stomach of Mary Ann Nichols had been punctured, which would have released the odour, thus permeating the clothes, the smell of alcohol would have persisted in her stomach for some hours after death. Why Dr. Llewellyn had felt obligated to report that there had been no smell of alcohol in her stomach had been beyond me. Unless, of course, he wanted to doggedly express his opinion that Mary Ann Nichols had not been intoxicated at the time of her death. If so, why?

Dr. Llewellyn should not be censured for having failed to notice the awful wounds inflicted upon the abdomen of Mary Ann Nichols when he had first examined her in Buck's Row. Our pious society scarcely advocates the raising of a woman's skirt in public, does it? What is indefensible is that, having satisfied himself of the cause of death; the cuts to the throat, he had failed to accompany the body to the mortuary, where he would have had ample time to determine if other injuries had been inflicted. He had, of course, finally observed the cuts made to the abdomen, but only after Inspector Spratling had discovered the injuries and had sent for him, requesting his presence for a second time.

The investigative initiative shown by Constable Neil after he had found the body had been admirable. However, his initiative seems to have deserted him in the mortuary yard, where the ambulance containing the body had been left unattended. Perhaps Sergeant Kirby had taken charge, thus overruling him? The action taken by Constable Mizen, upon being informed of the body in Buck's Row by Charles Cross and Robert Paul, had been inexcusable. He had, in fact, taken their story at face value, allowing them to continue their journey to work. It had never occurred to Mizen that perhaps Cross or Paul, or both, might have murdered the woman and were dutifully reporting the incident to clear themselves of suspicion.

When Charles Cross had pulled down the skirt of Mary Ann Nichols, had it been to preserve her honour or had it been to conceal the dreadful wounds he might have just inflicted upon her abdomen? Had Robert Paul actually stumbled upon Charles Cross with his victim? It had been dark. If Robert Paul had been unable to see the blood, flowing from a cut throat, then equally he would not have seen the bloody hands of Charles Cross. Pure conjecture, I know, but due to the feeble reaction of Constable Mizen, Charles Cross had been permitted to freely pass, perhaps to gain refuge, conceal his weapon, and clean himself, before offering himself to the police again as an untainted, innocent witness.

Although Constable Thain later denied having told the three men at Barber's Slaughter Yard that a murder had just taken place in Buck's Row, the probable route or routes taken by him to fetch Dr. Llewellyn suggests he had.

Having been instructed by Constable Neil to fetch Dr. Llewellyn, whose surgery had been at 152 Whitechapel Road, Constable Thain had dashed around the Board School, corner of Buck's Row, and entered Winthrop Street, intent on going down a dingy alleyway, Woods Buildings, which led directly into Whitechapel Road. Almost opposite Woods Building, he had paused at Barber's Slaughter Yard to retrieve his recently deposited uniform cape and had hurrledly told the slaughtermen of the murder.

Having retrieved his cape, Thain dashed from the yard, darted across Winthrop Street and entered Woods Buildings, hurrying towards Whitechapel Road. Emerging from the dingy alleyway into Whitechapel Road, he would have immediately turned left, about one hundred and forty-five yards away from Dr. Llewellyn's surgery. It is entirely possible that he had not taken this route, but continued right along Winthrop Street, passing the night watchman, Patrick Mulshaw, who perhaps had been napping at the time. Turning right into Brady Street and then right again into Whitechapel Road, he would have been merely three doors away from Dr. Llewellyn's surgery.

Whichever of the two routes Constable Thain had taken, he had undoubtedly used the moment, while retrieving his cape, to tell the slaughtermen of the murder in Buck's Row. Why Thain's cape had been deposited at Barber's Slaughter Yard that night, and why he had denied having spoken to the slaughtermen, must remain a mystery. Perhaps he had feared chastisement by his superiors for having associated with three possible murder suspects?

The man of the hour had undoubtedly been Inspector John Spratling. Despite the awful disregard for police procedure by the mortuary keeper Robert Mann and his assistant James Hatfield, Inspector Spratling had diligently obtained the evidence that had led to the identification of Mary Ann Nichols within less than twenty-four hours. An admirable achievement when you consider the size of the female population of East London. It was this dutiful pursuit of evidence that had also led him to uncover the appalling wounds inflicted upon the abdomen of the body. Something that Dr. Llewellyn should had discovered for himself.

In the absence of genuine clues to the identity of the murderer, police suspicion fell upon the slaughtermen, Henry Tomkins, James Mumford and Charles Britton. It had been an obvious reaction by the police. Noticeably foolish and to no avail.

At 3. 20 a. m. that morning and barely five minutes after he had passed through Buck's Row, Constable Neil had entered Winthrop Street and observed the three men working in Barber's Slaughter Yard. It was, of course, highly improbable but indeed possible that, having secured an alibi from the unsuspecting Neil, one or two of the men had quietly slipped out of the yard, scurried along Wood's Buildings and accosted Mary Ann Nichols in Whitechapel Road. Ushering her back through Wood's Buildings, the murderer, or murderers, would have taken her to Buck's Row and murdered her before returning to the yard, prior to Charles Cross stumbling upon the body at 3. 40 a. m.

Allowing a few minutes either way, the entire deed could have been accomplished in the available twenty minutes. But its success would have depended on the participation of Mary Ann Nichols herself. It seems improbable that she would have been standing at the end of Wood's Building in Whitechapel Road, waiting to be enticed to her death. Though she had been desperate for her bed money and decidedly drunk, which itself can lend to stubborn behaviour, it would have taken a little time from the onset to gain her confidence. She had last been seen alive at 2. 30 a. m. and had died about 3. 30 a. m., which supports the fact that she had

*been amiably persuaded to enter Buck's Row, where she was then
callously murdered and viciously mutilated.*

5 SEPT. 88

A49301

Whitehall
4th September 1888

Gentlemen,

In reply to your letter of the 31st ultimo, expressing the opinion
that a reward should be offered for the detection of the
Whitechapel murderer, I am directed by the Secretary of State to
inform you that the practice of offering rewards for the discovery
of criminals has for some time been discontinued and that so far as
the circumstances of the present case have at present been
investigated, they do not in his opinion disclose any special ground
for departure from the usual custom.

I am,
Gentlemen,
Your obedient Servant,
E. Ruggles-Brise.

Messrs. Walter & Son
11, 12 & 13 Church-street
Spitalfields.

*Before 1884, it had been the normal practice of the Secretary of
State to offer rewards, sometimes large amounts, for information
leading to the arrest of notorious criminals, especially murderers.
On the 6th May 1882, Lord Cavendish and his under-secretary, Mr.
Burke, were sliced to death with long surgical knives whilst walking
in Phoenix Park, Dublin. Although a reward of £10,000 had been
offered for the identities of the assassins, the offer had proved
ineffective, producing no evidence of any value. Four years later,
a conspiracy to blow up the German Embassy in London and then
to subsequently plant incriminating papers on an innocent person
in order to collect a sizeable reward had been uncovered. The
disclosure of the conspiracy had led the Gladstone government to
question the validity of rewards, ultimately deciding that rewards
produced no practical result whatsoever, beyond that of satisfying
the public's demand for action. Hence, in 1884, the custom of
offering government rewards had been abandoned. However, it
has recently been whispered in aristocratic circles that if a lady*

had been slain in the streets of Whitechapel instead of a common whore, the government would have most definitely offered a reward for the immediate capture of her murderer.

METROPOLITAN POLICE
J Division
5th September 1888

I beg to report that no information to point to the offender of the crime can be obtained. A man named "Pizer alias Leather Apron" has been in the habit of ill-using prostitutes in various parts of the Metropolis for some time past, and careful inquiries have been made to trace him, but without success. There is no evidence against him at present. Enquiries are being continued.

J. Spratling Inspr.
J. Keating Supt.

My bouts of melancholy had increased, with each spell more intense than the last. I had neglected everyone and everything, including my hygiene and health. My body had became rancid, my mind without purpose. I had slipped into a lethargic void of emptiness, knowing that my only chance of deliverance had lain in the hands of an unknown, mysterious murderer. I had scoured the newspapers, greedily consuming each and every speculative morsel on a probable motive for the crimes. It mattered not to me what had driven him to kill, so long as he did it again and released me from my wretched existence.

East London Observer Newspaper – 7 September 1888

WHITECHAPEL
MOURNS

The arrangements were of a very simple character. The time at which the cortège was to start was kept a profound secret, and a rouse was perpetrated in order to get the body out of the mortuary where it has lain since the day of the murder. A pair-horsed closed hearse was observed making its way down Hanbury-street and the crowds, which numbered some thousands, made way for it to go along Old Montague-street, but instead of doing so it passed into Whitechapel-road, and, doubling back, quietly entered the mortuary by the back gate in Chapman's-court.

Not a soul was near other than the undertaker and his men, when the remains, placed in a polished elm coffin, bearing a plate with the inscription 'Mary Ann Nichols, aged 42; died August 31, 1888' were removed to the hearse, and driven to Hanbury-street, there to await the mourners. These were late in arriving, and the two coaches were kept waiting some time in a side street. By the time the news had spread that the body was in the hearse, people flocked round to see the coffin, and examine the plate. In this they were, however, frustrated, for a body of police, under Inspector Ellisdon, of the H Division, surrounded the hearse and prevented their approaching too near.

At last the cortège started towards Ilford, where the last scene in this unfortunate drama took place. The mourners were Mr. Edward Walker, the father of the deceased, and his grandson, together with two of the deceased's children. The procession proceeded along Baker's-row and passed the corner of Buck's-row into the main-road, where police were stationed every few yards. The houses in the district had the blinds drawn, and much sympathy was expressed for the relatives.

The following night, and again in a dream, I had returned to Spitalfields. In a darkened backyard, I had risen from the body of the old toothless hag, bloodied knife in my hand. She had lain upon the ground in a recess between a few steps and a wooden fence. She had looked grotesque. Blood flowed from her slashed throat and her intestines lay above each shoulder. Suddenly from behind, I had felt a hand upon my shoulder. I had quickly turned and once more looked upon the face of the Gorgon, "Come on, dearie, prove you're a man." I had raised my arm and, with a single sweep of my knife, had sliced through her throat to the vertebrae. Her head had instantly wobbled but, to my utter horror, slowly corrected itself, resuming its former position with no outward sign that I had ever cut her throat. She had thrust an accusing finger at me and cackled, "Arthur, no dick, eh?" I swiped at her again, cutting at nothing. She had become a phantom. I sprang forward, went straight through her and pitched to the ground. She eerily turned, stood over me and had raised her skirt, "Come on, dearie, prove you're a man." I awoke, my entire body soaked in perspiration. The horror! Oh, the horror! When might it end?

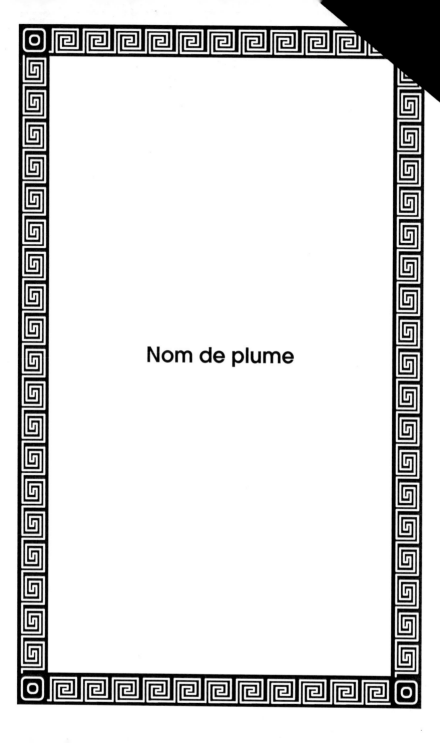

Nom de plume

Nom de plume

The Times Newspaper – 9 September 1888

ANOTHER ATROCITY IN
WHITECHAPEL

A third atrocity, the most diabolical yet and attributed to the same hand that slew the women Martha Tabram and Mary Ann Nichols, murdered another woman yesterday. The mutilated body was found in the back-yard of No. 29 Hanbury-street, Spitalfields, at 6 a. m. by John Davies of that address. The police were called and Dr. Phillips examined the body and pronounced life extinct. A common lodging housekeeper, Timothy Donovan, 35 Dorset-street, Spitalfields, later identified the body as that of Annie Chapman, who, up and until her death had resided at the same address.

The inhabitants of 29 Hanbury-street were seen by the police and their rooms searched. Statements were taken as well as those from the inhabitants of adjoining houses. Mrs Long of 32 Church-street, Bethnal-green, reported to the police that at 5. 30 a. m. she saw the deceased talking with a man outside 29 Hanbury-street. She heard the man say "Will you?" and the deceased answered "Yes." Mrs Long saw only his back and would be unable to recognise him again. He appeared to be a little taller than the deceased and looked like a foreigner. The police are making every possible enquiry to trace the man but up to now without success.

It is thought that Inspector Abberline of the Criminal Investigation Department will take charge of the enquiry along with the Buck's-row murder enquiry which he had earlier advised upon.

Oh, my spirit had soared. My mysterious benefactor had not deserted me. I had felt the yoke of misery begin to lift. I had eagerly bathed and groomed myself. I ate heartily, amazed that he had committed another murder so soon after his last. He had been utterly audacious to the extreme. Scarcely eight days had lapsed between this murder and the previous one. Though I knew his present victim had not been the whore of Babylon that I had desired to see dead, I wanted to believe that he had sensed my plea for help and had indeed acted on my behalf. Might he be a kindred spirit? Was he indeed my other-self? And if this be true, then I alone knew his identity. He was the merciless Edward Hyde.

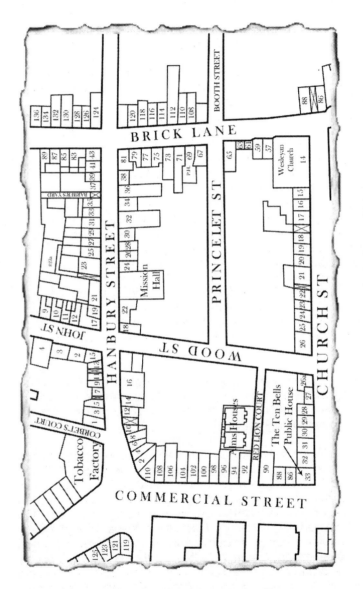

Hanbury-street, Spitalfields 1888

METROPOLITAN POLICE
H Division
10th September 1888

I beg to report that a man named "John Pizer alias Leather Apron" was arrested this morning at his home, 22 Mulberry-street, Commercial-road. A police search was made of his house, where five long-bladed knives were found concealed under his bed. These, along with suspect, were taken to Leman-street Police Station, where suspect is now detained for further questioning.

E. Ellisdon Insp.
T. Arnold Supdt.

Hanbury Street began at Commercial Street, Spitalfields, and had cut through Whitechapel, ending at Baker's Row. It had been here, at the junction with Old Montague Street, that Charles Cross and Robert Paul had told Constable Mizen about finding the body of Mary Ann Nichols in Buck's Row. Close to the main thoroughfare of Commercial Street, number 29 Hanbury Street was on the north side, situated between John Street and Brick Lane. Oddly enough, having had left Constable Mizen in Baker's Row, Robert Paul would have ambled past number 29 on his way to work in Corbet's Court, a dingy side-street just before Commercial Street.

Number 29 was three storeys high, two rooms deep, with eight rooms providing sanctuary for seventeen souls. The house had two street doors, one opening into a Cat's Meat shop; the other, with a sign; 'Mrs. A. Richardson, rough packing-case maker', gave entry to a long dismal, grubby passageway which sliced straight through the house to an equally dingy backyard. Harriet Hardiman ran the Cat's Meat shop, and with her sixteen-year-old son, also slept in it. Attached to the shop, with a clear view of the backyard, was the rear kitchen used by the landlady, Mrs. Amelia Richardson, to cook meals and hold weekly prayer meetings. Amelia also used the cellar for her packing-case business, which could only be entered from the backyard. Along with her fourteen-year-old grandson, Thomas, Amelia had occupied the front room on the first floor above the Cat's Meat shop as well.

Overlooking the backyard, the rear room on the first floor had been occupied by a boot-maker, Mr. Walker, and his retarded

71

adult son, Alfred. Above them on the second floor, cigar makers Mr. and Mrs. Copsey had lived in another rear room, again with a view of the backyard. The adjoining front room was inhabited by a carman, Mr. Thompson, his wife and their adopted daughter, whilst above them on the third floor, in the attic, had lodged another carman, John Davis, his wife and three sons. Finally, a widow, Sarah Cox, had occupied the rear room in the attic, also with an unhindered view of the backyard.

Seen from the street door and situated to the left of the dingy passageway, a rickety communal staircase offered the only way to the six rooms above. Slightly further along, on the right-hand side of the passageway, was the door to the rear kitchen used by Amelia Richardson, whilst immediately ahead was the self-closing door to the backyard. When pushed, this door opened out to the left, revealing a backyard, some five yards by four. Partially paved with flat stones, the yard was overlooked by similar shabby houses, paint peeling from their woodwork like a skin disease.

Three worn stone steps led from the back door down into the gloomy yard. To the left of the steps was a small recess and then a wooden paling fence about five and a half feet high, which ran the entire length of the yard, separating it from that of number 27. Opposite the back door, in the far left-hand corner was Amelia Richardson's woodshed, whilst in the far right-hand corner, a privy. Directly to the right of the self-closing back door and just below the kitchen window was the padlocked cellar. Slightly beyond that, and jutting from the brickwork, was a solitary tap, which had supplied the entire household with water.

Just after midnight on the morning of 8th September, William Stevens had seen Annie Chapman in the grimy communal kitchen of Crossingham's doss-house at 35 Dorset Street. Unwell, she had removed a small battered box of pills from her pocket but the box had split apart in her hands. Picking-up a piece of discarded paper from the kitchen floor near the fireplace, she had wrapped the pills in the piece of paper and then left the kitchen, going to the Britannia public house, corner of Dorset Street and Commercial Street, for a drink. At 1. 45 a. m., she had returned to the kitchen and was seen eating a baked potato by the doss-house deputy manager, Timothy Donovan. Unable to pay Donovan the pennies for her bed, she again left the kitchen, crowing to Donovan that she would before long return with the money. Crossingham's night watchman, John Evans, had seen Annie leave the doss-house, totter along Little Paternoster Row into Brushfield Street and then turn towards Spitalfields Church in the direction of Hanbury Street.

At about 3. 30 a. m., Mr. Thompson had quietly left his room on the second floor of 29 Hanbury Street, passing Amelia Richardson's front room on the first floor. Hearing him descending, Amelia had greeted him through her closed door, whilst he had continued on down to the grubby passageway. Seeing nobody loitering in the passageway, Mr. Thompson had left by the street door and strolled off along Hanbury Street towards his place of work in Brick Lane.

More than an hour later, at 4. 45 a. m., Amelia Richardson's son, John, who lived around the corner in John Street, had entered the house through the street door, looking for uninvited vagrants who occasionally slept rough in the passageway. Easing open the door to the backyard and standing on the steps, John had taken out a table knife and trimmed a piece of leather from a boot that had been hurting him. It had now been getting light. Having been on the step for just over three minutes and noticing nothing suspicious, he had turned away from the backyard door, walked along the passageway, leaving the house and closing the street door behind him.

Forty minutes later, at 5. 25 a. m., Albert Cadosch, who lived next door at number 27, had gone to use the backyard privy and had heard muffled voices, apparently coming from the yard of number 29. The only word he had been able to catch was "No!". Some three minutes later, at 5. 28 a. m., and returning to use the privy once more, he had heard a noise, again coming from the yard of number 29, of someone or something falling against the wooden paling fence. Impatient to use the privy, he had paid no further attention and heard no more noises. He had left for work and, passing Spitalfields Church, had noticed the time was about 5. 32 a. m.

Now daybreak and having just heard the clock of the Black Eagle Brewery chime 5. 30 a. m., Mrs. Elizabeth Long had turned from Brick Lane into Hanbury Street and had hastily walked along the northern side of the street, heading towards her intended destination, Spitalfields Market. Halfway along the street, she had noticed a man, his back towards her, talking with a woman just outside the street door of number 29. Drawing closer to the couple, Elizabeth had heard the man say, "Will you?" to which the woman had replied, "Yes." Hardly giving the couple a second glance, Elizabeth had hurriedly continued her journey to Spitalfields Market.

At 5. 45 a. m., John Davis had risen from his bed in the attic room on the third floor and began to dress for work. Fifteen minutes later, and intent on using the privy in the backyard, Davis had hurried down the stairs to the passageway, noticing that the street door to the house had been left wide open. Undoing his belt and hastily pushing open the door to the backyard, he had suddenly halted, instantly horrified by what he saw. Below him, upon the ground, was the hideously mutilated body of a woman, partially lying in the recess between the stone steps and the wooden paling fence. Quickly turning away, Davis had hurtled along the passageway and, rushing through the open street door, had slid to a halt on the pavement, his belt dangling by his side.

Waiting just outside their place of work at 23a Hanbury Street, James Kent and James Green had seen Davis hurtle out of number 29, holding his belt by his side. Approaching from the opposite direction, Henry Holland had also witnessed Davis' rapid exit from the house. Breathing heavily, Davis called upon the three men to follow him back into the house, which they had. Reaching the end of the passageway, the four men had crowded together in the doorway of the backyard and peered down at the body, aghast. Henry Holland had nervously ventured down the steps, taken a closer look at the woman but had refrained from touching her. Having seen enough, the four men had raced back along the passageway and, upon reaching the street, had dashed off in four different directions.

James Kent had gone directly into the Black Swan public house and had gulped down a large brandy to calm his nerves. James Green had returned to 23a Hanbury Street, intent on finding a piece of canvas with which to cover the body. Henry Holland had found a policeman in Spitalfields Market but the constable refused to help because he was on fixed-point duty, which meant that he could not leave his post under any circumstances. Perhaps the imbecile would have responded differently had he known that our illustrious queen had been murdered instead of a whore. In the meantime, John Davis had gone straight to the Commercial Street Police Station where he had reported his gruesome discovery.

At 6. 02 a. m. and not long on duty, Inspector Joseph Chandler had paused at the corner of Hanbury Street and Commercial Street and had immediately been faced by several men rushing towards him. Hastily informed of a likely murder, Chandler had hurried along Hanbury Street and entered number 29, pushing his way through morbid bystanders who had since gathered in the passageway. Stepping down into the deserted backyard, he saw the horrendously mutilated body of a woman, lying on her back upon the ground.

Her head was towards the back wall of the house, but it was some 2 ft. from the wall, and the body was not more than 6 in. or 9 in. from the steps. The face was turned on the right side, and the left hand rested on the left breast. The right hand was lying down by the left side, and the legs were drawn up. The body was lying parallel with the fencing, and was about two yards distant.

Having sent for a police surgeon, a handcart ambulance and further police assistance from Commercial Street Police Station, Chandler had obtained some sacking from a neighbour and covered the body. At 6. 20 a. m. and, with the arrival of extra police constables, the entire passageway, including the street door and the immediate front of the house, had been cleared of bystanders. Chandler had also gone to great lengths to ensure that no one, not even the police, touched the body. Summoned from his surgery at 2 Spital Square, Dr. George Bagster Phillips, a police surgeon for the past twenty-three years, had entered the backyard at about 6. 30 a. m. Removing the sacking, he had knelt beside the body.

I found the body of the deceased lying in the yard on her back, on the left hand of the steps that lead from the passage. The head was about 6 in. in front of the level of the bottom step, and the feet were towards a shed at the end of the yard. The left arm was across the left breast, and the legs drawn up, the feet resting on the ground, and the knees turned outwards. The face was swollen and turned on the right side, and the tongue protruded from the front teeth, but not beyond the lips; it was much swollen. The small intestines, and other portions were lying on the right side of the body on the ground above the right shoulder, but attached.

There was a large quantity of blood, with a part of the stomach above the left shoulder. The body was cold, except that there was a certain remaining heat, under the intestines, in the body. Stiffness of the limbs was not marked, but it was commencing. The throat was dissevered deeply. I noticed that the incision of the skin was jagged, and reached right around the neck.

Although Dr. Bagster Phillips would in time acknowledge that the coolness of the morning and the loss of blood meant that his timing was less accurate than desired, he nonetheless pronounced life extinct, stating that the woman had died at 4. 30 a. m. and no later. The body was carefully removed from the backyard, placed in the handcart ambulance and, under the supervision of Sergeant Edward Badham, wheeled to the mortuary, where only eight days earlier the body of Mary Ann Nichols had been taken. Meanwhile, Inspector Chandler had begun a careful search of the backyard.

On examining the yard, I found on the back wall of the house, close to the where the head of the woman had lain and about 18 inches from the ground, 6 patches of blood varying in size from a sixpenny piece to a pencil point, and on the wooden palings, to the left of where the body had lain, smears of blood about 14 inches from the ground.

A small piece of coarse muslin, a small tooth-comb, the type worn in the hair, and a pocket comb in a paper case were found lying where the feet had been and near the paling fence. They had apparently been placed there in order or arranged there.

A portion of an envelope was found lying near where the head had lain, and a piece of paper containing two pills. On the back of the envelope was the seal of the Sussex Regiment embossed in blue. On the front of the envelope, in a man's hand-writing, was the letter "M", and lower still the letters "Sp", possibly the remaining part of the first two letters of "Spitalfields". There was no postage stamp on this portion, but it had been postmarked in red, "London, 28 Aug. 1888". Beneath the water tap, I found a pan of clear water and, about 2 ft. from the pan and lying upon the ground, a leather apron saturated in water. A box, commonly used by packing-case makers, a piece of flat steel and a spring were also found lying close to where the body was found. There were no drops of blood in the passageway or outside the street door, and the bloodstains found were only in the immediate neighbourhood of the body.

At 7 a. m., Mrs. Fiddymont, wife of the landlord of the Prince Albert Tavern, corner of Brushfield Street and Stewart Street, had been talking to two customers, Mary Chappell and Joseph Taylor, when a man, 'shabby genteel appearance', had hastily entered the public house and ordered half a pint of ale. Serving him the drink, Mrs. Fiddymont had noticed that he had spots of blood on his right hand and dried blood between his fingers. The man had gulped down his drink and quickly left. Joseph Taylor had then followed the man, finally losing sight of him near Half Moon Street, adjacent to Bishopsgate Police Station.

At about the same time, Robert Mann, the mortuary keeper, had received the body from Sergeant Badham, whilst Detective Sergeant William Thick gave a verbal description of the deceased, which Badham wrote down. Minutes later, Inspector Chandler had hastily arrived and was relieved to see that the body, still lying in the ambulance, had not been disturbed. He had then searched the clothes of the deceased, finding nothing. Instructing Mann that the body was not be tampered with until Dr. Bagster Phillips arrived to perform his post mortem, Inspector Chandler had left the mortuary, leaving Police Constable Barnes on duty and in charge.

At some stage in the morning and in the absence of both Mann and Barnes, two infirmary nurses, Elizabeth Simonds and Frances Wright, acting upon the instructions of the clerk of the Guardians, had removed the deceased from the ambulance and laid her on a table. They had then proceeded to strip the body. Although they removed all the clothes and piled them in the corner of the mortuary, they left a white cotton handkerchief that the deceased had worn in life around her throat. Washing the body, they had noticed that a large amount of blood had flowed down from the throat to the chest. At 2 p. m. that afternoon, Dr. Bagster Phillips arrived and, after protesting loudly to Robert Mann that the body should not have been disturbed, had begun his post mortem.

Supposedly in charge, Police Constable Barnes had once more been noticeable by his absence.

There was a bruise on the right temple, another on her upper eyelid and two more, each the size of a man's thumb, on the fore part of her chest, but these appeared not to be fresh. Below the lower jaw on the left side, one and a half to two inches below the lobe of the ear, were three scratches. They ran in the opposite direction to the incisions in the throat. There were also evidently two recent bruises on the right side of the head and neck, one on the cheek and the other at a point corresponding with the scratches on the left side. This would indicate that the woman had been seized by the chin and partially suffocated before her throat had been cut.

The throat has been ferociously severed from left to right. The incisions of the skin indicate that they were made from the left side of the neck on a line with the angle of the jaw, carried entirely round and again in front of the neck, and ending at a point about midway between the jaw and the sternum or breast bone. The muscular structures between the side processes of the bone of the vertebrae had an appearance as if an attempt had been made to separate the bones of the neck. I believe that the murderer had tried but failed to remove the head from the body.

There were the distinct marks of one or more rings on the proximal phalanx of the ring finger of the left hand. An abrasion over the head of the proximal phalanx indicated that the murderer had indeed wrenched the rings from the finger.

The abdomen had been entirely laid open; the intestines, severed from their mesenteric attachments, had been lifted out of the body, and placed by the right shoulder of the corpse; a portion of the stomach had been placed by the left shoulder, whilst from the pelvis the uterus and its appendages, with the upper portion of the vagina and the posterior two-thirds of the bladder, had been entirely removed. No traces of these parts could be found. The incisions were cleanly cut, avoiding the rectum, and dividing the vagina low enough to avoid injury to the cervix uteri. Obviously the work was that of an expert, of one, at least, who had such knowledge of anatomical or certain pathological examinations as to be enabled to secure the pelvic organs with one sweep of a knife.

I myself could not have performed all the injuries, and effected them, even without a struggle, in under a quarter of an hour. If done in a deliberate way, such as would fall to the duties of a surgeon, it would probably have taken the best part of an hour. The whole inference seems to me that the operation was performed to enable the perpetrator to obtain possession of these parts of the body.

The injuries to the throat and abdomen were certainly inflicted with the same knife. The weapon must have been very sharp, probably with a thin, narrow blade at least six to eight inches long. It was not a bayonet or the type of knife commonly used by cobblers and the leather trades. These knives would not be long enough in the blade. However, a slaughterman's knife, well ground down, might fit the bill.

Due to the circulated police description of the body and the intense public interest in the murder, identification of the woman had been rapid. Amelia Palmer, also known as Farmer, who lived at 30 Dorset Street and had been a close friend of the deceased, had identified her as Annie Chapman. Timothy Donovan, who had initially recognised the white and red bordered handkerchief that Annie had worn, later confirmed the identification. "It was folded 'three-corner ways' and was tied in front of her neck with a single knot", he had exclaimed.

How on earth the murderer had not sliced through Annie's handkerchief when he had tried to sever her head had indeed been a conundrum. Perhaps after clamping his right hand over her mouth and, at the same time gripping her throat with his left hand, he had asphyxiated her, allowing her to collapse to the ground. Then with both hands freed, he had pulled down the handkerchief with his left hand and sliced open her throat, using his right hand.

30o/1

Commercial Street
METROPOLITAN POLICE
H Division
10th September 1888
I beg to report that every possible enquiry is being made with

a view of tracing the murderer, but up to the present without success. Local Inspector Reid being on annual leave, the enquiries have been entrusted to Inspector Chandler, and P.S's Thick & Leach C.I.Dept. I respectfully suggest that Inspector Abberline, Central, who is acquainted with H. Division be deputed to take up this enquiry as I believe he is already engaged in the case of the Buck's-row murder which undoubtedly would appear to have been committed by the same person as the one in Hanbury-street.

Jno.West ActgSupt.

Although, of course, I had not wanted my unknown benefactor apprehended, I nonetheless could not refrain from the temptation of evaluating the facts of the crime, along with the ineptitude of a few of the individuals involved. Whilst I had pondered the murder, it had become evident that my benefactor had deliberately left behind a significant clue, thus revealing his motive for the recent murders, along with a paltry theft, which undeniably had offered a clue to his social standing. Similar to Inspector Spratling, Inspector Chandler had been the man of the moment, ensuring that every piece of physical evidence had not been inadvertently disturbed and that the discovery of its whereabouts had been meticulously recorded. Though hindered by unwarranted stupidity, Dr. Bagster Phillips had diligently performed his duties, providing at least two significant clues that had indicated the probable part of London where the murderer lived.

But at what time on that fateful morning had Annie Chapman been murdered? Dr. Bagster Phillips had placed the time of her death at no later than 4. 30 a. m. But if the good doctor had been mistaken and the inquest testimonies of John Richardson, Albert Cadosch and Elizabeth Long had indeed been correct then Annie Chapman had been murdered a little after 5. 30 a. m. Meaning that the murderer had thrown the protective cloak of darkness aside and butchered Annie Chapman in broad daylight. However, the crucial witness whose dubious testimony perpetuated such a ludicrous assumption had been himself quite unreliable. In one breath, John Richardson had testified,

When I got to the house I found the front door closed. I lifted the latch and went through the passage to the yard door. I did not go into the yard, but went and stood on the steps. The back door was closed when I got to it. I stood on the steps and cut a piece of leather from off one of my boots. I cut it with a table knife about 5in. long.

Whilst in the next breath, he had said,

I did not sit upon the top step, but rested my feet on the flags of the yard. That would be quite close to the spot where the woman was found.

In a criminal court of law, I would have demanded that the witness clarify such a contradiction. Had he indeed stood on the steps? Or had he sat on the steps with his feet in the yard? If he had stood on the steps, using both hands to trim a piece of leather from his boot, he would have kept the self-closing door ajar, using either his left foot or left shoulder. Thus he would have seen only the padlocked cellar and its immediate vicinity and not the darkened recess, paling fence or the body obscured by the door. If on the other hand, Richardson had actually sat on a step with his feet partially in the yard, how did he prevent the self-closing door from slamming shut whilst trimming his boot? Again, and whilst sitting on the middle step with his feet in the yard facing the cellar, he would have used the upper part of his back and shoulders to keep the door open. Once more, he would not have seen the recess, paling fence or the body behind him.

Mr. Thompson had left 29 Hanbury Street at 3. 30 a. m., noticing nothing suspicious. Richardson had visited the house, principally the backyard, at 4. 45 a. m., seeing only the padlocked cellar. Dr. Bagster Phillips had placed the likely time of death at 4. 30 a. m. but no later. Therefore, it was quite credible that Annie Chapman had been murdered and mutilated between 3. 30 a. m. and 4. 30 a. m., corroborating Dr. Bagster Phillips' post mortem comment,

I myself could not have performed all the injuries, and effected them, even without a struggle, in under a quarter of an hour. If done in a deliberate way, such as would fall to the duties of a surgeon, it would probably have taken the best part of an hour.

The testimonies of Albert Cadosch and Elizabeth Long should be considered, but with the utmost caution. For a fleeting moment,

Cadosch thought he heard voices and a sinister noise originating from the backyard of number 29. I had reasoned that the sounds he had heard could have indeed originated from a number of places: Barber's Yard, neighbouring houses, backyards or the Black Swan public house adjacent to his backyard. Identifying the origin of a momentary sound can be enormously difficult at the best of times, especially when you are in a hurry to relieve yourself.

The eyewitness testimony of Mrs. Elizabeth Long totally collapses when one carefully weighs it against the medical evidence of Dr. Bagster Phillips. Under normal conditions, stiffness of the skeletal muscles appears soon after death, usually within the first four hours. Upon examining the body of Annie Chapman for the first time at 6. 30 a. m., Bagster Phillips had stated,

The body was cold, except that there was a certain remaining heat, under the intestines, in the body. Stiffness of the limbs was not marked, but it was commencing.

It had been the start of rigor mortis that had persuaded Bagster Phillips of the approximate time of Annie's death, which he had estimated, had occurred about 4. 30 a.m. at the very latest. If, on the other hand, Annie had been murdered at 5. 30 a. m., rigor mortis would not have been evident. Therefore, Elizabeth Long could not have seen Annie Chapman at 5. 30 a. m., as she had stated, because Annie had undoubtedly been murdered an hour earlier, if not before. The description given by Elizabeth Long of the man she saw with the woman outside 29 Hanbury Street is also worthless because he could not have possibly been the murderer. Quite obviously, Mrs. Elizabeth Long had unconsciously misled the police with an unfortunate case of mistaken identity. However, might the unknown man she described as having a 'shabby genteel appearance' have been the same individual served by Mrs. Fiddymont in the Prince Albert Tavern at 7 a. m.? It mattered not. Because if he was, he was most definitely not the murderer.

Circulated leaflet – 11 September 1888

IMPORTANT NOTICE. – To the Tradesmen, Ratepayers, and Inhabitants Generally, of Whitechapel and District. Finding that in spite of Murders being committed in our midst, and that the Murderer or Murderers are still at large, we the undersigned have formed ourselves into a Committee, and intend offering a substantial REWARD to anyone, Citizen, or otherwise, who shall give such information that will bring the Murderer or Murderers to Justice. A Committee of Gentlemen has already been formed to carry out the above object, and will meet every evening at nine o'clock, at Mr J. Aarons, the 'Crown', 74 Mile End-road, corner of Jubilee-street, and will be pleased to receive the assistance of the residents of the District.

George Akin Lusk, President
1 – 3 Alderney-road,
Mile End-road, E.

It had been evident to me that the Committee's sole purpose of offering a substantial reward for the apprehension of the murderer had been to protect tense local businessmen against the likely decline in trade and, of course, profits. Whitechapel traders had indeed begun to suffer, especially public houses. With people reluctant to venture out into the foggy streets at night, little or no money was being spent in those hushed dens of iniquity. Perhaps the Mile End Vigilance Committee had also begun to suspect, as I had already contemplated, that the murderer might be an East Londoner intent on running amok until either he was caught or slipped into obscurity, having satisfied his bloodlust.

After asphyxiating Annie Chapman and slicing deeply through her throat to the vertebrae, the murderer had wrenched three brass rings from the fingers of her left hand, ripped open a large pocket under her black skirt, removed a small piece of coarse muslin, a small tooth-comb and a pocket comb in a paper case, and had discarded the items, methodically placing them to the right of her left foot, upon the ground near the paling fence. The absence of blood on the latter three objects had clearly signified that they were removed, like the rings, by fairly clean hands before any disembowelment had taken place. However, it mattered not at what particular moment during the murder the objects had been removed. What had been of importance had been the revelation that the murderer had robbed his victim of three brass rings and perhaps other items he may have taken from her pocket at the time. But what manner of person would consider three brass rings valuable? A person accustomed to poverty would. A person familiar with perpetual starvation would. A person who sold stolen items for food would. A person born and raised in the East End of London would. During his post mortem report, Dr. Bagster Phillips had said,

However, a slaughterman's knife, well ground down, might fit the bill.

Needless to say, I had been somewhat disappointed to learn that my benefactor might prove to be a slaughterman residing in the slums of East London. Given the choice, I would have preferred someone befitting my own class. An elegant thoroughbred with a touch of panache, perhaps? But beggars cannot be choosers. If you wish to catch a thief then first employ a thief. But why had the murderer removed parts of the uterus, vagina and bladder and then taken them away? A nauseating thought had struck me, which had chilled me to the bone. Surely he could not have been that ravenous?

Commercial Street
METROPOLITAN POLICE
H Division
11th September 1888

Murder of
Annie Chapman
8. 9. 88

I beg to report having made enquiries at the Depot of the 1st Battn. Surrey Regiment, North Camp, Farnborough, 11th inst, the piece of envelope found near the body of the deceased was identified by Capt. Young Actg Adjutant, as bearing the official stamp of the Regiment, and stated that the majority of the men used this paper which they purchased at the canteen. Enquiries were made amongst the men but none could be found who corresponded with anyone living at Spitalfields, or with any person whose address commencing with "2" The pay books were examined and no signature resembled the initials on the envelope. I made further enquiries at the Lynchford Road, Post Office, and was informed by the Proprietors Messrs. Summer & Thirkettle, that the letter was posted there also they had a large quantity of the envelopes & paper in stock, and retailed them to any person.

Mr. William Stevens stated that he saw the deceased pick up the portion of envelope at 35 Dorset-street and put some pills into it. The witness was mistaken. The pills were found wrapped in another piece of paper beside the body of the deceased after it had been discovered that she had been murdered. Further enquiries are still being made.

J. L. Chandler Inspr.
Submitted Jno. West Actg Supt
To Ch Inspr Swanson 3.50 pm.
12. 9. 88   J.Shore, Supt.

The murderer had slipped a piece of envelope beneath Annie's head before he had departed from the backyard. How the police had discerned that the letter 'M' had been written by a man was beyond me. But more importantly, what had 'M' signified? And the postmark 'London, 28 Aug. 1888'? Had it been part of a riddle or a mere coincidence? These had been enigmas that had dominated my mind for days.

METROPOLITAN POLICE
H DIVISION
12th September 1888

Suspect
John Pizer

I beg to report that after extensive enquiries "John Pizer alias Leather Apron" was discharged from Leman-street Police Station last night at about 9. 30 pm. Suspicion that Pizer may have been the Whitechapel murderer proved to be groundless. The five knives found under his bed did not offer any evidence of guilt. No blood was found to exist on the blades and they were only found as would be used by a man of his trade as boot-maker. Enquiries into the Buck's-row & Hanbury-street murders are to be increased in the hope that the police will obtain further information that may lead to the arrest of the murderer.

E. Ellisdon Insp.
T. Arnold Supdt.

For days I had pondered the mystery of the piece of envelope found under Annie Chapman's head. It had become obvious to me that 'Sp' had indeed been the first two letters of 'Spitalfields' and that the envelope had probably been posted from another part of London to an address in Spitalfields. Hence the postmark 'London, 28 Aug. 1888'. Supposing the inhabitants of Spitalfields could write in the first place, an individual might have addressed it to another in Spitalfields but the postage would have been a prohibited luxury for those existing on a paltry income. Spitalfields was so small an area that it would have made far more sense to deliver the letter by hand. Therefore, an individual, business or professional person must have posted the envelope from another part of London. But why use an envelope embossed with the seal of the Sussex Regiment? It was a conundrum that I had been unable to answer. Perhaps it was insignificant?

Indirectly, the 'London, 28 Aug. 1888' postmark had revealed to me the startling significance behind the initial 'M' which had been written upon the piece of envelope. At first, I had observed the postmark as a mere stamp of postal information, until its date had prompted me to recall that Mary Ann Nichols had been murdered only three days later on 31st August. The date of her death had largely been unimportant but the first initial of her Christian name had certainly not been. Mary Ann Nichols' Christian name had begun with 'M'. And before her, Martha Tabram's had begun with an 'M'. Annie Chapman's Christian name had not begun with the same initial, but the murderer had undoubtedly christened her 'M'. I could scarcely believe what I had stumbled upon. The placing of the piece of envelope with the initial 'M' scrawled upon it had revealed that the past three murders had been somehow related. It was then that a plausible reason for the murders had struck me like a thunderbolt. The three victims were not actually 'M' but the equivalent of 'M'. 'M' was someone else. Almost certainly another woman. Probably another whore. Perhaps my benefactor wanted to butcher 'M' but loathed the idea. Perhaps he equally adored and despised her. Perhaps he was effectively telling 'M' to mend her ways or else he would murder her as well.

East London Observer Newspaper – 14 September 1888

DISCREET
WHITECHAPEL
FUNERAL

The family had paid the funeral expenses and had kept all the arrangements a profound secret. Apart from themselves only the police and the undertaker, Mr. Hawes of 19 Hunt-street, knew when it would take place. At seven o'clock this morning a hearse was sent to the Workhouse

Infirmary Mortuary. Quietly, expeditiously, the undertaker's men collected the body. It rested in an elm coffin draped in black. The coffin-plate read: 'Annie Chapman, died Sept. 8, 1888, aged 48 years.' Driven to Hunt-street, the hearse remained there until nine, when it set off for Manor-park cemetery. There were no mourning coaches because the relatives, in order to avoid attracting attention, had arranged to meet the hearse at the cemetery. All the arrangements were carried out most satisfactorily and there was no hindrance of any kind.

My most recent nightmare had bizarrely shown the recess in the backyard where Annie Chapman's body had been found. It had also depicted the mutilations inflicted upon her body and where her intestines had lain. In my nightmares, had my mind somehow become an ethereal being, going beyond the physical realm of actuality and experiencing the metaphysical world of ghastly tragedies? But why in my nightmares had it appeared as if I had committed the murders? Since I was perhaps the ethereal essence of my benefactor, I might have mimicked whatever he had done in reality. Or had the opposite really been true? Might my ethereal thoughts have motivated him to mimic me in the physical world? Whatever the truth, I had hungered for my next nightmare. I had, by now, convinced myself that the accursed whore of Babylon was indeed 'M'. I had wanted to look her in the eye. I had wanted to tell her that she was going to die horribly.

Daily Telegraph Newspaper – 17 September 1888

ANOTHER
WHITECHAPEL
OUTRAGE

An alarming story was told to our reporter yesterday, and it is understood that the Metropolitan police are aware of its details. If this statement be true, and there appears to be no reason to question it, then the bloodthirsty maniac who is now terrifying Whitechapel unsuccessfully attempted another outrage two days ago. The woman, Susan Ward of 25 Hollybush-gardens, Bethnal-green, who so narrowly escaped death is married, but admits having entered into conversation with a strange man for an immoral purpose. She alleges that he tripped her up, so that she fell upon the pavement. He made an effort to cut her throat, but she shielded herself with her arm, and in doing so received a cut upon it.

Alarmed by his failure, and fearing her shrieks, the attacker ran off, and the woman, when discovered, was removed to the London Hospital, Whitechapel-road. She has since been discharged, and the wound upon the arm is still to be seen. The occurrence is alleged to have taken place in Red Lion-court, Commercial-street, which is just around the corner from Hanbury-street. Unfortunately, Mrs. Ward was so much in liquor when she was assaulted that she cannot recollect the man's face or dress, and has been unable to give a description of him, which may account for the secrecy which has been maintained in regard to the attack.

Such had been the fear, panic created by the Whitechapel murders that an attack upon any woman within the district had been instantly attributed to my mysterious benefactor. However, and as I had done previously, other institutions had now begun to broach the question of his occupation.

Star Newspaper – 20 September 1888

WHAT WE THINK.

Meanwhile, theories as to the crimes are setting steadily in one direction. This is the slaughterman theory. The most startling facts in its favour are these:- (1) The knowledge of rough anatomy shown by the murderer, who was able to remove vital organs whole. (2) The resemblance between the method employed, and the manner of slaughtering a sheep. (3) The probability that the knife employed was larger than a leather-cutter's weapon, and not larger than a slaughterman's. (4) The extreme rapidity with which the crimes was accomplished, and the rude violence of the cuts. (5) The near neighbourhood of slaughterhouses to the scenes of the last two crimes. (6) The fact that no other workman but a slaughterman could walk through the streets of London in the early morning soiled with blood without arousing suspicion. We don't ask the police to accept the theory; we only suggest to them, to follow up such clues as it suggests.

After unwisely avoiding the continuing infatuation of my puerile boarding school boy, I had taken him aside one night, informing him that our transient association was at an end. He had wept in my arms, sobbing for a reprieve. His appeal had fleetingly touched my cynical heart, but I had relented not. Oh, the absence of love is the most abject of pain. I had gazed upon his pale face, staring into his wet hazel eyes. Desiring to kiss me upon my lips, he had stubbornly raised his head but I had callously pushed him away. My rejection of him had been complete. Spurned, he had rushed from my room, seeking solace elsewhere.

Daily Telegraph Newspaper – 24 September 1888

FINAL PERFORMANCE

In response to the gruesome murders in Whitechapel, Mr Russell Sullivan's theatrical adaptation of the Strange Case of Dr. Jekyll and Mr. Hyde will be withdrawn this week from the Lyceum-theatre in the Strand. The final performance will be on Saturday. Some critics have suggested that the Whitechapel murderer's dementia was inflamed by seeing a performance of the production. Another critic urges that our detectives should consider how Mr. Hyde would have acted – for there may be a familiar pattern associated with the demonic actions of the Whitechapel murderer.

I had laid my head upon my pillow and wearily closed my eyes. I had slipped blissfully into the void and returned to Spitalfields, or so I had thought. In a gloomy gas-lit square, I had risen from the body of the old toothless hag, bloodied knife in my hand. She lay upon the pavement, in a corner. Blood flowed from her slashed throat and her mutilated face. Suddenly I heard a cackle from behind. I had spun on my heel but saw only the emptiness of the square. Again, I heard the cackle. Again, I spun on my heel. The toothless hag rose from the ground and stood before me. She thrust an accusing finger at me, "Arthur, no dick, eh?" Horrified, I had stepped back from the abomination. Raising her skirt, she revealed intestines oozing from her slashed abdomen, "Come on, dearie, prove you're a man." I dropped my knife, which clattered noisily to the ground, echoing throughout the square. She threw back her head, cackling incessantly. Something had slid from her abdomen and plopped into the gutter. She stooped, retrieved the bloody organ and threw it at me. It struck me in the face. Swiping my face with my hands, I awoke, sat upright, breathing heavily. I slumped back upon the pillow, exhausted. She lay beside me, cackling, "Come on, dearie, prove you're a man." I had uttered a fearful scream and then truly awoke. And had screamed again.

THE CENTRAL NEWS LIMITED

5, New Bridge-street,
London, 29 Sep 1888
E. C.

The editor presents his compliments to Mr. Williamson & begs to inform the enclosed was sent the Central News two days ago, & was treated as a joke.

Yours truly
T. J. Bulling
A. F. Williamson Esqr.

Letter enclosed – 2 pages

25 Sept. 1888

Dear Boss

I keep on hearing the police have caught me but they wont fix me just yet. I have laughed when they look so clever and talk about being on the <u>right</u> track. That joke about Leather Apron gave me real fits. I am down on whores and shant quit ripping them till I do get buckled. Grand work the last job was. I gave the lady no time to squeal. How can they catch me now. I love my work and want to start again. You will soon hear of me with my funny little games. I saved some proper <u>red</u> stuff in a ginger beer bottle over the last job to write with but it went thick like glue and I cant use it. Red ink is fit enough I hope <u>ha. ha.</u> The next job I do I shall clip the ladys ear off and send to the police officers just for jolly wouldnt you. Keep this letter back till I do a bit more work then give it out straight. My knife's so nice and sharp I want to get to work right away if I get a chance. Good luck.

Yours truly
Jack the Ripper

Don't mind me giving the trade name

Wasnt good enough to post this before I got all the red ink off my hands curse it. No luck yet. They say I'm a doctor now <u>ha. ha.</u>

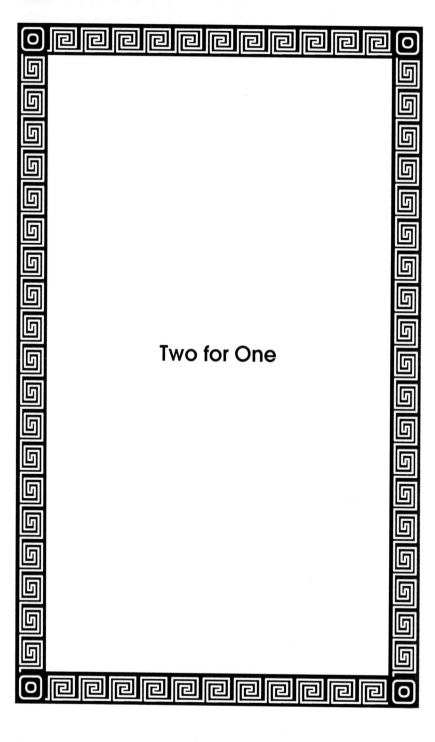

Two for One

Two for One

THE CENTRAL NEWS LIMITED

5 New Bridge-street,
London, 1 Oct 1888
E. C.

Dear Mr. Williamson,

We received the following postcard of which I enclose by which you will see resembles the previous communication dated 25 Sept 1888.

Yours truly
T. J. Bulling
A. F. Williamson Esqr.

Postcard enclosed.

I wasn't codding
dear old Boss when
I gave you the tip.
youll hear about
saucy Jack's work
tomorrow double
event this time
number one squealed
a bit couldn't
finish straight
off. had not time
to get ears for
police thanks for
keeping last letter
back till I got
to work again.
Jack the Ripper

The Times Newspaper – 1 October 1888

TWO HORRIBLE MURDERS
IN WHITECHAPEL

All of the Metropolis is aghast at the latest two atrocities committed in Whitechapel in the early hours of yesterday morning. At 1 a. m., Louis Diemschutz discovered the body of a woman in Dutfield's-yard, Berner-street with her throat cut. Half an hour later, Police Constable Watkins of the City Police discovered yet another body in Mitre-square. The body of the woman found in Dutfield's-yard had not been mutilated thus leading the police to think the murderer had been disturbed and fled the scene of the crime. The same could not be said of the poor woman found in Mitre-square; her face had been mutilated almost beyond recognition.

A piece of her blood-stained apron, presumed to have been taken away by the murderer, was found shortly afterwards by Police Constable Long in Goulston-street, Whitechapel. It is reported that the murderer chalked an anti-Semitic message on a wall above the piece of apron, his intent, it is believed, to induce racial disquiet among the inhabitants of the district. If that was his intention then he failed. The message was copied down by the police and then removed from the wall before daybreak. A number of witnesses, predominately Jewish, are being questioned by both the London Metropolitan Police and the London City Police. Both forces have doubled their efforts in order to identify the two murdered women.

Like the entire populace of the country, I had been stunned by the sheer audacity shown by my benefactor. In less than one hour, and within a short distance of each other, he had seemingly slaughtered two women, preceding the event by identifying himself with a name. Or had he? What had instantly struck me as being quite odd was that the letter and postcard had been posted to the Central News Agency and not directly to a specific newspaper or the police. If the writer of both communications had indeed been an ordinary individual, he would have undoubtedly known of the latter two, but not of the former. As a news gathering organisation, the Central News Agency was unknown outside the journalistic fraternity of Fleet Street where, along with Reuters, it had supplied most of the prominent newspapers with international news stories, especially major political speeches. It had also developed a reputation for supplying stories of a dubious nature, its correspondents using their imaginations when the facts were deemed dull or uninteresting. Supported by his manager, John Moore, an alcoholic journalist Thomas John Bulling had become a deft hand at fabricating stories where little or no news existed.

Inscribed with red ink, the two-page letter had been written by a neat copperplate hand, using curious American colloquialisms such as 'Boss', 'quit' and 'buckled'. Although the writer had made a noticeable attempt to appear illiterate, he had, in fact, shown himself to be an educated person who wrote frequently, possibly for a living. The postmark on the envelope revealed that the letter had been posted in East Central London, which comprised of Fleet Street and New Bridge Street, home to the Central News Agency. Inscribed with a red crayon, smeared with blood and apparently written in the same revealing hand as the letter, the postcard boasted of the two murders and had again been unquestionably a journalistic prank. However, the author's undeniable stroke of genius had been in the creation of the sobriquet, Jack the Ripper. A chilling pseudonym that might attain mythical prominence in the years to come.

The Times Newspaper – 3 October 1888

TWO WITNESSES
THE WHITECHAPEL MURDERER SEEN

The two women found murdered in Dutfield's-yard, Berner-street and Mitre-square have been identified as Elizabeth Stride and Catharine Eddowes. Both women were of the 'unfortunate' class and lived a miserable existence. The startling news is that two witnesses may have seen both women with the murderer moments before their deaths. Israel Schwartz of 22 Ellen-street, Back Church-lane, reported to the police that he had seen a man throw Elizabeth Stride to the ground outside Dutfield's-yard minutes before her body was discovered by Louis Diemschutz.

Another witness, Joseph Lawende of 45 Norfolk-road, Dalston, also reported to the police that he and two friends had just left the Imperial Club, Duke-street, when he saw Catharine Eddowes standing with a man at the corner of Church-passage, minutes before her mutilated body was discovered by Police Constable Watkins in Mitre-square. Church-passage is one of three entrances that lead into the square. Mr. Schwartz and Mr. Lawende are being closely questioned by the police with regards to a description of the man they both allegedly saw. Great anxiety is felt by the residents of Whitechapel for they fear that the murderer may strike again.

Five days earlier, on the 29th September, at about 6. 30 p. m., Elizabeth Stride and Elizabeth Tanner, deputy of the doss-house where Stride was lodging, had left the Queen's Head public house on Commercial Street and returned to the lodging house situated at 32 Flower and Dean Street. Several minutes later, Stride had been seen in the doss-house kitchen by Charles Preston, who had loaned her a clothes brush, noticing that she was dressed to go out. At 7 p. m., Stride had left the kitchen, showing charwoman Catharine Lane the sixpence that she had earlier been paid for cleaning two rooms in the lodging house. She had given the charwoman no indication where she was going and at what time she might return to the doss-house.

Some ninety minutes later, Police Constable Louis Robinson had noticed a small crowd outside Henry Phillip's Warehouse, 28 Aldgate High Street. Pushing his way through the crowd, Robinson had found Catharine Eddowes lying upon the pavement, drunk and incapable. Assisted by a fellow officer, Police Constable George Simmons, Robinson had pulled Eddowes to her feet and taken her to Bishopsgate Police Station. At about 8. 45 p. m. she had been placed in a cell and left to recover.

At 9. p. m., less than a mile away and south of Commercial Road, Philip Kranz had started work in the printing office of the Hebrew paper 'Worker's Friend', located behind the International Working Men's Educational Club at 40 Berner Street. A cheerless street in the parish of St George-in-the-East, Berner Street began at Commercial Road, cut straight through Fairclough Street and ended at Ellen Street. On the west side of Berner Street, between Fairclough Street and Commercial Road and directly opposite the London School Board building, was Dutfield's Yard. Shielding its entrance, two large wooden gates had displayed the discoloured painted letters of its two former businesses: 'W. Hindley, sack manufacturer' &' A. Dutfield, van & cart builder'. The right-hand gate had been fitted with a wicket for use when the gates were closed, which had been very seldom.

The yard began as a narrow alley and then widened slightly into a darkened court, flanked on the right by the International Working Men's Educational Club, 40 Berner Street, and on the left by number 42 Berner Street. Behind this grimy house were a row of shabby cottages and, at the rear of the yard, a partially disused sack shed and stable. Access to the International Working Men's Educational Club, which overlooked the dismal yard, had been through a front door in Berner Street or by a right-hand side door in

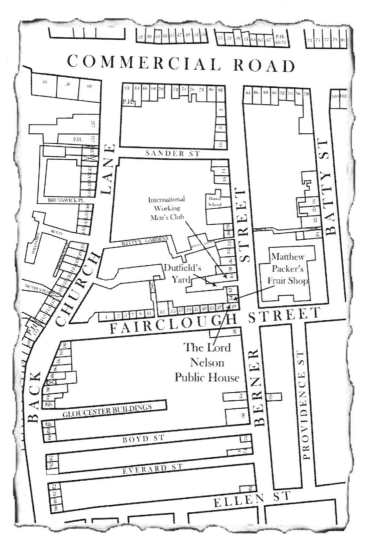

Berner-street, Dutfield's-yard, St-George-in-the-East 1888

Dutfield's Yard. It had been customary practice for members of the club to use this side door to avoid knocking and waiting at the front door in the street.

At 9. 45 p. m., Police Constable George Hutt had started duty at Bishopsgate Police Station and, upon checking one particular cell, had noticed that Catharine Eddowes was sound asleep. Some fifteen minutes later, Police Constable William Smith had also come on duty and began his beat, which meant patrolling part of Commercial Road, Berner Street, Fairclough Street and Grove Street. An hour later, two dockside labourers, John Gardner and John Best, had almost collided with Elizabeth Stride leaving The Bricklayer's Arms public house in Settles Street, accompanied by a man wearing a morning suit and a billycock hat. Teasing Stride that her companion could be 'Leather Apron', Gardner and Best had watched Stride and the man walk away, heading towards Commercial Road and Berner Street just beyond.

Thirty minutes later, at 11. 30 p. m., the majority of the members of the International Working Men's Educational Club had left the club for the night, leaving behind a small group of individuals in a first-floor meeting room, chatting and singing. Fifteen minutes later, at Bishopsgate Police Station, Catharine Eddowes awoke from her stupor and was heard by Constable Hutt to be softly singing to herself. At approximately the same time, William Marshall, loafing in the doorway of his house at 64 Berner Street, south of Fairclough Street, had seen Elizabeth Stride being kissed by a man who said, "You would say anything but your prayers." Stride had chuckled and sauntered along the middle of the road with the man, passing Marshall and continuing towards Ellen Street. The man had worn a peaked cap, black cutaway coat and dark trousers. He had been rather stout, possibly clean shaven and middle-aged.

Fifteen minutes later, at about 11. 45 p. m., Matthew Packer, a greengrocer, had sold half a pound of black grapes to Stride and a man, standing outside his shop at 44 Berner Street, situated just one house away from Dutfield's Yard. Packer had continued to observe Stride and the man loitering about Berner Street for the next forty minutes, until he had lost interest in them when he closed his shop at about 12. 30 a. m. The man had worn a wideawake hat and dark clothes. He had been stout, five feet seven inches tall and aged twenty-five to thirty. He had the appearance of a clerk.

At about 12. 10 a. m., William West had stepped out of the club by the side door, taking some literature to the printing office at the rear of Dutfield's Yard. Quickly returning to the side door, he had noticed that the gates to the yard were open but had seen nothing suspicious. Some five minutes later and, using the Berner Street front door, West and his brother had left the club, again seeing nothing unusual in the street. In the meantime, at about 12. 30 a. m., Catharine Eddowes had asked Constable Hutt when she would be released. Hutt had curtly answered, "Shortly." At about the same time, Charles Letchford, who had lived at 30 Berner Street, arrived home and in doing so had not seen anything irregular in the street.

Visiting London from the United States and desiring a breath of fresh air, Joseph Lave, a printer and photographer, had stepped out of the side door of the club, walked through the yard to the open gates and paused, noticing nothing unusual in Berner Street. Five minutes later, Police Constable William Smith had entered Berner Street from Commercial Road and passed Elizabeth Stride in the presence of a man, standing opposite Dutfield's Yard, close to the wall of the London Board School. The man had worn a dark felt deerstalker hat, black diagonal cutaway coat and had held a parcel wrapped in newspaper, which had been about eighteen inches long and six inches wide. Aged about twenty-eight, five feet eight inches tall, he had a dark complexion and a small dark moustache. Although Joseph Lave had been standing outside the open gates to Dutfield's Yard, it seemed odd that neither he nor Constable Smith had seen each other. Stranger still, Lave had also failed to observe Elizabeth Stride and the man standing across the street, opposite him. Apparently seeing nobody in the street, Lave had retraced his route back through the yard, entering the club by the side door. Aroused by the measured footsteps of Constable Smith, Fanny Mortimer had stood in the doorway of her house at 36 Berner Street, seeing no one in the street except Leon Goldstein, carrying a black shiny Gladstone bag. Walking past Mortimer, Goldstein had taken an immediate left into Fairclough Street and had continued onto his lodgings at 22 Christian Street, noticing nothing unusual.

Having escorted his lady friend home, Morris Eagle had returned to the club in Berner Street at about 12. 40 a. m. He had also failed to notice Elizabeth Stride and the man standing opposite the open gates to Dutfield's Yard. Might Stride and her companion have moved away? Or had both Joseph Lave and Morris Eagle got their times wrong? Trying the Berner Street door and finding it closed, Eagle had walked into the yard and entered the club through the side door, joining his friends on the first floor, singing. Five minutes later, at about 12. 45 a. m., James Brown of 35 Flairclough Street, had popped out of his lodgings to go to the chandler's shop on the corner of Berner Street and Fairclough Street for his supper. Hurriedly crossing Berner Street, Brown had seen Stride and a man standing close to the wall of the London School Board, opposite Dutfield's Yard. Brown had heard Stride say to the man, "No, not tonight, some other night." The man had been stout, 5 feet 7 inches tall and had worn a long coat that had reached almost to his heels. At about the same time and deemed to be sober by Constable Hutt, Catharine Eddowes had been removed from her cell and presented to the duty officer, Sergeant Byfield, for formal release. It was almost 12. 45 a. m.

Similar to Constable Smith, Israel Schwartz had entered Berner Street from Commercial Road and had walked along the street towards Dutfield's Yard, not far behind a man who was clearly drunk. Formally discharged by Sergeant Byfield and shown the street door by Constable Hutt, Eddowes had said, "Good night, old cock," then had turned left towards Houndsditch, merely an eight minute walk to Mitre Square. Nearing Dutfield's Yard and still behind the drunken man, Israel Schwartz had seen Elizabeth Stride standing alone outside the entrance to the yard. The drunken man had stopped, spoken to her and, placing his hand on her shoulder, had pushed her back into the yard. Not wanting to get involved in an argument, Schwartz had immediately stepped across to the other side of the street, passing both Stride and the man. Before he had gone just a few feet, however, he had heard them quarrelling. Turning to see what the argument was about, Schwartz had seen another man, knife in hand, rush from the Nelson beer shop, corner of Berner Street and Fairclough Street, and shout some sort of a warning to the man with Stride and then rush forward as if to attack him. Might the opposite have been true? Had a jealous rival, a jilted suitor, in fact, aimed the warning at Stride and then rushed forward to attack her and not the man as Schwartz had thought? Schwartz had not waited to find out. He fled as fast as his legs would carry him, timidly joining his wife at their new lodgings in Back Church Lane. The man with Stride had worn a black cap with *a peak and dark clothes. Aged about thirty, he had been stout and had a brown moustache. The man with the knife had been slightly taller and had a brownish moustache. It seemed that both men were inhabitants of the neighbourhood.*

HOME OFFICE 2 OCT. 88 RECEIVED and METROPOLITAN POLICE RECEIVED 1. OCT. 88 CRIMINAL INVESTIGATION DEPT.) A51202/123
METROPOLITAN POLICE.
CRIMINAL INVESTIGATION DEPARTMENT
SCOTLAND YARD
1st day of October 1888

SUBJECT Israel Schwartz
Com. To Home Office
Re Berner-street Murder.

I beg to report that at 12. 45am 30th Sept. Israel Schwartz of 22 Helen-street, Back Church-lane stated that at the hour on turning into Berner-street from Commercial-road & having got as far as the gateway where the murder was committed he saw a man stop & speak to a woman, who was standing in the gateway. The man tried to pull the woman into the street, but he turned her round & threw her down on the footway & the woman screamed three times, but not very loudly. On crossing to the opposite side of the street, he saw a second man standing lighting his pipe. The man who threw the woman down called out apparently to the man on the opposite side of the road 'Lipski' & then Schwartz walked away, but finding that he was followed by the second man he ran as far as the railway arch but the man did not follow so far. Schwatrz cannot say whether the two men were together or known to each other. I respectfully submit it is not clearly proved that either of the men that Schwartz saw was the murderer, although it is clearly probable that one was.

Donald S Swanson
Chinspr.
J. Shore Supt.

A Hungarian Jew, Israel Schwartz had spoken little or no English. Therefore, a local interpreter had been engaged, who then gave his account to both the police and the Star newspaper of what he believed Schwartz had seen outside Dutfield's Yard that fateful morning. I had promptly reasoned that this type of second-hand interpretation of the facts explained the variance contained within the two versions. Whatever the truth, however, Israel Schwartz had most certainly witnessed the last remaining minutes of Elizabeth Stride's life.

6095/11   3 OCT.88
Pressing A51202/123   WHITEHALL
                                         2 October 1888

Sir,

With reference to previous correspondence. I am directed by the Secretary of State to inform that since a Jew named Lipski was hanged for the murder of a Jewess in 1887 the name has very frequently been used by persons as mere ejaculation by way of endeavouring to insult the Jew to whom it has been addressed.

I am,
Sir,
Your obedient Servant
E. Ruggles-Brise.

The Commissioner
of the Metropolitan Police.

Some ten minutes later, at about 1 a. m., Louis Diemschutz, a hawker of cheap jewellery, had approached Dutfield's Yard from Commercial Road. Driving his two-wheeled cart into the darkened yard, his pony had immediately shied to the left, away from the right-hand club wall. Peering down, Diemschutz had discerned a dark object. Prodding the object with the handle of his whip and getting no response, he jumped down from the cart and struck a match. The feeble flame had instantly revealed the dim outline of Elizabeth Stride, lying prone upon the ground. Dashing into the club, Diemschutz had found his wife and had uttered, "There's a woman lying in the yard but I cannot say whether she's drunk or dead." Obtaining a candle and accompanied by young tailor machinist Isaac Kozebrodski, Diemschutz had returned to the yard, noticing blood before he had reached the body. Having followed her husband as far as the side door, Mrs. Diemschutz had peered out into the yard.

Just by the door, I saw a pool of blood, and when my husband struck a light I noticed a dark heap lying under the wall, I at once recognised it as the body of a woman, while, to add to my horror, I saw a stream of blood trickling down the yard and terminating in the pool I had first noticed. She was lying on her back with her head against the wall, and the face looked ghastly. I screamed out in fright, and members of the club hearing my cries rushed downstairs in a body out into the yard.

Diemschutz and Kozebrodski had made no attempt to disturb the body. Instead they had immediately bolted from the yard, turned right into Berner Street, left into Fairclough Street, shouting, "Murder!" "Police!" Seeing the blood and the body for himself, Morris Eagle had also darted from the yard. Turning left into Berner Street, he had frantically run towards Commercial Road in search of a policeman. Standing outside the Beehive Tavern, corner of Fairclough Street and Christian Street, a horse-keeper, Edward Spooner, had watched, utterly dumbfounded, as Diemschutz and Kozebrodski had tore past him, abruptly halting at Grove Street. The two men immediately turned about and had rushed back towards him. Stopping them, Spooner was told of their discovery and instantly returned with them to Dutfield's Yard. Upon reaching the yard, Spooner had found a small crowd clustered around the body. Someone had struck a match. Spooner had bent down and lifted up the chin of the dead woman, feeling that it was scarcely warm. Looking closely at the body for the first time, Diemschutz had seen the terrible wound in her throat.

I could see that her throat was fearfully cut. There was a great gash in it over two inches wide. In one hand she had some grapes, and in the other a packet of cachous. She was grasping them tightly.

Turning right into Commercial Road from Berner Street, Morris Eagle had immediately bumped into Police Constables Henry Lamb and Albert Collins walking towards him, patrolling the section of Commercial Road between Christian Street and Batty Street. Informed of the murder by Eagle, the two constables had dashed to Dutfield's Yard, whereupon Constable Lamb had dispatched both Constable Collins to fetch Dr. Blackwell from his surgery and Morris Eagle to Leman Street Police Station for further assistance. Lamb had then knelt beside the body, placed his hand against Elizabeth Stride's face and found that it was slightly warm. He had held her wrist to see if he could detect a pulse but had found none. Some minutes later, at about 1. 10 a. m., Constable Collins had pounded on the door of Dr. Blackwell's surgery at 100 Commercial Road. Whilst the doctor had struggled to get into his clothes, his assistant, Edward Johnston, had hurriedly gone with Collins back to Dutfield's Yard. Johnston had felt the body and found it warm except the hands, which were quite cold. He had then unfastened the dress at the neck to obtain a clearer view of the wound. The deep gash in Elizabeth Stride's throat had ceased bleeding and the stream of blood that had flowed along the yard had clotted. Dr. Blackwell arrived at 1. 16 a. m. and by the light of a policeman's lantern had thoroughly examined the body.

Her dress was unfastened at the neck. The neck and chest were quite warm, as were also the legs, and the face was slightly warm. The hands were cold. The right hand was open and on the chest, and was smeared with blood. The left hand, lying on the ground was partially closed, and contained a small packet of cachous wrapped in tissue.

What, I wondered, had become of the few grapes that Louis Diemschutz had seen in Elizabeth Stride's hand?

There were no rings, nor marks of rings, on her hands. The appearance of the face was quite placid. The mouth was slightly open. The deceased had round her neck a check silk scarf, the bow of which was turned to the left and pulled very tight. In the neck there was a long incision which exactly corresponded with the lower border of the scarf. The border was slightly frayed, as if by a sharp knife. The incision in the neck commenced on the left side, 2½ inches below the angle of the jaw, and almost in a direct line with it, nearly severing the vessels on that side, cutting the windpipe completely in two, and terminating on the opposite side 1½ inches below the angle of the right jaw, but without severing the vessels on that side. I could not ascertain whether the bloody hand had been moved.

Free scraps of food were a rarity in Whitechapel. Might a callous hungry person have taken advantage of the commotion in the darkened narrow alleyway and snatched the grapes from Stride's right hand, devouring them unseen?

The deceased had bled to death comparatively slowly because only the vessels on the left side of the neck had been cut and even then the carotid artery had not been completely severed. In my opinion, the woman could not have been dead for more than twenty minutes, half an hour at the most. Therefore, the murder probably took place at about 12. 55 a. m.

Meaning some minutes after Israel Schwartz had witnessed the assault on Elizabeth Stride and barely five minutes before Louis Diemschutz had discovered her body. Hurriedly leaving Dutfield's Yard and determined to avoid most of Berner Street, Fairclough Street and Commercial Road, the murderer had probably turned left into Berner Street and then left again into Batty's Gardens, thus bringing him into Back Church Lane. Turning left once more, he would have hastened along Back Church Lane, passing Mundy's Place on the right. At the junction with Fairclough Street, but still in Back Church Lane, he would then have turned right and entered Cherry Tree Passage that led into Gower's Walk. Turning right into Gower's Walk, he would have hurried along the street, crossing over Commercial Road and then taken the first right into Church Lane.

Star Newspaper – 1 October 1888

WHITECHAPEL
MURDERER SEEN

From two different sources we have the story that a man, when passing through Church Lane at about half past one, saw a man sitting on a doorstep and wiping his hands. As everyone is on the look-out for the murderer the man looked at the stranger with a certain amount of suspicion, whereupon he tried to conceal his face. He is described as a man who wore a short jacket and a sailor's hat.

Less than half a mile away from Church Lane and just within the eastern boundary of the City of London was Mitre Square. About twenty-four square yards in size, Mitre Square had three entrances: a carriageway and two narrow dismal passageways. Leading from Mitre Street into the dull cobbled square, the carriageway passed between the warehouse of Walter Williams & Co. on the left and Taylor's picture-frame shop on the right. At the eastern corner of

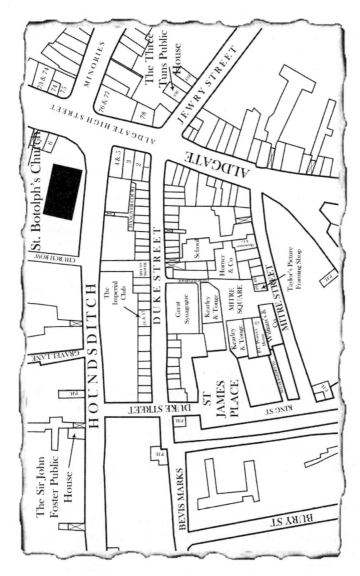

Mitre-square, City of London 1888

the square was Church Passage, which had led into Duke Street. Running alongside one of two Kearly & Tonge's warehouses, the northern unnamed passageway led into St. James' Place. Though near to the major thoroughfares of Leadenhall Street, Aldgate and Houndsditch, Mitre Square had been a gloomy place and almost deserted after dark. Two gas lamps had illuminated its entire area, a lamppost in the northwestern part of the square and a lantern affixed to the wall by Church Passage.

Except for a City of London policeman, Richard Pearce, who had lived with his family at number 3, the few remaining dreary houses had been empty, dwarfed by the tall gloomy warehouses that dominated the entire square on every side. Situated between another row of empty houses and the warehouse of Horner & Co. had been a backyard, which had belonged to general merchants Heydeman & Co. of 5 Mitre Street. To the rear of 5 Mitre Street and overlooking the backyard and most of Mitre Square, had lived a resident caretaker, George Clapp, his wife and an elderly nurse who attended to Mrs. Clapp. By 1. 30 a. m., all three had been sound asleep, having retired for the night at 11 p. m. Likewise, Richard Pearce and his family had also been asleep in 3 Mitre Square, having retired at the later time of 12. 30 a. m. The only soul that had been awake that morning had been George James Morris, a night watchman, who had been cleaning the ground floor offices of Kearly & Tonge's warehouse alongside the northern passageway and opposite the darkened southern corner of the square.

At about 1. 30 a. m, some forty-five minutes after Catharine Eddowes had been released from Bishopsgate Police Station and a mere thirty minutes after Elizabeth Stride's body had been found in Dutfield's Yard, Police Constable Edward Watkins had stepped from Mitre Street into Mitre Square, seeing and hearing nothing unusual. Turning about, Watkins had left the square and resumed his beat in Mitre Street. Five minutes later, at 1. 35 a. m., Joseph Lawende, Joseph Levy and Harry Hyam Harris had stepped out of the Imperial Club, 16-17 Duke Street, directly opposite the Great Synagogue, which forms one side of Church Passage. As the three men had walked away from the club, they had seen Catharine Eddowes with a man standing at the corner of Duke Street and Church Passage, about sixteen feet away. Passing the couple, Lawende had seen that Catharine was facing the man with one hand resting upon his chest. Catharine and the man had spoken very quietly. Thus, Lawende had not overheard anything of their conversation. The man had worn a peaked grey cloth cap, a reddish neckerchief tied in a knot and a pepper-and-salt coloured loose jacket. Aged thirty, with fair complexion and moustache, he had been five feet seven inches tall and of medium build. He had looked like a sailor.

Six minutes later, at 1. 41 a. m., Police Constable James Harvey had approached the corner of Duke Street and Church Passage and had seen no one in particular. Entering the passage and walking its entire length, he had halted at its end, peering into the gloomy square before him. The darkened southern corner had lain directly in front of him but he had seen nothing unusual. Turning about, he had retraced his route back to Duke Street and had then entered Aldgate. Four minutes later, Constable Watkins had again stepped from Mitre Street into the square.

I came round to Mitre Square again at 1. 45, and entering the square from Mitre Street, on the right-hand side, I turned sharp round to the right, and flashing my light, I saw the body in front of me. The clothes were pushed right up to her breast, and the stomach was laid bare, with a dreadful gash from the pit of the stomach to the breast. On examining the body I found the entrails cut out and laid round the throat, which had an awful gash in it, extending from ear to ear. In fact, the head was nearly severed from the body. Blood was everywhere to be seen. It was difficult to discern the injuries to the face for the quantity of blood which covered it. The murderer had inserted the knife just under the left eye, and, drawing it under the nose, cut the nose completely from the face, at the same time inflicting a dreadful gash down the right cheek to the angle of the jawbone. The nose was laid over on the cheek. A dreadful sight I never saw; it quite knocked me over.

Unlike the argumentative, domestic murder of Elizabeth Stride, there had been no doubt in my mind that the same hand that had slain Annie Chapman had butchered Catharine Eddowes. Whilst I had read Constable Watkins' account on finding the body, I had smiled to myself, convinced that my benefactor had left behind a clue, indicating entire responsibility for the crime.

Running across the square to Kearly & Tonge's warehouse, Watkins had found its door ajar. Throwing open the door, he had encountered George Morris, sweeping down some steps. Watkins had gasped, "For God's sake, mate, come to my assistance." Morris, a police pensioner himself, had dropped his broom and grabbed a lamp, "What's the matter?" Watkins had despairingly shaken his head, "Oh dear, there's another woman cut up to pieces." Standing guard over the body, Watkins had sent Morris off for help. Rushing out into Mitre Street and then into Aldgate, Morris had blown his whistle, attracting the attention of Police Constables James Harvey and James Thomas Holland.

At about 1. 55 a. m, the news of the murder had reached the ears of Inspector Edward Collard at Bishopsgate Police Station. Telegraphing the news through to headquarters at Old Jewry, Collard had sent a police constable to fetch the divisional police surgeon, Dr. Frederick Gordon Brown, whilst he had hurried off to Mitre Square. Arriving in the square at about 2. 03 a. m., Collard had found several policemen and Dr. George William Sequeira, who had been called out by Constable Holland eight minutes earlier at 1. 55 a. m. Fifteen minutes later, at about 2. 18 a. m., Dr. Frederick Gordon Brown had arrived and, assisted by Dr. Sequeira, had begun an immediate examination of the body.

The body was on its back, the head turned to the left shoulder. The arms were by the side of the body as if they had fallen there, both palms upwards. The clothes were drawn up above the abdomen, the thighs were naked, left leg extended in a line with the body, right leg bent at the thigh and knee. The bonnet was at the back of the head. Great disfigurement of face, the throat cut across, below the cut a neckerchief. The upper part of the dress was pulled open a little way. The abdomen was all exposed. The intestines were drawn out to a large extent and placed over the right shoulder. They were smeared over with some feculent matter.

My heart had missed a beat. Had not part of Annie Chapman's intestines been placed over her right shoulder? Surely this had to be the diabolical handiwork of my benefactor again?

I draw the only conclusion that the mutilations were made

after death by someone on the right side of body, kneeling below the middle of the body. A detached portion of intestine, two feet long, had been placed between the body and left arm, apparently by design. The left kidney and part of the womb had been cut out and taken away. These parts would be of no use for any professional purpose. The face had been savagely mutilated. I am of the opinion that the murderer intended to obliterate the identity of the victim but due to lack of time had failed. The lobe and auricle of the right ear had been cut off. There was a cut about ¼ of an inch through the lower left eyelid. The right eyelid was cut through to about ½ an inch. The tip of the nose was quite detached from the nose by an oblique cut from the bottom of the nasal bone to where the wings of the nose join on to the face. There was on each side of the cheek a cut which peeled up the skin forming a triangular flap about an inch and half.

I had scarcely been able to breathe. An inverted 'V' had been cut into each cheek. Placed together, they had formed the letter 'M'. Now I had been in no doubt. Catharine Eddowes had been christened Mary because, like Martha Tabram, Mary Ann Nichols and Annie Chapman, she had been representative of Mary – the whore of Babylon.

Due to the severance of the left carotid artery, death may have resulted from loss of blood. It is conceivable, however, that the deceased was suffocated, or partially suffocated, before the mutilations were inflicted. About one half of the woman's apron had been severed by a clean cut and had been taken away. The injuries were inflicted by a sharp, pointed knife with a blade at least six inches long. I am of the opinion that the degree of knowledge and skill shown does not suggest a medical man. A slaughterman, for example, would have known enough to have inflicted the injuries.

Completing his initial examination, Dr. Frederick Brown had the body removed from the square and taken to the City Mortuary in Golden Lane. Mitre Square had now become the hub of a frantic police investigation with detectives dashing from the square to search adjacent lodging houses and neighbouring streets.

Several men had been stopped by the police and searched in Middlesex Street and Wentworth Street but with no actual arrests. At about 2. 20 a. m., Police Constable Alfred Long, temporarily drafted to H Division, had walked past Wentworth Model Dwellings, Goulston Street, seeing nothing unusual. By 2. 45 a. m., two major murder investigations were now underway. The Metropolitan Police Force had jurisdiction over the Elizabeth Stride investigation whilst the City of London Police Force had jurisdiction over the Catharine Eddowes murder inquiry. Neither force seemed to assist the other. Ironically, the two forces would ultimately agree that the same hand had murdered both women when the opposite had indeed been true. Jack the Ripper, my benefactor, had ruthlessly claimed only one victim that dreary morning – Catharine Eddowes.

At about 2. 55 a. m., or seventy minutes after Constable Watkins had first stumbled upon the mutilated body of Catharine Eddowes, Constable Long had again walked along Goulston Street, curiously peering into the entrance of Wentworth Model Dwellings.

A49301C/8c

6th November, 1888

HOME OFFICE 6 Nov. 88 RECd. DEPt.

I was on duty in Goulston-street on the morning of 30th Sept: at about 2. 55 A. M. I found a portion of an apron covered in blood lying in the passage of the door-way leading to Nos. 108 to 119 Model-dwellings in Goulston-street.

Above it on the wall was written in chalk "The Juwes are the men that will not be blamed for nothing." I at once called the P.C. on the adjoining beat and then searched the stair-cases, but found no traces of any persons or marks. I at once proceeded to the Station, telling the P.C. to see that no one entered or left the building in my absence. I arrived at the Station about 5 or 10 minutes past 3, and reported to the Inspector on duty finding the apron and the writing.

The Inspector at once proceeded to Goulston-street and inspected the writing. From there we proceeded to Leman St., and the apron was handed by the Inspector to a gentleman whom I have since learnt is Dr. Phillips.

I then returned back on duty in Goulston-street about 5.

Alfred Long PC 254A.

To fully understand the importance of those tantalising clues discovered by Constable Long, I had promptly consulted a map of the district and had reasoned the probable route taken by my benefactor, upon leaving Mitre Square and slipping back towards Spitalfields. Jack the Ripper had but only three avenues of escape from Mitre Square. First, back out into Mitre Street and then into Aldgate. Second, along Church Passage and into Duke Street from whence he first came. And finally, across the square and along the northern unnamed passage, leading into St. James' Place. With the exception of this passageway, the other two exits would have invited capture, regularly patrolled by both Constable Watkins and Constable Harvey. Hurrying along the northern passage into St. James' Place, my benefactor had turned right, hastened through the end section of Duke Street and entered Houndsditch. Crossing Houndsditch, he had hurried along Gravel Lane, taking a right into Stoney Lane and heading towards Middlesex Street. It was at the junction of Stoney Lane and Middlesex Street that I had paused for thought, troubled by the seemingly illogical rationale of the night's events. Try as I might, I had found it increasingly hard to believe that my benefactor had remained within the vicinity of the murder for more than an hour before discarding the piece of apron and chalking an enigmatic message upon a wall in Wentworth Model Dwellings, Goulston Street.

At about 2. 20 a. m., some thirty-five minutes after Catharine Eddowes' mutilated body had been found, Constable Long had walked past Wentworth Model Dwellings, seeing neither her piece of apron nor the chalked message upon the wall. But had he been mistaken? Had he entirely missed both bits of evidence? Had the piece of apron and the chalked message already been there? If so, then my benefactor had certainly walked across Middlesex Street, hurried along New Goulston Street where, at its junction with Goulston Street, he had crossed the street and entered Wentworth Model Dwellings opposite. Though this had seemed quite plausible, relying as it did on the premise that Constable Long had not seen the two bits of evidence, I could not envisage that Jack the Ripper had calmly paused to chalk a message and discard a piece of apron that had held part of a womb and a kidney. Nay, Constable Long had not been mistaken. Both bits of evidence had yet to be displayed. Therefore, at the junction of Stoney Lane and Middlesex Street, my benefactor had turned immediate left and then right into Wentworth Street, passing Goulston Street on the right-hand side of Wentworth Street. His place of refuge had been extremely close at hand. In fact, mere minutes away.

Between 2. 20 a. m. and 2. 55 a. m., after having cleaned and rid himself of the portion of womb and kidney, my benefactor had undoubtedly returned and entered Wentworth Model Dwellings, chalking the message upon the wall and discarding the piece of apron below it. I had surmised that the piece of apron had been deliberately placed to draw attention to the anti-Semitic message and not the other way round. In addition to his incredible hatred of whores, particularly Mary, Jack the Ripper had revealed that he had despised another minority group – Jews. In doing so, he had inadvertently revealed his own persuasion. He had not been a deprived foreigner, but a Gentile. But why, amidst such a hue and cry, had he partially returned in the direction of Mitre Square? Perhaps he had merely paused at Goulston Street. Perhaps he had returned to Mitre Square and mingled with the swelling crowd of morbid spectators, amongst whom he would have appeared entirely innocuous. Staring at the corner where he had recently butchered Catharine Eddowes, he would have gloated, relishing his moment of infamy.

At about 4. 30 a. m., Elizabeth Stride's body was removed from Dutfield's Yard and taken to St. George's Mortuary, Cable Street. Twenty-five minutes later, at 4. 55 a. m., the Metropolitan Police Commissioner, Sir Charles Warren, had arrived at Leman Street Police Station and had been briefed by Superintendent Thomas Arnold, H Division, on the two murders, particularly the chalked message found in Wentworth Model Dwellings. Arnold proposed that the message be washed from the wall. Considering the decision his responsibility, Warren had decided to visit Goulston Street and see the chalked message for himself.

I went to Goulston-street before going to the scene of the murder: it was getting light, the public would be in the streets in a few minutes, in a neignbourhood very much crowded on Sunday mornings by Jewish vendors and Christian purchasers from all parts of London.

There were several police around the spot when I arrived, both Metropolitan and City.

The writing was on the jamb of the open archway or doorway visible to anybody in the street and could not be covered up without danger of the covering being torn off at once.

A discussion took place whether the writing could be left covered up or otherwise or whether any portion of it could be left for an hour until it could be photographed; but after taking into consideration the excited state of the population in London generally at the time, the strong feeling which had been excited against the Jews, and the fact that in a short time there would be a large concourse of people in the streets, and having before me the report that if it was left there the house was likely to be wrecked (in which from my own observation I entirely concurred) I considered it desirable to obliterate the writing at once, having taken a copy.

I do not hesitate myself to say that if that writing had been left there would have been an onslaught upon the Jews, property would have been wrecked, and lives would probably have been lost; and I was much gratified with the promptitude with which Superintendent Arnold was prepared to act in the manner if I had not been there.

Detective Constable Daniel Halse of the City of London Police had vigorously protested and suggested a compromise by which only the top line that had included the word 'Juwes' would be wiped out. But Warren's word had been quite final. According to Constable Long who had been present at the time, the message was sponged from the wall at about 5. 30 a. m. At about the same time, Constable Albert Collins had also washed the last vestiges of gore from Dutfield's Yard. Although Grand and Batchelor, two private detectives engaged by the Mile End Vigilance Committee, would later discover a grape-stalk amidst the assorted filth of the yard, no weapon, no clue to who might have murdered Elizabeth Stride had been discovered. Shortly afterwards, Dr. Frederick Brown would confirm that the bloodstained piece of apron found by Constable Long had indeed been part of the garment which had been worn by Catharine Eddowes.

POLICE NOTICE
TO THE OCCUPIER.
On the mornings of Friday, 31st August, Saturday 8th, and Sunday, 30th September, 1888, Women were murdered in or near Whitechapel, supposed by some one residing in the

immediate neignbourhood. Should you know of any person to whom suspicion is attached, you are earnestly requested to communicate at once with the nearest Police Station.

Metropolitan Police Office, 30th September, 1888.

As I had previously reasoned for myself, the police had by now recognised the fact that my benefactor was indeed a local man who most certainly resided in the area. In a flurry of activity, the police had descended upon an assortment of common lodging houses, interviewing over two thousand occupants and distributing eighty thousand handbills appealing for information. However, common sense had dictated that if the murderer had indeed lived in a doss-house, he could not have remained inconspicuous for long. Thus, he must have retreated elsewhere. Private lodgings had been thought of as a possibility but would have been expensive for someone earning a meagre wage and hardly very secure from the inquisitive eyes of resident landlords and other tenants. Nay, my benefactor had retired to a haven in Spitalfields altogether unknown. But where in Spitalfields?

On Monday, 1st October, Mrs. Mary Malcolm of 50 Eagle Street, Red Lion Square, Holborn, had mistakenly identified the body of Elizabeth Stride as her sister, Elizabeth Watts. The real Elizabeth Watts, formerly Elizabeth Stokes and living at 5 Charles Street, Tottenham, had miraculously appeared three weeks later, feeling unwell with a crippled foot but very much alive. The next evening, Tuesday, 2nd October, John Kelly, a middle-aged labourer, had gone into Bishopsgate Police Station, saying that he thought he knew the Mitre Square victim. Shown the mutilated body, Kelly had identified the woman as Catharine Eddowes, whom he had lived with for the past seven years at 55 Flower and Dean Street. Less than fourteen hours later, Elizabeth Tanner, deputy of the lodging house at 32 Flower and Dean Street, had formally identified the Dutfield's Yard victim as Elizabeth Stride. I had been astounded. Although both women had been murdered in different parts of the district they had, in fact, resided in the same street in Spitalfields. Perhaps just doors from each other. Had they known each other? Or more intriguing had my benefactor known them? Disregarding Elizabeth Stride as a victim, Martha Tabram's last known address had been at 19 George Street, off Flower and Dean Street. Mary Ann Nichols had lodged at 18 Thrawl Street, parallel with Flower and Dean Street, whilst Annie Chapman had lived at 35 Dorset Street, barely a five minute walk from Flower and Dean Street. Had this not implied that my benefactor had known all the four victims, prior to murdering them? Doubtlessly, he had been somewhat familiar with them. Intimately, perhaps? The description of the man that Joseph Lawende had seen with Catharine Eddowes some six minutes before her death had also been intriguing.

He was aged about 30, 5ft 7in or 5ft 8in, tall with a fair complexion and moustache. He wore a pepper-and-salt loose jacket, red neckerchief and peaked grey cloth cap. He had the appearance of a sailor.

Undoubtedly, this had been my benefactor. He had been of my age, my height and, similar to myself, had a fair complexion and moustache. Curiously enough, Mitre Square had also been close to the Minories, where my cousin had his surgery. My benefactor was most certainly partially illiterate, hence the misspelling of the word 'Jews', whom he appeared to detest as much as he hated whores. Given that the murders had been committed either at the weekends or on public holidays, he had a regular job, worked in the district and was probably a slaughterman or had been one. He lived somewhere in Spitalfields and had access to a second place of refuge, where he could change his clothes and clean himself before he had returned to his initial dwelling, probably a common lodging house. Although he utterly loathed whores, he had been familiar with his four victims, butchering them because they had personified Mary, a particular individual whom he equally adored and despised. The mutilations inflicted upon his victims had steadily increased and were indicative of his rage, suggesting that he was nearing his final act: the destruction of an unattainable obsession. All of this had explained a great deal about my benefactor, but a repugnant, chilling question had remained unanswered. Why had he removed and taken away Annie Chapman's and Catharine Eddowes' organs and what had become of them?

Whore of Babylon

Whore of Babylon

East London Observer Newspaper – 9 October 1888

WHITECHAPEL
MOURNS YET AGAIN

At half-past one o'clock yesterday afternoon, the remains of the unfortunate woman Catharine Eddowes, victim of the Mitre-square tragedy, were removed from the City mortuary in Golden-lane to Ilford Cemetery, for interment. Mr. Charles Hawkes, undertaker, of Banner-street, St. Luke's defrayed the entire cost of the interment, which had been readily accepted by the deceased's relatives. The body of the deceased woman, which had been placed in a polished elm coffin, surmounted with a plate in gilt letters, with the following inscription "Catharine Eddowes, died September 30th, 1888, aged 43 years" was then brought out of the mortuary and placed in the funeral car.

Never perhaps, has Golden-lane and the precincts of the mortuary presented a more animated appearance. The footway was lined on either side of the road with persons who were packed in rows five deep. Manifestations of sympathy were visible everywhere, many among the crowd uncovering their heads as the hearse passed.

A strong body of City police, under the supervision of Mr. Superintendent Foster and Inspector Woollett kept the thoroughfare clear, and conducted the cortege to the terminus of the City boundary. The route taken was along Old-street and Great Eastern-street into Commercial-street. On reaching Old-street the funeral car was met by a body of Metropolitan Police, who, under the direction of Inspector Burnham, of the G Division, kept the roadway clear for its passage.

Emerging into Whitechapel-road, the cortege passed slowly through a densely packed mob, which lined the roadway on either side, and extended as far as St. Mary's Church. The sympathy shown here was more marked than at any other point of the route, the majority of rough-looking labouring men removing their caps as the body passed.

Opposite Whitechapel parish church a number of policemen were drawn up, it being rumoured that a demonstration might be attempted. Beyond the marks of sympathy referred to, nothing whatever occurred and the services of the police were consequently not brought into requisition.

The cortege then proceeded along the Mile End-road, almost unobserved, and after passing through Bow and Stratford it turned into Ilford main road, reaching the cemetery shortly before half-past three.

Whilst the majority of the country had relentlessly discussed the infamous deeds of Jack the Ripper, my boarding school boy had begun to assail me with puerile letters, imploring me to reconsider my rebuttal of him. At first, I had merely looked upon his messages as nothing more than mournful appeals from a spurned child, but I soon became alarmed when he had implied that death would be preferable to absolute rejection. It mattered not to me if he wanted to dispose of himself but the impulsive death of a pupil might possibly embroil me in an unfashionable scandal and bring about my own ruin. I had therefore decided to placate him, responding to his juvenile messages with a prudent letter, feigning eternal love. I had declared that I had acted hastily, begged his forgiveness and suggested that we should no longer meet in my room but away from the boarding school. His written response had been almost immediate and cheerful. Agreeing to my proposal, we had met eight days later amidst the ruins of a medieval abbey. Elated to see me, he had occupied the entire afternoon dutifully kissing and stroking my manhood, his malleable hands causing me to spend numerous times. Although I had wallowed in the physical pleasure, I had felt very uneasy. I was no longer in control, having unwisely surrendered to the infantile impulses of a thirteen-year-old boy. I had foolishly allowed myself to be snared. My predicament was utterly hopeless. I had become a slave, and now a hapless victim of my own shameful desires. I could only hope that he would soon weary and ultimately cast me aside for someone else. For once in my life, I had longed for rejection.

He had succumbed to that terrible disease eight years ago and every subsequent year, on the anniversary of his untimely death, I had stood by his grave, troubled that I may have defiled the memory of our union. But in my mind, and only on such solitary visits, I had always heard his gentle voice absolving me of guilt and tenderly assuring me of his love. But had he truly spoken to me? An ethereal voice originating from the grave was quite absurd. Might it have been my own inner voice that had exonerated me, thus justifying my decadent life? If so, I had been horrendously wicked. I had dishonoured his memory and entirely debased the purity of his soul for my own loathsome existence. The thought had disturbed me immensely. I had instantly thrown aside my preoccupation with the whore of Babylon and hurried to his grave, fearing reproof but nonetheless intent on confronting the truth. It had been bitterly cold and raining heavily as I had knelt beside his grave. Similar to a flurry of snowflakes, autumn leaves had swirled through the air, creating a damp carpet upon the ground. I had waited for what seemed like an eternity, hearing nothing but the doleful wind moaning through the trees. My anxiety had intensified. I had heard neither his nor my inner voice. Nothing. I had despairingly slumped to the ground, staring at the headstone of his grave. Had he truly forsaken me? A sudden chill had gnawed at my body and then the terrible truth had struck me like a spear. I had scarcely been able to breathe. The sound of my thumping heart had resonated in my ears. Nay, he had not forsaken me. How could he? He was dead. The voice that I had heard on those past visits had been my own. And now even that was absent. I had lowered my head and, for the second time in my life, wept. I had forsaken myself. I could not sanction my own existence. I had indeed rejected myself. I had spiritually ceased to be.

The Times Newspaper – 19 October 1888

A CHILLING MESSAGE FROM
THE WHITECHAPEL MURDERER

Not satisfied with the butchery of 'unfortunates' in Whitechapel, the murderer has succeeded in horrifying the Metropolis once again by dispatching to Mr. George Lusk, 1 Alderney-road, Mile-end, a ghastly reminder of his atrocities.

Our readers may recall that when Catharine Eddowes was horribly murdered her left kidney was removed and taken away by the murderer. On Tuesday last Mr. Lusk received a small cardboard box by post which contained a kidney. The appalling reminder was also accompanied by a letter which indicated that it was the same kidney that the murderer had removed from the deceased.

Dr. Openshaw, curator of the London Hospital Museum, Whitechapel, has since pronounced it to be a woman's kidney infected with Bright's Disease, which is caused by excessive consumption of 'ardent spirits' such as gin. The organ was at once handed over to the City Police who arrived at the opinion that the kidney had indeed come from the body of the deceased. Mr. George Lusk is Chairman of the Mile End Vigilance Committee which was formed to assist the police in their hunt for the murderer.

93305/28
HOME OFFICE 24 OCT. 88 RECd. DEPt.
Confidential   4 Whitehall Place, SW,
                                                24th October, 1888

Sir,

I beg to report that the portion of kidney sent to Mr. Lusk would appear to be of that removed from the Mitre-square victim, Catharine Eddowes. If this is indeed correct then the murderer must have penned the letter that accompanied the portion of kidney. The hand-writing of the Lusk letter is not dissimilar to a previously undisclosed letter received by the police dated 17th Sept. 1888 and signed Jack the Ripper.

The police are therefore of the opinion that the letter dated 25th Sept. 1888 & the postcard dated 1st Oct. 1888, whose hand-writing is altogether different from the Lusk letter, are hoaxes. A view held by most of the Detective Branch who has thought all along that a misguided journalist penned the two communications.

The postmark upon the parcel sent to Mr. Lusk is so indistinct that it cannot be established whether the parcel was posted in the E. or E. C. districts. The City Police are therefore unable to prosecute any enquiries upon it.

All enquiries of the City Police are now merged into those of the Metropolitan Police with each Force cordially communicating to the other daily the nature and subject of their enquiries.

I am,
Sir,
Your most obedient Servant,
C. Warren

The Under Secretary
of State
Home Office.

ATTACHED
Letter dated 17th Sept. 1888

17th Sept. 1888

Dear Boss
So now thay say I
am a Yid when will thay
lern Dear old Boss? You an
me know the truth don't we.
Lusk can look forever hell
never find me but I am rite
under his nose al the time.
I watch them looking for me
and it gives me fits ha ha. I
love my work an I shant stop
until I get buckled and even
then watch out for your old
pal Jacky.

Catch me if you can
Jack the Ripper

Sorry about the blood still
messy from the last one. What
a pretty necklace I gave her.

ATTACHED
Lusk letter
sent with portion
of human kidney

From hell

Mr Lusk
Sor
I send you half the
Kidne I took from one woman
prasarved it for you tother piece I
fried and ate it was very nise I
may send you the bloody knif that
took it out if you wate a whil
longer
signed   Catch me when
you can
Mishter Lusk.

Seemingly sent by my benefactor, this latest affront to human decency had shaken me from my despondent mood. Nine days earlier, on Monday 15th October, a tall clerical man had cagily entered a leather shop at 218 Jubilee Street, Mile End, enquiring after the address of George Lusk, who actually lived at 1 Tollet Street, though he ran a builders merchant business just around the corner in Alderney Road. The furtive manner and appearance of the man had so worried the shop assistant, Emily Marsh, that she had instructed a shop boy, John Cormack, to follow the man after he had left. Cormack had done so, but had rapidly lost sight of the stranger in the crowded neighbouring streets. Aged forty-five and six feet tall, the man had a sallow face, a dark moustache and beard and had spoken with an Irish accent. Hardly the same man that Joseph Lawende had seen with Catharine Eddowes at the corner of Duke Street and Church Passage some fifteen days before. In fact, the man had been much more interested in the reward notice posted in the leather shop window by the Mile End Vigilance Committee than he had been about the address of its president, George Lusk. Perhaps the stranger had information that he thought might lead to the reward and hence had warily sought the address of George Lusk from an alert but nervous Emily Marsh.

The next evening, at about 8 p. m., George Lusk had received through the post a cardboard box, 3½ inches square, wrapped in brown paper. Contained within the box had been half a kidney. It had stunk. Heralded by the two shocking words 'From hell', a derisory note had accompanied the organ. At first, Lusk thought it had been a hoax but then had been persuaded by the treasurer of the Mile End Vigilance Committee, Joseph Aarons, to take the half of kidney to Dr. Frederick Wiles at 56 Mile End Road. Finding the doctor out, Lusk had handed the kidney to his assistant, Mr Reed, who had opined that it was most certainly human and had been preserved in spirits of wine. Reed had then submitted the portion of organ to Dr. Thomas Horrocks Openshaw of the London Hospital, who had promptly examined it under a microscope. Openshaw affirmed that it was part of a left kidney that may have belonged to a woman who had been an habitual drinker and who may have died about the time that Catharine Eddowes had been murdered. Without further ado, George Lusk had presented the grisly piece of evidence to Inspector Abberline at Leman Street Police Station who, in turn, had dispatched the gruesome item to the City Police where Dr. Gordon Brown had duly examined it.

I cannot see that it is the left kidney. It must have been cut previously to its being immersed in the spirit which exercised a hardening process. It certainly had not been in spirit for more than a week. As has been stated, there is no portion of the renal artery adhering to it, it having been trimmed, so therefore, there could be no correspondence established between the portion of the body from which it was cut. As it exhibits no trace of decomposition, when we consider the length of time that has elapsed since the commission of the murder, we come to the conclusion that the probability is slight of its being a portion of the murdered woman of Mitre-square.

It had appeared to me that two members of our medical fraternity had been at loggerheads and had reached an impasse. Dr. Gordon Brown had stated at Catharine Eddowes' inquest,

The peritoneal lining was cut through on the left side and the left kidney carefully taken out and removed – the left renal artery was cut through – I should say that some one who knew the position of the kidney must have done it.

The left renal artery, about three inches in length, had been cut through, leaving two inches joined to the corpse, whilst the other inch, attached to the kidney, had been removed. Dr. Brown had clearly admitted that the portion of kidney sent to George Lusk, and then later examined by him, had been trimmed to remove any attachments, including a piece of the renal artery. Due to this, it had been quite obvious to me that Dr. Brown would have found it nigh on impossible to establish any physical connection with the trimmed kidney and the remaining two inches of renal artery found in Catharine Eddowes' body. I had therefore reasoned that Dr. Brown's ruling had been nothing more than calculated guesswork and that Dr. Openshaw's analysis had been closer to the truth. Curiously enough, Dr. Brown had unwittingly corroborated part of Dr. Openshaw's analysis at the inquest of Catharine Eddowes.

The sigmoid flexure was invaginated into the rectum very tightly – right kidney pale bloodless with slight congestion of the base of the pyramids.

These right kidney symptoms had clearly indicated that Catharine

Eddowes had indeed been suffering from an advanced stage of Bright's Disease. Meaning, that had she not been murdered, she would have ultimately died of kidney failure.

93306/29
HOME OFFICE 2 NOV. 88 RECd. DEPt
Confidential   4 Whitehall Place, SW,
                                          2nd November, 1888

Sir,
   I beg to report that the attached letter was received by Dr. Thomas Horrocks Openshaw who is the pathological curator of the London Hospital Museum, Whitechapel. You may recall that Dr. Openshaw examined the portion of kidney sent to Mr. George Lusk and affirmed his belief that it was part of the missing left kidney of the Mitre-square victim, Catharine Eddowes.

   The hand-writing of the attached Openshaw letter is not dissimilar to the letter received by the police dated 17th Sept. 1888 and the letter received by Mr. George Lusk. The three letters seem to suggest that the writer is partially illiterate and knows of Mr. Lusk and Dr. Openshaw, which indicates that he resides in the area where these appalling murders have been committed.

   The police are of the opinion that the word "me" contained within the Openshaw letter indicates local residency. The people of East London habitually use the word "me" instead of "my" and the expression is not found anywhere else in the country but East London. It is entirely possible that a misguided person tried and failed to imitate the East London dialect as in the case of the 17th Sept. 1888 letter where the word "my" is used correctly, suggesting that this letter is probably a hoax.

   However, the police are of the opinion that the Lusk and Openshaw letters are undoubtedly genuine and were indeed penned by a local inhabitant, possibly by the Whitechapel murderer himself.

                         I am,
                         Sir,
              Your most obedient Servant
                      C. Warren

The Under Secretary
of State
Home Office.

ATTACHED
Envelope:

London
E   6
OC29
88

Dr Openshaw
  Pathological curator
 London Hospital
  Whitechapel

Openshaw letter – 1 page.

> Old Boss you was rite it was
> the left kidny I was goin to
> hopperate agin close to your
> ospitle just as I was goin
> to dror me nife along of
> er bloomin throte them
> cusses of coppers spoilt
> the game but I guess I wil
> be on the job soon and will
> send you another bit of
> innerds
>   Jack the ripper

> O have you seen the devle
> with his mikerscope and scalpul
> a lookin at a kidney
> with a slide cocked up

6215/18   6 NOV. 88
Pressing A93306/29
                                       WHITEHALL
                                       5 November 1888
Sir,
   With reference to previous correspondence. I am directed by
the Secretary of State to signify the utmost urgency that members
of the press should <u>not</u> be shown any police evidence. Mr.
Secretary Matthews is of the opinion that <u>if</u> the letter dated 25th
Sept. 1888 & the postcard dated 1st Oct. 1888 were indeed
penned by a journalist then such a person had prior privileged
access to the former undisclosed letter dated 17th Sept. 1888. Mr.

Secretary Matthews believes that such an irresponsible action may have provided the journalist of the two said communications with the name of Jack the Ripper. The Secretary of State wishes to inform you that it is the duty of your office to preserve the integrity of crucial police evidence at all times and negligence of these matters will not be tolerated.

> I am,
> Sir,
> Your obedient Servant
> E. Ruggles-Brise

The Commissioner
of the Metropolitan Police.

Feeling that my life had once more become intolerable, I had slid beneath the blankets of my bed and laid my head upon the pillow. My thoughts were dominated by failure. I had utterly failed as a barrister. I had also failed to restrain the snivelling affections of a thirteen-year-old boy, knowing that I had become nothing more than a mere bauble of his infantile obsession. But above all else, I had felt that my benefactor had totally failed me. In spite of four dramatic murders, he had yet to rid me of that 'shilling whore'. I had descended into the darkness and returned to Spitalfields in a dream. Rising from what seemed like the body of the old toothless hag, I had stood in a small sparsely furnished room, some twelve to fifteen feet square, bloodied knife in my hand. The floorboards were bare and filthy and the pattern of the wallpaper was hardly discernible beneath the dirt. Before me, upon the soiled mattress of a wooden bedstead, lay the disembowelled body of a woman. Her face had been so savagely slashed that she was quite beyond recognition. Parts of internal organs lay about her person. The bed clothing was saturated with gore whilst beneath the bed, upon the floor, was a large pool of blood. Recoiling from the grotesque spectacle, I had bumped into a bedside table, catching sight of a small pile of entrails upon its surface. I had retched. The entire room had resembled a charnel house. I had felt something moist and sticky pulsating in my left hand. It had been a bloodied heart, still beating. Nauseated, I had dropped it to the floor. I had heard a cackle. Spinning on my heel, I had seen no one but again heard the cackle. I had turned to the bedstead, instantly drawing back. The disembowelled corpse stood before me, hideously grinning. It raised a mutilated arm and pointed an accusing finger at me.

Trying to speak, it had mumbled incoherently. Appalled, I furiously stomped upon the pulsating heart on the floor, crushing it beneath my boot. The cackling ceased. The corpse immediately collapsed to the bed, resuming its grotesque position upon the mattress. I had instantly awoke, trembling. Oh the disgusting horror of it all. Madness run riot. What had it all meant? What had it signified?

The Times Newspaper – 10 November 1888

A SIXTH MURDER
ANOTHER CASE OF HORRIBLE
MUTILATION

Yesterday, a sixth murder, the most horrible yet, was committed in Spitalfields, Whitechapel. As in all previous instances, the victim was a woman of immoral character and humble circumstances. Unlike former victims she had not been murdered in the open street but obscenely mutilated in a room which the deceased had rented at 13 Miller's-court, which is the rear part of 26 Dorset-street. The deceased has since been identified as the Irish woman, Mary Jane Kelly. The unfortunate woman was twenty-five years of age and of attractive appearance. It is reported that she was married, but separated from a foreman employed at an iron foundry in Carnarvon, Wales.

Overcome with sheer excitement, I had hardly finished reading the newspaper article. I had doubted my benefactor but he had surpassed himself with this latest atrocity. Surely his fifth victim had been the same despicable Irish bitch I had previously met in the Ten Bells? It had to be Mary, the twenty-five-year-old whore of Babylon. I had leaned back in my armchair and had felt a huge sense of relief. I had been mercifully plucked from the abyss of despair. I had endured bouts of torment but I had survived. At last my dreadful ordeal was over. My benefactor, Jack the Ripper, had unwittingly freed me from bondage.

Considered to be the most perilous street in Spitalfields, where police constables cautiously patrolled in pairs, Dorset Street started at the Britannia public house, corner of Commercial Street, and ended at the Horn of Plenty beer shop, corner of Crispin Street. A dreary cobbled street, it had been entirely made up of common lodging houses, offering beds at fourpence and sixpence a night.

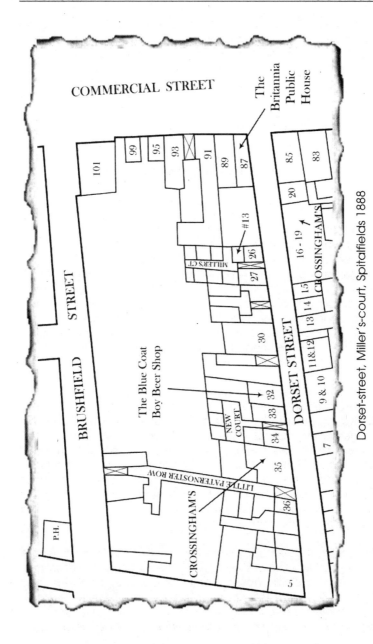

COMMERCIAL STREET

The Britannia Public House

Dorset-street, Miller's-court, Spitalfields 1888

Four dingy courts, mainly inhabited by prostitutes, led off the northern side of Dorset Street. A short distance from the Britannia public house was the first of these, Miller's Court. On the immediate left of its arched entrance was a chandler's shop, owned by the landlord of Miller's Court, John McCarthy. To its right was 26 Dorset Street, consisting of a storage space for costermongers barrows at the front and 13 Miller's Court to its rear. Access to the cul-de-sac court was gained through the arch, along a narrow twenty-foot gloomy covered passage. At the end of this passage, and to the left, was the chandler's shop rear window, giving a clear view of most of the court. In front of the window and, again to the left, was an overhead gas lamp attached to the wall. Directly opposite this solitary gas lamp was a shabby door, which opened directly into a single room, 13 Miller's Court.

Just inside the squalid room and to the left of the door, which opened inwards and to the right, were two grimy windows with faded curtains. The window nearest to the door had two broken panes of glass. In an attempt to block out any offending draught, an old coat had been draped in front of the damaged window. Both windows gave a general view of a dingy outer recess, where a water pump was positioned against a right-hand wall, whilst straight ahead, situated against another wall, was a small rubbish bin close to the communal lavatory in the far corner. Inside the room, in front of the window furthest from the door, was a wooden table. To the right of a small fireplace had stood a tall cupboard containing a few bits of cheap crockery and some empty beer bottles. Opposite this, and in the other corner, was the dominant piece of furniture, an old bedstead with a soiled mattress. Close by, between the bed and the door, stood a small bedside table. Immediately above the room, lived a prostitute, Elizabeth Prater, whose husband had deserted her five years ago. Directly opposite and below, Julia Venturney had lived in the ground floor room at number 1, whilst above her and opposite the outer recess, Mr. and Mrs. Keyler had occupied the room at number 2. On the same side but at the far end of the stone-flagged court, an elderly prostitute, Mrs. Mary Ann Cox, had occupied the upstairs room at number 5. Overlooking the dingy outer recess and the two grimy windows of 13 Miller's Court, Catherine Picket and her husband had inhabited the first-floor room at number 12.

Aged twenty-five, five feet seven inches tall and buxom, Mary

Jane Kelly had possessed light ginger hair, blue eyes and a fair complexion. This was undeniably the same odious siren that I had met in the Ten Bells public house. It had been her seductive luminous blue eyes that had first caught my attention. Born in Limerick, Ireland, she had in due course adopted the somewhat pretentious name of Marie Jeanette Kelly, after making several trips to Paris with a French woman who had resided in the wealthy neighbourhood of Knightsbridge, London. Having spent the past nine months of 1888 living at 13 Miller's Court with a fish porter named Joseph Barnett, Mary Kelly had found herself alone at the end of October, after fiercely quarrelling with Barnett about her return to prostitution. Infuriated by her repeated habit of providing temporary shelter for other prostitutes at 13 Miller's Court, Barnett could no longer endure the constant intrusions and had left her on the 30th October, finding refuge at a common lodging house in New Street, Bishopsgate. Barnett would ultimately divulge to the police that Mary had become apprehensive about the murders in Whitechapel and had frequently demanded that he read to her aloud everything that the newspapers had to say about them. Perhaps she had an inkling of the terrible motive that lay behind the slayings and that she was possibly being sought after by Jack the Ripper. Might this explain why she had begun to drink heavily, trying to numb the thought of her own death, perhaps? Shortly after Joseph Barnett had walked out on her, she had told a friend, Lizzie Albrook,

I'm afraid to go out alone at night because of a dream I had that a man was murdering me. Maybe I'll be next. They say Jack's been busy down in this quarter.

Had Mary actually seen me in her dream? Nay, the idea had been preposterous. Our individual dreams must have been merely coincidental. However, the very thought that she had endured a horrid nightmare similar to mine had been of some consolation. It had indeed been heartening to know that she had experienced a mild degree of punishment prior to her death. Burdened with rent arrears of some twenty-nine shillings and downcast about life, Mary had solicited the fogbound streets at night, etching out a meagre existence. Lizzie Albrook would later recall the last conversation that she had with Mary shortly before she had been murdered.

About the last thing she said to me was "Whatever you

do don't you do wrong and turn out as I did." She had often spoken to me in this way and warned me against going on the street as she had done. She told me, too, that she was heartily sick of the life she was leading and wished she had money enough to go back to Ireland where her people lived. I do not believe she would have gone out as she did if she had not been obliged to do so to keep herself from starvation.

Attached to H Division, Whitechapel, a young detective, Walter Dew, recalled having seen Mary Kelly whilst he had been on duty in the district. His final remark about her had been quite ominous.

I knew Marie quite well by sight. Often I had seen her parading along Commercial-street, between Flower and Dean-street and Aldgate, or along Whitechapel-road. She was usually in the company of two or three of her kind, fairly neatly dressed and invariably wearing a clean white apron, but no hat. A pretty, buxom girl. There was no woman in the whole of Whitechapel more frightened of Jack the Ripper than Marie Kelly.

On the afternoon of the 8th November, Mary had gone to the Ten Bells public house and met another prostitute, Elizabeth Foster, remaining with her in the pub until about 7. 05 p. m. As he had routinely done every day since he and Mary had parted company nine days earlier, Joseph Barnett had visited 13 Miller's Court that evening, finding Mary in her room with a laundress, Maria Harvey.

I last saw her alive between 7. 30 & 7. 45 the night of Thursday before she was found. I was with her about one hour, we were on friendly terms. I told her when I left her I had no work and had nothing to give her of which I was very sorry, we did not drink together, she was quite sober. There was a female with us on Thursday evening when we were together, she left first and I left shortly afterwards.

Maria Harvey had later confirmed the visit.

I was in the room when Joe Barnett called. I went away. I left my bonnet there. I knew Barnett. I left some clothes in the room. I have seen nothing of them since except the overcoat produced to me by the police.

The clothes that Maria had left behind in the room consisted of two men's shirts, one boy's shirt, a man's black overcoat, a child's white petticoat, a black crepe bonnet with black strings and a two-shilling pawn ticket for a shawl. She had also left her own bonnet behind, which was to mysteriously disappear along with the other items. But why had Maria left the clothes behind? She had been a laundress. Had she stolen the items from her place of work and left them behind for Mary to sell or pawn? Mary had been desperate for money. Perhaps Maria was merely providing for Mary in her hour of need? If so, then why did she admit to the police after the murder that she had indeed left the clothes behind? Perhaps she had sought to evade the charge of theft or had, in fact, simply left the items behind, including her own bonnet, intent on retrieving them later.

At about 11 p. m., Mary was apparently seen in the Britannia public house, drinking with a respectable young man with a dark moustache. She had been drunk. Walter Dew would later remark,

This was unusual, for normally Marie was a sober girl.

Forty-five minutes later, at about 11. 45 p. m., Mary Ann Cox had turned the corner by the Britannia public house and entered Dorset Street. Directly ahead of her and walking unsteadily had been Mary, accompanied by a man carrying a pail of ale. Mrs. Cox had followed the couple and entered Miller's Court, shuffling behind them along the darkened narrow passage. Seeing Mary about to enter her room with the man, Mrs Cox had said, "Good night, Mary Jane." Slurring, Mary had replied, "Good night. I'm going to have a song." Aged about thirty-five with a blotchy face and a carroty moustache, the man had been stout and had worn a billycock hat and a long overcoat. Upon reaching her room at the far end of the court, Mrs. Cox had heard Mary, from within her own room, start to sing a popular music hall song:

**A VIOLET
- FROM -
MOTHER'S GRAVE.**

———

Scenes of my childhood arise before my gaze,
Bringing recollections of by-gone happy days,
When down in the meadows in childhood I would roam,
No one's left to cheer me now within the good old home;
Father and mother they have passed away,
Sister and brother now lay beneath the clay,
But while life does remain to cheer me I'll retain,
This small Violet I plucked from mother's grave.

Chorus. – Only a violet
            I plucked when but a boy,
        And oftimes when I'm sad at heart
            This flow'r has giv'n me joy;
    But while life does remain in memoriam I'll retain,
    This small Violet I plucked from mother's grave.

Well I remember my dear old mother's smile,
As she used to greet me when I returned from toil,
Always knitting in the old arm chair.
Father used to sit and read for all the children there,
But now all is silent around the good old home,
They have all left me in sorrow for to roam.
But while life does remain in memoriam I'll retain,
This small Violet I plucked from mother's grave. – Cho.

Fifteen minutes later, Mrs. Cox had left her room and returned to the streets in search of a customer. At about 12. 15 a. m. and in her room overlooking the two windows of 13 Miller's Court, Catherine Picket had become increasingly irritated by the repetitive lyrics sung by Mary, but had been stopped by her husband from going across the gloomy court to protest. At about 1 a. m. it had begun to rain heavily. Mrs. Cox had again returned to her room, hearing Mary still singing. Landlord John McCarthy had also heard her, later saying that she had sounded very happy. Merrily drunk, no doubt? Quickly warming her hands, Mrs. Cox had again ventured out into the streets, desperate to find a customer. At about the same time, Elizabeth Prater had returned home and had stood at the arched entrance to Miller's Court for about thirty minutes, except for the ten minutes when she had popped into the chandler's shop next door for a quick chat. Resuming her position outside the entrance to Miller's Court, Elizabeth Prater, like Mrs. Cox, had hoped to snare one final customer before retiring. Curiously, she had heard no singing, which would have undoubtedly echoed along the gloomy passage to the entrance where she had stood. Having seen no one enter or leave the court, Elizabeth Prater had then retired to her room above number 13, securely wedging two chairs against her door. Without undressing, she had lain upon her bed and fallen into a deep, drink-induced sleep.

Thirty minutes later, at 2 a. m., Mary herself had seemingly taken to the wet dreary streets, casually accosting a labourer, George Hutchinson, in Commercial Street and asking him to lend her sixpence. Unable to oblige her, Mary had remarked to him, "I must go and look for some money." Hutchinson had watched her walk away towards Thrawl Street whereupon a man had approached her, tapped her on the shoulder and said something to her, which had made her laugh. The man had then put his arm around her shoulders and begun to walk with her back towards Dorset Street. Hutchinson, who by now had stood beneath a street gas lamp just outside the Queen's Head public house, watched as the couple had drawn near him. Aged about thirty-four, the man had been about five feet six inches tall, wore a long dark coat trimmed with astrachan, and a soft felt hat drawn down over his eyes. He had carried a small parcel, eight inches long, which had been covered in American cloth and had a strap around it. He had dark features, dark moustache and seemed to be a 'foreigner', which had been a euphemism for Jew. Curiously enough, this thorough description had matched the two men seen separately by Police Constable William Smith and James Brown in Berner Street just before Elizabeth Stride had been found murdered in Dutfield's Yard. The man that had been seen with Mary Kelly had appeared to be a composite of both those men. I had not been able to put my finger upon it, but something about George Hutchinson's detailed description of the man had struck me as being rather false. As the couple had passed him, Hutchinson had stooped and looked at the face of the man, who had glared back at him. The couple had then walked across Commercial Street and turned into Dorset Street. Another oddity about this episode, which had again struck me as being peculiar, was that Mary had undoubtedly been inebriated before she had met Hutchinson but, according to him, she had not been drunk but spreeish or partially drunk. Ignoring the pouring rain, Hutchinson had then curiously followed the couple and had halted at the corner of Commercial Street and Dorset

Street, observing Mary and the man as they had paused at the entrance of Miller's Court to talk for a few minutes. After kissing Mary, the man had jovially taken a red handkerchief from his pocket and given it to her. Edging his way along the other side of the street, Hutchinson had then seen the couple enter the court. Standing in the shadows of Crossingham's lodging house, opposite the entrance of Miller's Court, Hutchinson had begun a lonely, bone-chilling vigil, which he was to endure for the next three quarters of an hour. His reason for such a dutiful act was that he had known Mary for the past three years and had been extremely concerned for her safety. But what had caused his concern in the first place? Other than being very surly and seeming Jewish, what had Mary's male companion done to arouse suspicion? If the man had indeed been my unknown benefactor, intent on murder, then Hutchinson had hardly positioned himself effectively to prevent such an act. Why had he not sought the help of a policeman? The inhabitants of Spitalfields, nay Whitechapel, were awfully close to panic and Hutchinson, drenched to the skin, had stood inertly watching Miller's Court, where Mary Kelly was soon to die horribly. The apparent futility of his presence that rainy morning had defied belief.

After quarrelling with her husband at 24 Great Pearl Street, Spitalfields, Sarah Lewis had angrily stormed out of their lodgings into the teeming rain, determined to seek refuge with Mr. and Mrs. Keyler at 2 Miller's Court. Passing Christ Church and hearing its clock chime half-past-two, she had turned from Commercial Street into Dorset Street and, upon reaching Miller's Court, had noticed a man loitering in the shadows of Crossingham's, directly opposite.

I saw a man with a wideawake hat. There was no one talking to him. He was a stout-looking man, and not very tall. The hat was black. I did not take any notice of his clothes. The man was looking up the court; he seemed to be waiting or looking for someone. Further on there was a man and woman – the latter being drunk. There was nobody in the court.

About twenty minutes into his forty-five minute vigil, the man had undoubtedly been George Hutchinson. Although Sarah Lewis had certainly seen him, Hutchinson curiously had never disclosed that he had seen her. Perhaps he had a lapse of memory when he volunteered his statement to the police three days later. Warmly greeted by Mr. and Mrs. Keyler, Sarah Lewis had shaken the rain from her clothes, sat in a chair and had dozed. Twenty-five minutes later, at about 3 a. m., Hutchinson, obviously soaked to the bone and miserable, had decided upon a new course of action. He abandoned his watch and had scurried away, leaving the fate of Mary Kelly in the balance. This from a sympathetic man who had known her for the past three years and had been concerned for her safety. How Inspector Abberline of the Criminal Investigation Department had eagerly embraced George Hutchinson's flawed statement without recognising this noticeable contradiction had been quite beyond me. As Hutchinson had strolled away at 3 a. m. to inexplicably roam the dismal wet streets until 6 a. m., Mrs. Cox had returned and entered Miller's Court. Hurriedly passing number 13, she had seen that the light within the room was out and had heard nothing. Perhaps Mary and her newly acquired companion had been in bed, getting better acquainted. Half an hour later, at 3. 30 a. m., Sarah Lewis had awoke from her awkward slumber in her chair. Shortly before four o'clock she had heard a woman scream, "Murder!" At the same time, Elizabeth Prater, awakened by her pet kitten Diddles clambering across her neck, had heard a similar scream, "Oh! Murder!" Although the shrieks had come from the immediate vicinity of number 13, neither women had taken much notice because such cries had regrettably been a regular occurrence throughout Whitechapel.

At 5. 30 a. m., Elizabeth Prater had left her room above number 13, seeing no one in the court or Dorset Street, except for two or three carmen harnessing their horses. It had been a chilly morning and drizzling rain as she had hurried to, and entered, the Ten Bells public house, for a tot of rum. Fifteen minutes later, Mary Ann Cox had heard the heavy tread of a man leaving the court. She had been unable to determine from which room he had departed. Shortly after, and having left the Ten Bells public house, Elizabeth Prater had hastily returned to her room and once again had fallen asleep. Stirring at 7. 30 a. m, Catherine Picker had slowly dressed and left her room, descending into the court by 8 a. m. Feeling the chill in the air, she had knocked on the door of number 13, intent on asking Mary if she might borrow her shawl. Getting no reply, Catherine Picker had turned away and gone off to work. Half an hour later, at 8. 30 a. m., Caroline Maxwell, who had lived at 14 Dorset Street and was also the wife of doss-house deputy Henry

Maxwell, had seen Mary Kelly standing just outside the entrance to Miller's Court. Conversing across the street, Maxwell had asked, "What brings you up so early?" "Oh, Carrie, I've the horrors of drink upon me as I've been drinking for some days past," replied Mary. Maxwell glibly advised, "Why don't you go to Mrs. Ringer's and have half a pint of beer?" Mary had then pointed to some vomit upon the surface of the cobbled street, "I've been there and had it, but I've brought it up again." Anxious to get her husband's breakfast, Maxwell had turned away, remarking, "I can pity your feelings." Having known Mary for about four months and only spoken to her twice, Maxwell had nonetheless known her by name and that she had been a prostitute. At 9 a. m., Maxwell had again seen Mary, this time outside the Britannia public house, nicknamed 'Ringer's', talking with a stout man, dressed as a market porter.

Nearly two hours later, at 10. 45 a. m., John McCarthy had sent his chandler shop assistant, Thomas Bowyer, into Miller's Court to confront Mary on her rent arrears. Why McCarthy had permitted the arrears to escalate to such an impossible settlement would forever remain a mystery. Perhaps he had anticipated keeping Mary in servitude to service him personally? Knocking on the door of number 13 and getting no reply, Bowyer had tried the door, finding it locked. He had knocked again and then had peered through the keyhole, distinguishing nothing. Stepping around the corner to the first window, he had reached through the broken pane of glass and drawn aside the faded muslin curtain. Peering into the room, Bowyer had immediately recoiled and rushed back to McCarthy, stammering,

Governor, I knocked at the door and could not make anyone answer. I looked through the window and saw a lot of blood.

Fearing the worst, McCarthy had returned with Thomas Bowyer to number 13 and looked through the window. The sight that had greeted him had been more nauseating than he had expected.

The sight we saw I cannot drive away from my mind. It looked more like the work of a devil than a man. I had heard a great deal about the Whitechapel murders, but declare to God I had never expected to see such a sight as this. The whole scene is more than I can describe. I hope I

135

may never see such a sight as this again.

McCarthy had immediately sent Bowyer to Commercial Street Police Station, where Inspector Walter Beck, Detective Walter Dew and Sergeant Betham had been on duty. Overcome with fright, Bowyer had spluttered, "Another one. Jack the Ripper. Awful. Jack McCarthy sent me." Bursting into the police station shortly after Bowyer had reported the grisly news, McCarthy had confirmed the discovery. Quickly donning their hats and coats, Beck and Dew had hurriedly returned to Miller's Court along with McCarthy and Bowyer. Peering through the hole in the glass, Beck had reached forward and pulled aside an old black overcoat that had been hanging just inside the window. A moment later he had staggered back, his face as white as a sheet. He had stared at Dew, "For God's sake, Dew. Don't look." Dew had ignored the order and looked into the room.

When my eyes had become accustomed to the dim light I saw a sight which I shall never forget to my dying day.

Beck instantly had the court sealed off from the public, trapping the remaining hapless residents of Miller's Court in their rooms. Awoken by a commotion immediately below her, Elizabeth Prater had descended from her room and, allowed by the police to get some water from the water pump in the outer recess, had taken the opportunity and had peered through the window herself.

I'm a woman myself and I've got to sleep in that place tonight right over where it happened. I could bear to look at it only for a second but I can never forget the sight of it if I live to be a hundred.

At 11. 15 a. m., Dr. Bagster Phillips had arrived and was followed by Inspector Abberline fifteen minutes later. Both these men must shoulder some responsibility for the fiasco that had ensued. Having looked through the window and ascertained that Mary Kelly had been beyond help, Bagster Phillips had deemed it unnecessary to force the locked door at that particular time. Inspector Abberline, who had been in overall charge of the case, had later explained this bizarre decision.

I had an intimation from Inspector Beck that the dogs had

been sent for and Dr. Phillips asked me not to force the door but to test the dogs if they were coming.

Bred by Edwin Brough, the dogs in question had been two English bloodhounds affectionately known as Barnaby and Burgho. Since the murder of Annie Chapman, it had been suggested to the police that bloodhounds might be of more use than a hundred police constables in ferreting out criminals who had left no trace behind except their scent. Although dog breeder Edwin Brough had applauded the special qualities of the bloodhound, he had remained sceptical that they would be of any use in the crowded streets of London. However, after the murders of Elizabeth Stride and Catharine Eddowes, Sir Charles Warren had earnestly seized upon the bloodhound idea, partaking in a ludicrous experiment on Tooting Common, where he had been tracked by bloodhounds who had eventually got utterly lost in the fog. Undeterred, Warren had encouraged further trials, this time using Edwin Brough and two of his finest dogs, Barnaby and Burgho. On the 8th October, at 7 a. m., the first of these trials had begun in Regent's Park. Although the ground of the park had been thickly coated in frost, Barnaby and Burgho had successfully tracked a man who had been given a fifteen-minute start. That night, in total darkness, they had once more succeeded in another trial, tracking a man in Hyde Park. The following morning, 9th October, a further six trials were held with Warren acting the part of the hunted man on two occasions. Although the scented trail had been purposely tainted to deceive Barnaby and Burgho, they had successfully tracked him each time. After concluding the trials, Brough had cautioned Warren, explaining that even though Barnaby and Burgho had performed impressively on grass, there could be no certainty that they would repeat their success in the fetid streets of Whitechapel. Nonetheless, Warren had thought that the two bloodhounds had performed splendidly and, under the impression that Brough would loan Barnaby and Burgho to the police free of charge, had issued instructions that, in the event of another Whitechapel murder, the body should not be disturbed until the bloodhounds were allowed to take up the scent. Brough, of course, had expected the police to either purchase or hire his two valuable bloodhounds and insure them against accidents. When he had failed to get a firm financial pledge from Warren, Brough had reluctantly withdrawn Barnaby and Burgho, leaving the police at the end of the month with no trained bloodhounds in the metropolis. At the time of the murder of

Mary Jane Kelly, Barnaby and Burgho had been reunited with their owner in Wyndyate near Scarborough for at least nine days.

Shuffling from foot to foot in the drizzling rain and waiting for imaginary bloodhounds, the police had little to do in Miller's Court but to accumulate statements from local residents and arrange for a photographer to photograph the corpse. By now, news of the murder had begun to filter throughout the district, giving rise to disbelief. Among all the pomp and pageantry the wealthiest city of our Empire could have devised, the Right Honourable James Whitehead, the new Lord Mayor of London, had been travelling in state, heading towards the Royal Courts of Justice to take his oath of office. As the procession had turned from Ludgate Circus into Fleet Street, news of the murder had burst upon the crowds lining the route. Spectators soon deserted the show in their thousands and converged upon Dorset Street. Positioned at each end of the street, ranks of police constables had denied them access but the neighbouring streets soon became clogged with hordes of morbid, frightened people. Miller's Court had become besieged.

At 1. 30 p. m., Superintendent Thomas Arnold had arrived at the court, bringing news that the order regarding the bloodhounds had been countermanded. He had then given direct instructions to force the door. Wielding a pickaxe, John McCarthy had broken the door open. It had been an unnecessary act. The door had a spring lock that fastened when the door was pulled shut but could easily be unlocked by simply reaching through the broken window from the outside. Something the police had failed to contemplate, even though they had ample time to assess the simple procedure. A moment later Inspector Abberline and his men were inside the room. The sight that had met their eyes was to haunt all of them for the rest of their days. The horribly butchered mess that lay before them had been barely recognisable as a human being. Mary Kelly had been grotesquely mutilated to an extraordinary degree.

Aftermath

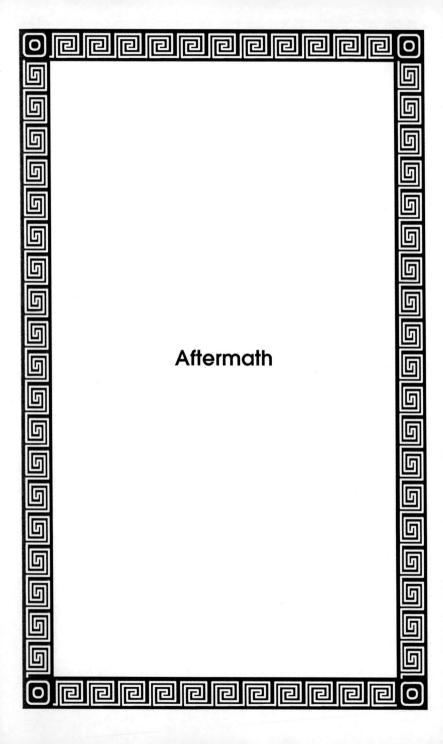

Aftermath

Upon seeing the carnage that greeted him in 13 Miller's Court, Superintendent Thomas Arnold had the room thoroughly searched.

The clothes of the woman were lying by the side of the bed, as though they had been taken off and laid down in the ordinary manner. The bedclothes had been turned down, and this was probably done by the murderer after he had cut her throat. There was no appearance of a struggle having taken place, and, although a careful search of the room was made, no knife or instrument of any kind was found. The fire grate contained an exceptionally large amount of ashes, including a few scorched remnants of clothing and the charred wirework of a bonnet. A copper kettle with a melted spout was close to the grate, signifying that a fierce fire may have melted the spout. Some tableware and empty beer bottles were found in a cupboard next to the fireplace. One piece of candle was found on a table by the second window and a black overcoat hung down by the first window. Whilst this search was being made of the room a photographer took two photographs of the body, including organs that had been placed on a small bedside table. Dr. Bagster Phillips examined the body of the dead woman along with Dr. Duke, from Spitalfields, Dr. Gordon Brown, from the City and Dr. Bond, from Westminster.

Arnold's detailed description of the virtual destruction of Mary Jane Kelly had made for a harrowing read.

A more horrible or sickening sight could not be imagined. The poor woman lay on her back on the bed, entirely naked, except for part of a chemise which covered her shoulders and upper arms. Her face was horribly hacked about, so the features of the poor creature were beyond all recognition. The ears and nose had been cut clean off. Her cheeks and eyebrows had been partially removed. The lips were cut with several incisions running down her chin at an angle. Her throat had been savagely cut from ear to ear, right down to the spinal column. The breasts had also been cleanly cut off. One breast was found under her head, the other by the right foot. Her heart had been removed and was found to be absent. The arms had been severely mutilated by several jagged wounds. The right thumb had a superficial cut about an inch long whilst the back of the right hand had several minor abrasions. The stomach and abdomen had been ripped open and emptied of its contents. The uterus & kidneys were found by her head. The liver was between her feet. The intestines by her right side & the spleen to her left side. The thighs and legs had been terribly mutilated. The left thigh was stripped of both skin & muscles as far as the knee. The left calf had a deep gash from the knee to just above the ankle. The left arm was bent at the elbow with its hand in the abdominal cavity. Some partially digested food, fish & potatoes, were found in the remains of the stomach attached to the intestines. The three large flaps removed from the abdomen and thighs had been placed upon the bedside table. The bed clothing was saturated with blood, whilst beneath the bed was a pool of blood about 2 feet square. After the examination was completed the body was placed in a shell, which was put on a cart and conveyed to the Shoreditch mortuary to await an inquest.

I recalled being taken aback. Had my previous nightmare been an omen for what had now become so hideously real? The thought had seemed quite preposterous until I remembered that Mary Kelly had also dreamt of being murdered. Had our emotional thoughts become so inexplicably intertwined that we had both foreseen her impending death? Yes, I had indeed hungered for her ultimate demise. Yes, I had indeed yearned that she should be obliterated from the face of the earth. But had my mania been so intense that I could have butchered her in my dream? Nay, the idea was utterly ridiculous. Surely two individuals, enduring a similar lurid dream, had to be pure coincidence. But then an unsettling thought had struck me. The duality of man. Henry Jekyll and Edward Hyde. Could my obsession with Mary Kelly have released an inner murderous self? In a somnambulous condition, had I silently returned to Whitechapel and slaughtered five women, recalling nothing of my nocturnal exploits afterwards? Again, the idea had seemed absurd. On the contrary, I had noticed nothing improper on my person or clothes to indicate otherwise. But a nagging doubt preyed upon my mind. If I had indeed committed the five murders I would have undoubtedly possessed a second place of refuge, where I would have washed and changed my clothes before returning to the boarding school. If this had truly been the case then my ethereal nightmares had been the only tangible confirmation that I was indeed my own benefactor.

To Marquis of Salisbury, Prime Minister – 10 November 1888

Balmoral Castle

10th inst

This new most ghastly murder shows the absolute necessity for some very decided action. All these courts must be lit & our detectives improved. They are not what they should be. You promised when the 1st murders took place to consult with your colleagues about it.

VR.

At what time had Mary Kelly actually been murdered? In his post mortem report Dr. Bond had stated,

The body was lying on the bed at the time of my visit at two o'clock quite naked and mutilated. Rigor Mortis had set in but increased during the progress of the examination. From this it is difficult to say with any certainty the exact time that had elapsed since death as the period varies from six to twelve hours before rigidity sets in.

The body was comparatively cold at two o'clock and the remains of a recently taken meal were found in the stomach and scattered about over the intestines. It was therefore almost certain that the woman must have been dead about twelve hours and the partly digested food would indicate that death took place about three or four hours after food was taken, so one or two o'clock in the morning would be the probable time of the murder.

Similar to some of his colleagues before him, the good doctor had obviously had a lapse of memory. The corpse had not been discovered quite naked. Mary Kelly had been found dressed in part of a chemise, which had covered her shoulders and upper arms. However, if Mary had indeed been killed between 1 a. m.

and 2 a.m. as Dr. Bond had declared, then Caroline Maxwell could not possibly have spoken with Mary at 8. 30 a. m. or seen her half an hour later at 9. a. m. Perhaps Caroline Maxwell had simply got her dates mixed up, innocently believing that she had indeed spoken with Mary that fateful, dreary morning when, in fact, the conversation had taken place on an entirely different morning. I nonetheless had felt a twinge of doubt about such a probability. Caroline Maxwell had given her statement to the police on the very same day that the body had been found in 13 Miller's Court. Could she have really got such a recent encounter muddled up with another time? Might her conversation with Mary Kelly have actually taken place at the exact hour she said it had? If so, Mary Kelly had been murdered after Caroline Maxwell last saw her alive at 9 a. m. and before Thomas Bowyer had first stumbled upon her mutilated body at 10. 45 a. m. But had the medical evidence supported such an improbable possibility? Definitely not. Thus, had Mary died between the hours of 1 a. m. and 2 a. m. as Dr. Bond had suggested? Probably not. According to Mary Ann Cox and John McCarthy, Mary had been alive at 1 a. m., gaily singing. At 2 a. m., she had then accosted George Hutchinson in Commercial Street, asking him to lend her sixpence. Due to the testimonies of these eyewitnesses, I had begun to regard Dr. Bond's medical opinion with extreme caution. Might it have been possible that Mary Kelly's body had lost heat more rapidly than usual, thus accelerating rigor mortis and signifying that she had actually died after 2 a. m.? Dr. Bagster Phillips, who had arrived at Miller's Court at 11. 15 a. m. and subsequently examined the body at 1. 30 p. m., considered this to have been the case.

There is no doubt that the body of a person who was "cut all to pieces" would get cold far more quickly than that of one who had died simply from the cutting of the throat; and the room would have been very cold, as there were two broken panes of glass in the windows. Again, the body being entirely uncovered would very quickly get cold. I am, therefore, of the opinion that the murder was committed at about 5 a. m. or 6 a. m.

The extraordinarily large amount of ashes that had been found in the fire grate of the room were undoubtedly the remains of the clothes left behind by Maria Harvey. Fierce enough to melt the spout of a copper kettle, a blazing fire would have kept the body fairly warm, thus delaying rigor mortis and undermining Dr. Bagster Phillips' estimated time of death. I had therefore reasoned that the murder had taken place between both the estimated times stated by Dr. Bond and Dr. Phillips; somewhere, I thought, between 2 a. m. and 5 a.m. The shriek of "Murder!" or "Oh! Murder!" heard by both Sarah Lewis and Elizabeth Prater indicated that Mary Kelly had probably died between these times, shortly before 4 a. m. Aware of the broken pane of glass and having reached through the window from the outside, my benefactor had unbolted the door and had stealthily entered the room. Stepping past Mary Kelly, asleep in her bed alone, he had lit the candle upon the table by the second window, causing her to stir and suddenly awake. Blearily recognising him, she had raised her right hand in her defence, screaming, "Murder!" Instantly drawing his knife, he had lunged at her, grabbing her by the right hand and nicking her thumb as he savagely sliced through her throat down to her spinal cord. Soaked to the bone and shivering, he had immediately thrown some of the clothes left behind by Maria Harvey into the grate and made a fire, thereby warming himself. Rolling back the bedclothes and exposing the almost naked body of Mary Kelly, he had then begun to butcher her beyond reason. Some forty-five minutes later he had extinguished the flame of the candle and, with her heart securely wrapped in a white petticoat, had left the room, pulling the door shut behind him. At 5. 45 a. m. and alone in her room, Mrs. Cox had heard the heavy tread of his footsteps as he had left Miller's Court.

MURDER. – PARDON. – Whereas on November 8 or 9, in Miller's Court, Dorset Street, Spitalfields, Mary Jane Kelly was murdered by some person or persons unknown: the Secretary of State will advise the grant of Her Majesty's gracious pardon to any accomplice, not being a person who contrived or actually committed the murder, who shall give such information and evidence as shall lead to the discovery and conviction of the person or persons who committed the murder.
CHARLES WARREN, the Commissioner of Police
of the Metropolis
Metropolitan Police Office, 4 Whitehall Place,
S. W., Nov. 10, 1888.

I had been, of course, completely aware that my hypothesis on the murder of Mary Jane Kelly could have been interpreted as mere conjecture. But having studied the numerous newspaper reports of the physical evidence found within the room, I had ultimately arrived at the only probable course of events that had shown me as to how she had been murdered. More importantly, I had also inadvertently learnt that Jack the Ripper, my benefactor, had been seen that morning, thus enlightening me to his identity. A revelation that I had not been ready to disclose to any Scotland Yard official. Shown the horrendously mutilated corpse the day after the murder, Joseph Barnett, himself an instant suspect, had managed to identify Mary Kelly by her light ginger hair and blue eyes. The police had quickly absolved Barnett of any involvement in the crime when it had been found that he had an alibi for the time of the murder. He had, in fact, been with other lodgers in his lodging house at 24 - 25 New Street, Bishopsgate, playing a game of whist. Shortly after 12. 30 a. m., he had retired to his bed and, falling asleep, had risen some hours later, prior to Thomas Bowyer discovering the body.

The Secretary of State
Home Office – 13 November 1888

Balmoral Castle

13th inst.

    The Queen fears that the Detective department is not so efficient as it might be. No doubt the recent murders in Whitechapel were committed in circumstances which made Detection very difficult. Still the Queen thinks that in a small area where these horrible crimes have been perpetrated a great number of detectives might be employed and that every possible suggestion might be carefully examined, and if practicable followed. Have the cattle boats & passenger boats been examined? Has any investigation been made as to the number of single men occupying rooms to themselves? The murderer's clothes must be saturated with blood and must be kept somewhere. Is there sufficient surveillance at night? These are some of the questions that occur to the Queen on reading the accounts of this horrible crime.

                                              VR.

Although I had at first been elated by the fact that the whore of Babylon had finally ceased to exist, I had soon experienced an inner emptiness, similar to a torturous rapid decline after a brilliant career. I would awaken each morning feeling relieved, but mindful that I possessed no sense of purpose. In an attempt to remedy this apparent futility, I had again turned to my beloved cricket club, proposing as its Honorary Treasurer that a further acre of land be purchased by the club to enlarge its present sporting field. The following day, in the ruins of the medieval abbey, I had furtively accommodated the whimsical infatuation of my boarding school boy, who persisted with bodily stimulation, although it had been a somewhat chilly afternoon.

That evening and feeling fatigued, I had slipped beneath the blankets of my bed, eager for a restful night. Alas, it was not to be. Having slowly closed my tired eyes, I had drowsily slipped into a darkened void to be gradually engulfed by an ominous fog. Steadily, the fog had dissipated and, to my utter bewilderment, I had found myself in a gloomy court, thoroughly drenched to the skin. In the drizzling rain, seemingly waiting for someone, I had stood in the shadows, looking at the two rear windows of a small room. The flickering flame of a solitary candle had shone within the room, but then had been quickly extinguished by a silent shadowy figure. I had then heard the unmistakable sound of a door bolt withdrawing. The door of the room had opened and a man, wearing a wideawake hat and with his back to me, stealthily emerged from the room, clutching something in his left hand. He quietly pulled the door shut and then, as if feeling my presence, had paused. Suddenly turning, he had stared at me. The light from an overhead gas lantern revealed his face. I shuddered. The face had been mine. I then awoke, perspiring. After calming myself, I had risen from my bed, dressed and taken a nocturnal stroll to ponder the eerie dream. Had I actually emerged from 13 Miller's Court, with a wrapped human heart in my hand? Had I in due course disposed of the organ but had no recollection where? Nay, the thought had been abhorrent. However, many other anomalies about the five murders had perplexed me immensely. I had also to be convinced beyond all doubt that my repetitive nightmares were nothing more than imaginary creations of my unconscious mind. Only my benefactor could resolve such a conundrum. I knew his identity. I would therefore return to Spitalfields and seek him out. I had been exuberant. Unexpectedly, my morbid dreams

had released me from my melancholy malady and had given me
an entirely newfound sense of purpose.

The Times Newspaper – 16 November 1888

RESIGNATION OF SIR CHARLES WARREN

As will be seen from our Parliamentary report, Sir Charles Warren, Commissioner of the Metropolitan Police, tendered his resignation on Thursday last – the day before the Irish woman Kelly was found murdered. A News Agency learns on the highest authority that the relations between Sir Charles Warren and the Home Office have for some time been strained. In spite of the remonstrances of Sir Charles Warren, the control of the Criminal Investigation Department has been withdrawn more and more from Whitehall-place. Every morning for the last few weeks, conferences have been held at the Home Office between Mr. Monro, Mr. Anderson, and principal Detective Inspectors, and the information furnished to Sir Charles Warren in regard to these conferences has been, he states, of the scantiest character.

The reproof of the Home Secretary, Mr. Henry Matthews, last week in response to an article that Sir Charles had published in Murray's magazine completed the rupture. Sir Charles thereupon took counsel and immediately tendered his resignation, which was accepted by Mr. Matthews. Yesterday morning, Sir Charles removed all his books and papers from his office, and this was the first intimation in Whitehall-place that he had relinquished the position.

Continuously taunted by both the press and the public for his failure to apprehend the Whitechapel murderer, might Sir Charles Warren had been made a scapegoat by an equally besieged government? True, Warren had been an aristocratic authoritarian who had arrogantly thought that he should retain complete authority over the Metropolitan Police, but he had nonetheless believed that the British police should become much more like the continental police, who were far less answerable to the press and politicians. This explosive opinion, contained in an terse article and printed in Murray's magazine, enabled his long term adversary, the Home Secretary, to write a supercilious letter, reminding Sir Charles of an edict that forbade serving police officers from writing to the press without due clearance from the Home Office. Sir Charles had replied that such a ruling did not apply to the Commissioner of the Metropolitan Police, and if it had he would be forced to tender his resignation, which the Home Secretary had eagerly accepted. However, it had been interesting to note that if Jack the Ripper had actually been caught, the Home Secretary would have never dared to accept Sir Charles' resignation. Therefore, there is a grain of truth in the theory that my benefactor had actually assisted in his downfall. Albeit indirectly.

The Times Newspaper – 17 November 1888

A PROFILE OF
THE WHITECHAPEL MURDERER

Dr. Thomas Bond, who made a post mortem examination of the mutilated remains of the Irish woman Mary Jane Kelly and has read the reports of the other 4 victims, is of the opinion that the murderer is a man of physical strength and of great coolness and daring. He is a man subject to periodical attacks of Homicidal and erotic mania. The character of the mutilations indicate that the man may be in a condition sexually, that may be called satyriasis. It is of course possible that the Homicidal impulse may have developed from a revengeful or brooding condition of the mind.

Assuming the murderer to be such a person as described he would probably be solitary and eccentric in his habits, also he is most likely to be a man without regular occupation, but with some small income or pension. He is possibly living among respectable persons who have some knowledge of his character and habits and who may have grounds for suspicion that he is not quite right in his mind at times. Such persons would probably be unwilling to communicate suspicions to the Police for fear of trouble or notoriety, whereas if there were a prospect of a reward it might overcome their scruples.

Dr. Bond's mental and physical portrait of my benefactor had rather intrigued me. I had to admit that it had never once crossed my mind that the murders may have been committed because of the result of an erotic affliction. A sexual craving, if you will. Having initiated the murders as an act of revenge, had my benefactor inadvertently released a dormant inner sexual desire that had peaked and abated whilst he had gutted his victims? Or had the murders been intended initially to placate a sexual desire, which then developed into diabolical acts of revenge? Or might the depraved motive behind the murders have been a combination of both? Whilst I had been deliberating Dr. Bond's article, an altogether different thought about the murder of Mary Kelly had come to mind. Why had she been the last victim and not the first and only victim? What had prevented, delayed my benefactor from murdering her until very recently?

The Times Newspaper – 20 November 1888

THE WHITECHAPEL MURDER

The remains of the unfortunate woman, Marie Jeanette Kelly, who was murdered on November 9th, in Miller's-court, Dorset-street, Spitalfields, were carried yesterday, Monday, from the Shoreditch mortuary to the Roman Catholic Cemetery at Leytonstone, for interment, amidst a scene of turbulent excitement. On the afternoon of the murder the body of the murdered woman was conveyed to the mortuary attached to St. Leonard's Church, Shoreditch, and there it remained until yesterday.

Since the inquest, held on the 12th November, which concluded the same day, a great amount of sympathy for the fate of the unhappy creature has been created, but it remained for Mr. H. Wilton, the sexton attached to Shoreditch Church, to put sympathy into a practical form, and as no relatives have appeared he incurred the total cost of the funeral himself. Mr. Wilton has been sexton for over 50 years, and he provided the funeral as a mark of sympathy with the poor people of the neighbourhood, in whose welfare he is deeply interested.

The body was enclosed in a polished elm and oak coffin, with metal mounts. On the coffin plate were engraved the words: 'Marie Jeanette Kelly, died 9th Nov. 1888, aged 25 years'. Upon the coffin were two crowns of artificial flowers and a cross made up of heartsease. The coffin was carried in an open car drawn by two horses, and two coaches followed. An enormous crowd of people assembled at an early hour, completely blocking the thoroughfare, and a large number of police were engaged in keeping order.

The bell of St. Leonard's began tolling at noon, and the sound drew all the residents in the neighbourhood together. As the coffin appeared, borne on the shoulders of four men, at the principal gate of the church, the crowd appeared to be greatly affected. Round the open car in which it was to be placed men and women struggled desperately to touch the coffin. Women with faces streaming with tears cried out "God forgive her!" and every man's head was bared in token of sympathy. The sight was quite remarkable, and the emotion natural and unconstrained. Two mourning coaches followed behind, one containing three, and the other five persons – mourners who had been fortifying themselves for the journey at a public house close to the church gates. Joseph Barnett was among them, with someone from McCarthy's, the landlord; and the others were women who had given evidence at the inquest.

The traffic was blocked, and the constables had great difficulty in obtaining free passage for the small procession through the mass of carts and tramcars. The cortège made its way by way of Hackney-road, to Leytonstone, where beneath a stormy sky, Marie Jeannette Kelly was finally laid to rest.

No one's left to cheer me now within the good old home;
Father and mother they have passed away,
Sister and brother now lay beneath the clay,
But while life does remain to cheer me I'll retain,
This small Violet I plucked from mother's grave.

> 'A Violet from mother's grave'
> Music hall song.
> 1888

It had been the mention of Joseph Barnett in the newspaper article that had prompted me to take a closer look at him and his association with Mary Kelly, which I had hoped would ultimately explain the reason why she had been the final victim. The year before, on 8th April, 1887, Joseph Barnett had first met Mary Jane Kelly in a public house in Commercial Street, Spitalfields. Unlike Mary, Barnett had been born and raised in the East End of London and had been employed as a fish porter at Billingsgate market, an attribute that would have undoubtedly impressed the impetuous

Mary, who had constantly sought the financial security offered by men. The following day, they had met again and had decided to remain together, promptly moving into a lodging house in George Street, Commercial Street. Later the same year, they had moved from George Street into another common lodging house in Little Paternoster Row, Dorset Street, seventy yards from Miller's Court. Often drunk and behind with the rent, they were eventually thrown out of the lodging house in Little Paternoster Row and had moved to another lodging house in Brick Lane. The following year, towards the end of February, 1888, they had left the lodging house in Brick Lane, finally moving into 13 Miller's Court.

It had been during this point of my research that an unsettling thought had struck me. Annie Millwood had been cruelly attacked on Saturday, 25th February, in an alleyway beside her lodging house at 8 White's Row, running parallel with Dorset Street. Joseph Barnett and Mary Kelly had moved into 13 Miller's Court on or about the time of the attack. Might the two separate events have been connected? Six months later, at the end of August, Joseph Barnett had been without regular work, having been dismissed by his employer for theft. Without any income, Mary had returned to her former line of work, prostitution. On Friday, 31st August, Mary Ann Nichols had been found brutally murdered in Buck's Row. On or about the time of her murder, Mary Kelly had returned to ply her trade in the streets. Again, had the two separate events been connected? While Barnett had been gainfully employed, Mary had no reason to walk the fog-shrouded streets at night. Besides, even when Barnett had become unemployed, he had ample time to involve himself with her whereabouts and safety.

Some two months later, Tuesday, 30th October, the couple had a heated argument, breaking a pane of glass in the window nearest the door of their room. Unable to endure her repeated practice of providing brief shelter for other prostitutes at 13 Miller's Court, Barnett had left Mary, taking refuge in a lodging house at New Street, Bishopsgate. I had at last learnt what had initially delayed Jack the Ripper from murdering Mary Kelly and why she had become his final victim. Up and until he had left Mary, Joseph Barnett's continual presence had prevented my benefactor from murdering her, which he had ultimately achieved a mere nine days after Barnett had departed 13 Miller's Court. I had also learnt something else about Jack the Ripper. Something quite unnerving.

Martha Tabram had been murdered at the end of a public bank holiday on a Tuesday morning. Mary Ann Nichols had died on a Friday morning, Annie Chapman on a Saturday morning, Catharine Eddowes on a Sunday morning. And finally Mary Kelly on a Friday morning. Prior to these five murders, Annie Millwood had been attacked on a Saturday morning. The murders had all occurred at the end of the week or at the weekend, indicating that they had not been random murders, but had been purposely planned. Far from simply being a lunatic running amok through the streets of Whitechapel, Jack the Ripper had shown that he was a ruthless individual skilled in premeditated murder. If I were to seek him out as I intended to do, then I would have to be very cautious and plan a practical strategy to protect myself. Unlike Dr. Bond, who had suggested that the murderer had no regular occupation, I had firmly believed that my benefactor had possessed regular employment. Hence he had only killed at the end of the week or the weekend.

The Times Newspaper – 21 November 1888

MURDEROUS OUTRAGE IN WHITECHAPEL

Considerable excitement was caused throughout the East-end yesterday morning by a report that another woman had been brutally murdered and mutilated in a common lodging-house in George-street, Spitalfields, and in consequence of the reticence of the police authorities all sorts of rumours prevailed. Although it was soon ascertained that there had been no murder, it was said that an attempt had been made to murder a woman, of the class to which the other unfortunate creatures belonged, by cutting her throat, and the excitement in the neighbourhood for some time was intense.

Whether the woman's assailant is the man wanted for the seven recent murders committed in the district of Whitechapel is not known, although his description tallies somewhat with that given by one of the witnesses at the last inquest; but should he be, the police are sanguine of his speedy capture, as a good and accurate description of him is now obtained, and if arrested he could be identified by more than one person.

The victim of this last occurrence, fortunately, is but slightly injured, and was at once able to furnish the detectives with a full description of her assailant. Her name is Annie Farmer, and she is a woman of about 40 years of age, who lately resided with her tradesman husband in Featherstone-street, City-road, but, on account of her dissolute habits, was separated from him. On Monday night the woman had no money, and, being unable to obtain any, walked the streets until about half-past 7 yesterday morning. At that time she got into conversation, in Commercial-street, with a man, whom she describes as 36 years of age, about 5ft. 6in. in height, with a dark moustache, and wearing a shabby black diagonal suit and hard felt hat. He treated her to several drinks until she became partially intoxicated. At his suggestion they went to a common lodging-house, 19, George-street, and paid the deputy 8d. for a bed. That was about 8 o'clock, and nothing was heard to cause alarm until half-past 9, when screams were heard coming from the room occupied by the man and Farmer.

Some men who were in the kitchen of the house at the time rushed upstairs and met the woman coming down. She was partially undressed, and was bleeding profusely from a wound in the throat. She was asked what was the matter, and simply said "He's done it!" at the same time pointing to the door leading to the street. The men rushed outside, but saw no one except a man in charge of a horse and cart. He was asked if he had noticed any person running away, and said he had seen a man, who he thought had a scar at the back of the neck, run down George-street and turn into Thrawl-street, but not thinking much of the occurrence, had not taken particular notice of the man and had made no attempt to detain him. By this time a considerable number of people had assembled, and these ran into Thrawl-street and searched the courts leading out of the thoroughfare, but without any success. While this was being done the police were communicated with and quickly arrived on the scene. In the meantime the deputy of the lodging-house had wrapped a piece of rag over the woman's wound, and, seeing that it did not appear to be a dangerous cut, got her to dress herself. Dr. George Bagster Phillips, police surgeon of the H Division, together with his assistant, quickly arrived, and the former gentleman stitched up the wound. Seeing that it was not a dangerous one, and in order to get the woman away from the crowd of inmates, who pressed round, he suggested that she should be removed to the Commercial-street Police-station, and that was quickly done on the ambulance.

Although none but police officers were allowed to interview her with regard to the attack, and consequently nothing definite is known as to the cause, it has transpired that she had previously met her assailant some 12 months since, and owing to this fact the officers are doubtful whether the man had anything to do with the recent Whitechapel murders. Owing to the excellent description given they are sanguine of securing the man's arrest within a very short space of time.

Superintendent T. Arnold, who was quickly apprised of what had happened, at once ordered Detective-officers Thicke, New, M'Guire, and others to endeavour to capture the man, and by about 10. 30 a full description of him was telegraphed to all police-stations in the metropolitan police district. It is stated that Farmer is able to converse freely, and that lodgings will be found for her by the police until the person who attacked her is captured. Directly the police arrived at the house in George-street a constable was stationed at the door, and no person was allowed to leave until his or her statement and full particulars concerning each one had been written down.

During the whole day a crowd collected in front of 19, George-street, apparently drawn thither merely out of curiosity to view the house, but none not belonging to it were allowed to enter.

Putting aside the possibility that my benefactor might have indeed attacked Annie Millwood, our reprehensible newspapers were still erroneously attributing seven murders to Jack the Ripper when, in actual fact, I had known he had committed but five. I had been under no illusion that, given a free rein, future, dishonest journalists would attempt to increase the figure to beyond the reported seven, shamelessly obscuring the actual murders with half truths and blatant fabrications.

Six days before the Annie Farmer incident and after nearly three months of self-imposed exile, I had at last returned to Whitechapel, initially visiting my cousin at his surgery in the Minories. Though he had been delighted to see me, my gaunt appearance and obvious loss of weight had once more perturbed him. Prescribing a tonic of Valentine's Meat Juice, he had implored me to take a holiday and regain my strength with regular wholesome meals. Thanking him for his attentive concern, I had further burdened him by handing him a sealed envelope, requesting that in the advent of my sudden disappearance or untimely death he was to deliver the letter to Inspector Abberline at Scotland Yard to whom it had been addressed. Unbeknown to my cousin, the letter had been a summary of the five Whitechapel murders, divulging the name of my benefactor, whom I thought to be Jack the Ripper. Whilst critical of such an unorthodox request and receiving no other explanation from me whatsoever, my cousin had nonetheless consented, politely agreeing that my letter would indeed be delivered if the need arose. Thanking him for his unquestionable support and bidding him good morning, I had then left his surgery, retracing my route back along the Minories to Aldgate High Street.

Upon reaching this busy major thoroughfare, I had inquisitively paused, knowing that just across the road, to my left and hardly three minutes away, had lain Mitre Square, where the penultimate victim, Catharine Eddowes, had been murdered. Possessed by a morbid curiosity, I walked across Aldgate High Street and, passing Houndsditch and Duke Street on my right, had turned from Aldgate into Mitre Street. I had been singularly excited by the thought that Police Constable Edward Watkins had walked along this very same street, prior to stumbling upon the mutilated body of Catharine Eddowes eight weeks earlier. I entered the square and had halted just inside its entrance. Except for an unattended pony and cart and a few pigeons pecking between the cobblestones for strewn granules of barley wheat, the grim square had been deserted. Stepping forward, I had studied the southern corner and had tried to imagine the ghastly sight that had greeted Constable Watkins that fateful morning, but to no avail. A cold wind had blown through the square, chilling my body and disturbing my concentration. I had shivered, instantly aware of someone behind me. I quickly turned and saw a bearded police constable standing at the entrance of the square, staring at me suspiciously. I offered a feeble excuse to explain my being there, but his disapproving silence informed me that my solitary presence was offensive and undesired. Not wishing to provoke him, I had bade him good day and had hastily left the square, passing through Church Passage into Duke Street and right into Aldgate. I then proceeded towards Whitechapel High Street, knowing I would get to Spitalfields by way of Goulston Street.

Strolling past Middlesex Street, known extensively as Petticoat Lane, I had promptly arrived at Goulston Street on my left. Nudged to one side by a surly drunken man lurching out of the grimy street, I had begun to question the wisdom of venturing forth into such a labyrinth of perilous streets to reach my intended destination, when a safer route might be had using the major thoroughfares of Whitechapel High Street and Commercial Street. However, my impulsive curiosity had again triumphed and compelled me forth. I had gone but only halfway along the foul stenching street when a wretched looking woman had drawn near, plying her trade. Her breath had smelt of gin, which was just as repulsive as the offensive odour of the street. She grabbed my arm, mumbling something incomprehensibly. I jerked my arm away and pushed her aside. To my sheer surprise and utter relief, a police constable appeared from New Goulston Street and, upon seeing my predicament, had immediately detained the woman, allowing me to continue my journey unhindered. Nearing Wentworth Model Dwellings, where the enigmatic message had been chalked on the wall above the piece of Catharine Eddowes' apron, I had been sorely tempted to halt and examine the inside of its dim entrance, but two untimely encounters with our police force had convinced me otherwise. Desiring no further attention that might delay my progress, I had promptly crossed over Wentworth Street and hurried along Bell Lane towards Brushfield Street.

My journey along Bell Lane was uneventful, but the presence of patrolling police constables had been particularly evident. In a feeble attempt to appear inconspicuous, I had deliberately worn my least appealing clothes, but the superior quality and cut of the material nonetheless attracted vigilant glances from every police constable I had passed. Increasing my pace, I had hurried past White's Row, where Annie Millwood had been attacked in the alleyway beside her lodging house, and then past Dorset Street, where the whore of Babylon had been butchered in Miller's Court. Strolling along Crispin Street, I had turned right into Brushfield Street and, passing Little Paternoster Row where Annie Chapman had last been seen alive, I at long last entered the major thoroughfare of Commercial Street. If the rabbit warren of foul side streets had been noticeable by a dismal lack of activity, then Commercial Street offered a stark contrast. Clogged with every conceivable type of horse drawn vehicle, stationary or travelling, the main road was a continuous bustling trade route reeking of horse dung and urine, which sliced right through Spitalfields, itself the degenerate heart of Whitechapel. Mechanised omnibuses, a recent novelty, hummed along iron grooves embedded in the cobbled street, frequently halted by horse drawn wagons heavily laden with goods. Opposite Christ Church, and warily navigating my way through the moving morass, I had crossed the chaotic road and had quickly arrived at my intended destination, the Ten Bells public house. Situated at the corner of Church Street and Commercial Street and directly opposite Spitalfields fruit and vegetable market, the Ten Bells had been an obvious choice from where to begin my search for Jack the Ripper.

Entering the virtually deserted public house and ordering a pint of dark ale, which had made me feel quite nauseous every time I swallowed a mouthful, I had diplomatically informed the brawny middle-aged publican that I sought a local man who might be the beneficiary of a substantial inheritance and that a reputable firm of solicitors had charged me to find him. Divulging the name of my benefactor, I had placed a florin coin upon the counter in front of him, hoping it would improve his memory or at best untie his tongue. Clearly agitated by my presence, he had sternly replied, "Best you leave, sir. He'll not be found here." Which implied that, whatever the temptation, he was reluctant to disclose information to a total stranger about a man whom he might or might not know. Somewhat irritated by his curt response, I had retrieved the florin and left the Ten Bells, tasting yet again the foul stench of Commercial Street. Strolling past Christ Church and feeling slightly fatigued, I had deliberately slowed my pace, peering through the cumbersome traffic at the Britannia public house across the road. Situated on the corner of Dorset Street, the Britannia was destined to be my next port of call, so to speak. But the very thought of having to once more steer a wearisome course through the hectic traffic to reach this den of iniquity was, to say the least, utterly off putting. I therefore had opted to stay on my side of the road, permitting me to proceed straight along to the corner of Fashion Street, where the Queen's Head public house had been located. Upon reaching its entrance, I had gazed along Fashion Street, recalling how Mary Kelly had brazenly taken me into New Court and contemptuously humiliated me, ultimately compelling my mind to the brink of madness. Had the despicable whore also derided my benefactor in a similar manner, thus igniting his fury and initiating the Whitechapel murders? Stepping through the doors of the Queen's Head, my heart had somewhat quickened. I was eager to locate my benefactor and hear for myself the actual motive that had driven him to commit such hideous atrocities.

Unlike the solemn mood of the Ten Bells, the Queen's Head had been crowded with boisterous men and women, the majority of them standing and drinking at the bar. Upon seating myself at a small wooden table by one of its amber glass windows, I was served a bowl of hot broth by a buxom barmaid, who had amiably queried my presence. I repeated the same story I had given to the publican of the Ten Bells, telling the barmaid that she could earn a small reward for any information. Raising an eyebrow and placing her hands on her hips, she had enquired, "Inheritance, eh? And what's in it for me?" I laid the florin upon the table. She gawked at the coin, stared at me and then grinned, "What's his name then?" I drew her closer and whispered the name of my benefactor in her ear. She grinned again, "Finish yer broth, sir. I'll be back in a tick." She turned away, hurried to the far end of the bar and promptly tapped an elderly man upon his shoulder. I tasted the broth, which had been quite delicious. So good, in fact, I had rapidly consumed it. Shoving the elderly man towards my table, the barmaid had ordered him, "Go on! Tell 'im! There's a fortune to be had." She eagerly indicated the florin upon my table and nudged him in the arm, "What yer fink of that then? Ain't a brass farthing, is it? Go on! Tell 'im!" The elderly man stared at me, "Ain't no odds to me one way or t'other. He's a barman at the Ten Bells but he don't drink there. Ask down at the Princess Alice. They'll set you right." I had been momentarily stunned. Now I knew why the publican of the Ten Bells had been so abrupt. I had unwittingly enquired after one of his own staff. Or had I? Might the publican have actually been a barman? My benefactor, perhaps? The unsettling thought was broken by the barmaid's shrill voice, "Have I earnt my reward, sir?" Standing, I had handed her the florin, which she instantly fingered. "Gawd, it's real! " she squawked. I had nodded in agreement and departed, impatient to get to the Princess Alice public house.

Passing Flower and Dean Street and then Thrawl Street on my left, I had slowed my pace, pausing at the corner of Commercial

Street and Wentworth Street and gazing across the road at the Princess Alice public house, situated on the other corner. Entering the sparsely occupied public house and politely presenting myself to its bored but congenial landlady, I had once more repeated my fictitious inheritance story, again disclosing the actual name of my benefactor as possible beneficiary. Upon hearing his name and to my utter delight, she had told me that he lived in the common lodging house directly opposite the Princess Alice in Commercial Street. Constraining my instant feverish excitement, I had rewarded her forthrightness with a sovereign coin and then had discreetly withdrawn from the public house to stand before the lodging house across the road. Named in honour of our illustrious monarch, the lodging house had provided accommodation only for single men who possessed regular employment. A singular characteristic that I had curiously noted when I had inadvertently learnt the true identity of my benefactor.

Boldly stepping into the grimy building, I had been confronted by a frail middle-aged man, who had haughtily revealed himself as the deputy. Surreptitiously handing him a shilling, I had enquired after my benefactor, naming him. Opening a thick ledger and fingering through its pages, the deputy had ultimately paused at a name, confirming that my benefactor was indeed a resident of the lodging house. Without further hesitation, I had then given the deputy a sealed note, insisting that he personally hand it to my benefactor and that I would return the next day to collect any reply. Cheered by my rapid progress, I had happily retired to an opium den in Limehouse and, whilst under the blissful influence of its narcotic substance, had pondered how my benefactor might interpret my somewhat obscure message.

Money is pledged for him who does not lie. Reveal the truth and escape the past. Signify your interest, where and when we should meet tomorrow. A place frequented by the public is greatly favoured.

Signify here:

Evil Emergent

Evil Emergent

Buoyant but somewhat weary, I had returned from Limehouse to the boarding school in the early hours of Friday morning only to find my thirteen-year-old boy still awake, impatiently desiring my attention. In an attempt to rid myself of his stifling infatuation, I had shunned our recently planned rendezvous at the ruins of the medieval abbey, hoping to distance myself from him. In doing so, I had not foreseen that he would have the audacity to waylay me at the school, especially at such an unholy hour. Powerless to rebuff him, I had taken him to my room and, during the next hour or so, had vigorously ravished him, thereby venting my anger and undoubtedly appeasing him. Exhausted by the events of the day, I had then foolishly fallen asleep, suddenly to awake at daybreak to find him still lying beside me in my bed. Anxiously rousing him, I had watched as he had hastily dressed, unaware that lurking nearby, Mrs. S. was about to witness his furtive departure from my room. An indiscretion, unbecoming a gentleman, that she would zealously exploit to ultimately disgrace me.

A few hours later, I left the school and had excitedly returned to Spitalfields, eager to know if my benefactor had indeed replied to my note. Obtaining the services of a shoeless street urchin and promising him a reward if he retrieved my note, I had discreetly strolled past my benefactor's lodging house whilst the grubby boy had promptly darted into the building. Minutes later, and waiting outside St. Jude's Church in Commercial Street, I had seen him triumphantly bound from the lodging house, clutching something in his hand. My heart had missed a beat. Was it indeed my note? And if so, had my benefactor accepted my invitation? Upon reaching the church and in return for a ha'penny coin, the boy had shoved the note into my hand and then dashed away. Feeling slightly vulnerable in the unfriendly street and desiring some privacy, I had retired to the entrance of the church and had slowly unfolded the note.

Money is pledged for him who does not lie. Reveal the truth and escape the past. Signify your interest, where and when we should meet tomorrow. A place frequented by the public is greatly favoured.

Signify here:

Ringers. 8 o'clock tonight.

I had been utterly thankful that my hand-written message had been returned to me. Though I was delighted by my benefactor's swift response, I was equally relieved that he had not retained my note, which could have conceivably been used to incriminate me in the Whitechapel murders. Briefly halting beside a chestnut brazier, I had rapidly disposed of the note, throwing it upon the hot coals and watching it burn. It had been a cold afternoon. In fact, bone chilling. A delicious bowl of hot broth, agreeably served at the Queen's Head, had beckoned. Upon entering the congenial tavern once more, I had decided to while away my time, relaxing in its warm atmosphere before venturing out again into the foul streets to meet my benefactor. An appointment, I must confess, which had filled me with a sense of trepidation.

I keep six honest serving men,
They taught me all I knew;
Their names are What and Why and When
And How and Where and Who.

Rudyard Kipling
(1865 – 1936)

Leaving the Queen's Head at precisely 7. 55 p. m., I had walked across Commercial Street, instantly observing that the usual hectic thoroughfare was now strangely quiet. Practically bereft of people, in fact. Thirteen days previously, Jack the Ripper had audaciously assailed the heart of the district, almost flaying Mary Kelly to the bone. By their noticeable absence, had the pitiful inhabitants of Spitalfields been paying homage to the slain woman or had they been utterly stricken with fear, believing that the dreaded killer might strike again with impunity? Of course, my benefactor and I had known differently. Jack the Ripper was still very much alive, but he had vented his fury. His murderous campaign was over. Totally aware that I was about to enter uncharted territory, I had cautiously pushed open the door and stepped into the Britannia public house.

Expecting boisterous activity, I had been quite taken aback to find myself standing alone in the pubic house, except for a solitary barman and an intoxicated old hag, slumped across a table, snoring. Gingerly walking across the sawdust floor to the bar, I had ordered a drink and then had cautiously retired to a small wooden table at the back of the tavern with an unhindered view of its doors. Producing my pocket watch and clicking open its etched metal cover, I had looked at the time, which had indicated 8 p. m. Snapping the cover shut and returning the watch to my waistcoat pocket, I had then looked ahead, my blood instantly chilling. He was sitting at my table, seated opposite me. Whilst I had looked at my pocket watch, he had appeared from nowhere. Instinctively, I knew who he was, my benefactor, Jack the Ripper. He was aged about twenty-eight with a slightly overweight Anglo-Saxon face, which was of a pale complexion, indicating that he had not spent much time outdoors. He had a straight nose, a brown moustache and wore a wide-brimmed black hat, jacket and trousers. He had appeared tired, drained of essence, in fact. The colour of his eyes were dark brown, almost black, and had an intensity about them that had made me feel quite uneasy.

Overcoming my initial shock at his sudden appearance, I had decided that his ominous presence demanded an immediate forthright approach, whereupon I told him of the precaution I had taken by naming him in the letter that I had deposited with my cousin. I had expected a somewhat menacing response from him, but he simply stared at me, "Yer not a copper then?" I had shaken my head and had added, "Nor a journalist." He tensely glanced over his shoulder and then had turned back to me, "Yer note mentioned money?" I nodded in agreement. He leaned forward, intently staring at me, "How much then?" Although I had been pleased that I had his attention, I was rather disappointed that, instead of characterising the cold calculated murderer that I had expected to meet, he had appeared to be a desperate individual simply seeking money.

I had taken two guinea coins from my pocket and placed them upon the table in front of him. His hand had instantly shot forward to claim them, but I had promptly stopped him, placing the palm of my hand over the coins. "Quid pro quo. A fair exchange is no robbery." I had snapped. With a bemused expression, he had slumped back in his chair, "What yer want then?" Leaning forward, I had whispered, "I want the truth and nothing but the truth." I then slid the guinea coins towards him, politely saying, "A token of my goodwill." He had snatched the coins, clenching them in his hand, "I'm all ears, guv'nor. Let's hear yer." For the next two hours or so, I had proceeded to enlighten him on everything I had learnt about *the murders, ultimately divulging that I thought he had indeed been the killer. Throughout my entire meticulous exposition, he had listened attentively, rising only once to relieve himself. However, upon the mention of his name, he had instantly pounced like a tiger, snarling, "Conjecture ain't admissible in an English law court, is it?" I had been briefly stunned, impressed by his rudimentary knowledge of our judicial process. I had calmed him, reassuring him that I had no desire to prove what I already knew to be true. I desired only to know what motive had driven him to murder the five women in such a horrendous fashion. Fidgeting in his chair, he squirmed like a tormented animal, his eyes revealing an inner sadness, "She ain't long lain in her grave." I leaned a little closer to him, "Mary Kelly?" He had nodded sadly. Seizing upon his forlorn vulnerability, I had then begun to cough hoarsely, immediately producing my handkerchief and covering my mouth. Startled, he had looked at me, "What ails yer?"*

I had then introduced another fictitious story, declaring that I had consumption and that I might not live beyond the next three months. Consequently, anything he might divulge to me about his involvement in the Whitechapel murders would go to the grave with me. I further added that hearsay was also inadmissible in an English court of law, thereby protecting him against any possible charge or conviction. I again cough hoarsely, wiped my mouth, returned my handkerchief to my pocket, hoping that my theatrical performance had convinced him to confide in me.

Swallowing the remainder of his drink, he had inquiringly stared at me, "What's in it for me then?" "Money! Escape from poverty," I had exclaimed. I further elaborated, telling him that I would award him fifty guineas, in five equal instalments, to hear what would be tantamount to a confession. At the end of his admission, I would furthermore retrieve and destroy the letter now deposited with my cousin. However, if during our five meetings, he attempted any deceit whatsoever, I would instantly withdraw from our agreement, which might also provoke the possibility that the deposited letter could be dispatched to the police authorities.

Providing him with the opportunity to ponder my proposal, I had risen from my chair, walked to the bar and ordered two drinks, feeling less uneasy but very conscious that I was associating with an extremely dangerous murderer who for the moment should not be trusted. My only armour against becoming a fetid corpse was that he required money, which I possessed and he did not. But would money be enough to loosen his tongue? I had returned to the table and placed a pint of ale upon its surface before him. He had broodingly sipped the drink and then had slowly raised his head, staring at me, "What if I refuse?" Taken aback, I had slowly sat, thinking how best to respond to his question. I had quickly decided to test him, "Then you have earnt two guineas tonight and I can now dispose of the incriminating letter, which is no longer required." Standing, I had curtly added, "Thank you for your time. Good night." He frowned and coldly stared at me, "Yer know the Northumberland Arms in Fashion Street?" I had nodded. He turned away from me and then had raised his glass to his lips, "Tomorrow night at six o'clock. Be outside."

Hastily leaving the Britannia, I had been instantly engulfed by a thick sinister fog that had swathed the entire neighbourhood whilst I had been with my benefactor. Hurrying along Commercial Street towards Whitechapel High Street and unable to distinguish one foggy street from the next, I had nonetheless been thankful that I had left my benefactor behind in the public house, thus averting the possibility that he could have gone ahead and lain in wait to brutally murder me. Upon reaching Whitechapel High Street, I had breathlessly hailed a Hansom cab, having decided not to return to the boarding school but to retire to my private chambers at the Inner Temple, which would make my return journey to Spitalfields the next day a relatively short one. Upon retiring for the night, I had found it extremely difficult to sleep, due largely to the constant rotating thoughts of my own brazen success.

Having persisted throughout the entire day and into the early evening, the thick fog had begun to somewhat dissipate as I had paused at the corner of Commercial Street and Fashion Street, exactly opposite the Queen's Head situated on the other corner. Walking along Fashion Street and conscious of my own echoing footsteps, I had once more observed that the area was unusually quiet, especially for a Saturday night. The degenerate whores of Spitalfields, who would have typically spewed out of their festering hovels to ply their trade in the murky streets, had been entirely noticeable by their absence. The spectre of Jack the Ripper and a possible unimaginable death at his hands had all but halted their licentious activities. I had chuckled to myself. Unbeknown to them *all, I was about to meet the architect of their fear for the second time. Halfway along the street and on the left-hand side, I found the Northumberland Arms public house. A dimly lit oasis in an otherwise gloomy street. Looking at my pocket watch, I had seen that I had arrived shortly before 6 p. m., leaving me little or no time to warm myself in the public house. I had become increasingly aware that my Inverness coat was beginning to feel rather damp, due no doubt to the moisture released by the dispersing fog. As he had done before in the Britannia, my benefactor had once more silently appeared, standing at the entrance to a darkened court across the narrow street, almost opposite from where I had stood. For the first time since I had met him, I had taken note of his build. He was about five feet seven inches tall and stout. He had worn the same wide-brimmed hat, which made him look quite ominous, particularly in the lingering fog. Hurriedly, he had beckoned to me with his hand. Rapidly walking across the street, I had followed him through the covered alleyway into the court.*

Uncertain of his ultimate intentions, I had remained a few paces behind him, ensuring that he could not strike me from behind. Due to the murkiness of the court, I had been totally unable to discern anything of any significance, hearing only the snorting of pigs in a nearby pen. We rapidly reached the end of the court, whereupon I had noticed a second covered alleyway, leading into another street, which I had reasoned had to be Flower and Dean Street.

Halting behind a dilapidated warehouse and unlocking its rear door, he had quickly seized my arm and, shoving me forward, had pitched me into the blackness of the building. Suddenly fearful for my own life, I had been instantly overwhelmed by the pungent smell of stale tobacco that had permeated right through the entire warehouse. I had heard the rear door slammed shut, expecting the swift thrust of cold steel to end my existence. Instead, a match was struck, igniting the wick of a lantern held by my benefactor. I had immediately begun to relax, knowing that if he had indeed intended to kill me, he would have undoubtedly pounced upon me in the darkness. He had beckoned again, indicating a flight of sodden wooden steps leading up to the top of the building. Slowly climbing the steps, the significance of the disused warehouse had struck me like a thunderbolt. My theory had been correct. It was his place of retreat, where he had at once retired after committing the murders. It had been an ideal choice, very close to where he lodged and restricted to the public. Upon reaching the top floor, he had led me to a back room, placing the lantern on a battered wooden table.

Positioning both hands upon the table and looming over the lantern, whose flickering light had made him look extremely sinister, he had quietly said, "The whole truth and nothing but the truth, eh?" I had nodded in agreement, "Quid pro quo. Fifty guineas." He then slid paper, pen and a pot of ink across to me, "Lest you forget." The sound of something shuffling in the darkness suddenly caught his attention. Instantly grabbing the lantern, he moved to a corner and slowly knelt, revealing a scrawny dog lying upon a filthy sack. Half of its left ear had been torn away, leaving a wound now encrusted with dried blood. The tip of the nose, which had suffered the same fate, had been a festering sore. My benefactor had stroked the head of the animal, who had whimpered, suggesting pain. He stood, returned to the table and once more placed the lantern upon its surface, "Happened nigh on three months ago. A pit terrier tore into 'im. Would have tore 'im apart if I hadn't been there." He had seated himself, opposite me, "Ain't long for this world neither."

In the darkened back room, lit by a solitary lantern and beset by the smell of stale tobacco, my benefactor began his story whilst a mauled dog lay dying in the corner. For ease of comprehension, I had decided to write down his admission in tolerable English, thus dispensing with his candid cockney dialect.

I was born in 1859, nearly twenty-eight years ago. My father had been a licensed victualler, who ran a public house in Shadwell, East London, the district of my birth. I never knew my mother and while my father lived he never spoke of her. Perhaps I was born out of wedlock. My father's pub was named the 'Ryde', situated at 43 King David Lane, a grimy cobbled street about one hundred and fifty yards in length, located between Shadwell High Street and Sun Tavern Fields, which eventually became known as Cable Street ten years later in 1869. About a mile from Spitalfields, Shadwell bordered the same poverty-stricken districts of Stepney just to the north and Wapping barely to the west. Despite the nearby presence of a police station situated on the corner with Juniper Row, the 'Ryde' still remained an

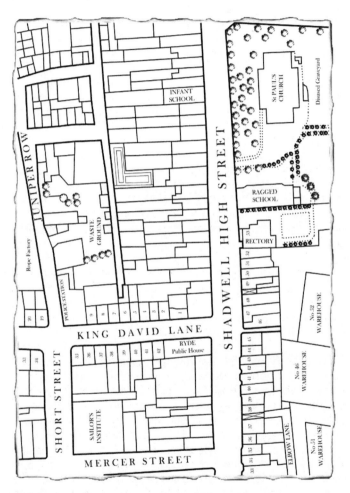

King David-lane, Shadwell 1859

iniquitous den of wickedness, continuously frequented by scheming scoundrels and vile prostitutes, whose immoral activities my father seemingly encouraged. Old before their time, some of these decrepit whores hankered after the lost innocence of their youth, which, of course, they never had in the first place.

When I was two-years-old, or maybe three, an elderly whore, known locally as Mother Hen, would perch me on her knee and try to suckle me with her sagging breasts. At the time, I thought she'd been my mother, but later I learnt otherwise. Poor old soul. Rumour had it, she'd never had sprats of her own, but had always dreamt of a little one sucking her teats. Hence, she'd often nab nippers like me to fulfil her pitiful dream. She was soft in the head. Simple, like. Got run over by an ale wagon in Shadwell High Street. Died before they got her to the infirmary. Another whore, Fanny Perkins, heartily gave her womanhood to her husband, who was blown to kingdom come during the Charge of the Light Brigade at Balaclava. After that and destitute, she just gave other men knee tremblers, declaring that her dear departed husband had been the only man worthy of her body. There were many more like these two. Hundreds of disease-ridden, gin-sodden women, dreaming of the past, fearful of the future, aware that only death could release them from their miserable bondage. My father had once said that rats were preferable to whores because he could at least rid the rodents of any disease by cooking them. I must have been about five-years-old when, after first knocking it senseless, I cut the throat of a rat and gutted it. The sight of its innards nigh on knocked me over. But slowly, and with time, I got a huge amount of pleasure from fingering their slimy insides.

My father was a tough, hardened man. Hence he ran the 'Ryde'. His shoulders and forearms bore several scars, proof of the frequent fights he'd had with knife-wielding ruffians who had tauntingly swallowed one drink too many before he had thrown them out into the street. Although he had a foul temper, he never struck or beat me as a nipper. In fact, he was an amusing, spirited man, often regaling regulars and me about past villains of our city. Jack Ketch, Jack Sheppard and Spring Heeled Jack were legendary scoundrels he repeatedly talked about. I would often go to bed at night and lay awake, my thoughts utterly captivated by the daring exploits of these extraordinary characters, especially the sheer terror created by the Ratcliff Highway Murders.

Richard Jaquet, alias Jack Ketch, had been a rogue and a liar, who had held the office of common hangman until he himself was hanged in May, 1718, at Bunhill Fields, London, for the murder of Elizabeth White, whom he had drunkenly beaten to death. Born in White's Row, Spitalfields, Jack Sheppard had been a handsome burglar who stole exclusively from the aristocratic wealthy, and upon being arrested numerous times, ingeniously escaped from every prison where the authorities had incarcerated him. Popular songs, books, pamphlets, pantomimes and even church sermons had hailed his exploits until he was caught by the treacherous 'thief taker', Jonathan Wild, and hanged on the 16th November, 1724, at Tyburn, London. Ironically, six months later, on the 24th May 1725, Jonathan Wild was also hanged at Tyburn, having previously been tried and found guilty of perverting the course of justice.

In December 1811 and very close to where my benefactor had been born, seven people had been murdered in two separate incidents, which eventually became known as the Ratcliff Highway Murders. Timothy Marr, a linen draper, his wife Celia, their baby son Timothy and James Gowan were found savagely murdered at 29 Ratcliff Highway, killed with a ripping chisel and maul. Twelve days later, John Williamson, a licensed victualler, his wife Elizabeth and Bridget Anne Harrington were discovered at the Kings Arms public house in Old Gravel Lane with their skulls crushed and throats cut. A lodger at the Kings Arms, John Turner, who had found the three bodies, became so distraught that he took his own life, leaping out of an upper window. The seven murders caused an uproar and, after numerous false arrests, John Williams was finally apprehended but hanged himself whilst in prison. Raised high on a cart, his corpse was paraded past the homes of the victims, with the local residents baying for blood. A wooden stake was hammered into his chest and his body hastily thrown into a pit dug at the corner of Back Lane and Cannon Street Road.

Some twenty-six years later, in 1837 and 1838, areas of London, including Limehouse and Commercial Road, had been plagued

by a mysterious figure named Spring Heeled Jack. Able to escape
any pursuer by bounding over high walls, gates and railings, this
frightening creature had pounced upon his female victims from
darkened alleyways, assaulting and rendering them unconscious.
Polly Adams, Mary Stevens, Lucy Scales, her sister Margaret Scales
and Jane Alsop had all testified to being utterly horrified by his
abrupt appearance and astonishing departure. Declared a public
threat by the then Lord Mayor of London, Sir John Cowan, the
police had begun to suspect Lord Henry Beresford, the Marquis of
Waterford, of being the perpetrator, but had soon abandoned the
idea when he had been tragically thrown from his horse, dying well
before the attacks of Spring Heeled Jack finally ceased.

Expected to earn my keep at a young age, much of my
boyhood was spent in the dank cellar, struggling to budge
kegs of ale and lugging wooden crates of bottled beer
upstairs to the bar. It was difficult, exhausting work but it kept
me fit and steadily toughened my body. My father had
never flinched from hard work and he insisted that I should
be his equal. Trouble was, I was only a nipper and some of
those kegs were big, bigger than me. With splintered fingers
and calluses on my hands, I persevered and, in due course,
was paid a small wage for my graft. Mind you, it wasn't
much, a few coppers, but it was something. I was thankful
for small mercies. My father could barely read or write but
oddly enough, he knew arithmetic backwards. He was a
deft hand with sums, quickly adding and subtracting figures
like a barrel organist churning out musical notes. He'd often
say to me, look after the pennies and the pound coins will
take care of themselves. Not that I had any pound coins to
worry about anyway. But he was right. Intent on buying a
particular item, I began to hoard my pennies.

When I was about eleven and much to the fury of my
father, the government of the day decreed that all children
from the age of five to thirteen had to attend day school.
Fortunate enough to escape the relentless daily toil of the
'Ryde', I went to St. Paul's schoolhouse in Shadwell High
Street. Commonly known as a 'ragged' school for orphans
and poor children, it was a grim building, quite bare except
for its single stove and aligned rows of wooden desks. Mrs.
Griffiths was our middle-aged teacher, who exercised her

cane as often as she scolded us with her caustic tongue. Lessons consisted of the three Rs. Reading, wRiting and aRithmetic. Like a group of bleedin' parrots, we learnt by repeating things until we were deemed word perfect. Paper was considered a luxury, so we had to write, scratching letters on slate boards with awkward bits of chalk. We were supposed to bring sponges from home to clean the boards but most of us just spat on the slates and rubbed them clean with our sleeves. Mrs. Griffiths would read aloud strange poems, which we were meant to write down word for word, but none of us could because we didn't have a clue what she was talking about in the first place. Annoyed by our ignorance, she would retaliate, caning boys across their backsides and girls across their hands or bare legs. Due to the fact that I continued to work in the pub at night, I sometimes went to school tired and nodded off during lessons, but the sharp pain inflicted upon the knuckles of my hands by Mrs. Griffiths' cane instantly revived my attention. Adhering to her two Fs, fear and flogging, Mrs. Griffiths finally taught us to crudely read and write the Queen's English. But after more than two years of her tyrannical outbursts, I'd had enough. Aged thirteen, I bade both Mrs. Griffiths and the school goodbye.

I had got it from a Jack Tar, lodging at the Sailor's Institute in Short Street. It had cost me a sovereign and was as good as new. Not daring to show it to my father, I had admiringly toyed with it that same afternoon in the cellar, fingering its horn handle and continuously opening and closing its six inch steel blade. It was a French clasp knife with a hinged, folding blade, which was safely housed in its handle when not in use. From the moment that an one-eyed sailor had first shown me his in the pub, I had wanted one. That's why I had hoarded my coppers. I've still got it.

Slowly taking the knife from his pocket, he had affectionately lain the item upon the table in front of me, insisting that I open it. The handle appeared to be honed from antler. Easing open the pointed blade, I had seen that it was extremely sharp, similar to a razor used by a barber. The surface of the blade had glistened, indicating that a light oil was present to prevent corrosion. My benefactor had indeed been correct. It still looked perfectly new.

But had this particular knife been used to murder and mutilate five women? Something inexplicably told me that it had not. He took the knife from me, carefully closed its blade and had returned it to his pocket.

Most boys of my age belonged to a local gang. Me? I chose to be alone. I liked it that way. Didn't have to answer to anyone except my father. I continued to catch the cellar rats, but now took them at night to the disused graveyard behind St. Paul's Church, where I beat them senseless with a wooden mallet, before slitting their throats and gutting them with my new knife. The sight of the dark blood spurting from their cut throats and oozing from their slit stomachs had thrilled me immensely. But cutting out their slimy innards and holding them in my hands had excited me even more. Whilst fingering their innards, I'd had a peculiar thought. If my throat had been slit open in the same manner, would I have heard the sound of my own blood gushing forth? If so, might that be the pleasure to end all pleasures? I became intoxicated by the thought, instantly yearning for something larger to kill. But what? However, the disused graveyard did solve the problem on how to dispose of the carcasses after I had finished with them. I simply left them where they were and walked away.

I had remained utterly speechless, shocked into silence whilst he had described his obscene butchery. He had been thirteen at the time of this incident, clearly shameless about his mania and totally obsessed with death and mutilation. Already a social aberration, he was a smouldering gunpowder keg yet to explode and fated to become the most heinous murderer of the nineteenth century, who would heartlessly walk away from his victims after he had slit their throats and gutted them. His early barbarous behaviour had been so appalling, so devilish and so inhuman that I had instantly shuddered, disturbed by what other horrors he had in store for me.

It happened when I was about sixteen. I'd had many chances to spend my seed with whores but had avoided them on account that any one of their contagious diseases could soften a man's brain. Her name was Ethel. About six years older than me. She often plied her trade in the 'Ryde', regularly picking up drunken customers and taking them to nearby courts to service them for sixpence. One particular evening she had found the fish in the sea rather sparse and feeling downcast, had offered herself to me in exchange for a meagre tot of gin. Instantly forgetting about infectious diseases and eager to exercise my organ for the first time, I had cheerfully obliged her with three tots of gin, swallowing two myself. She took me to a dingy alleyway and began to rapidly stroke my member which, after briefly stiffening, soon became limp again. Try as she might, my organ steadfastly refused to harden until I had angrily seized her by the throat, tightly squeezing it with my hands. Upon seeing her shocked expression, my member had instantly stiffened and in a mere second or so I had spent over her skirt. Shoving me aside and furiously rubbing her throat, she had cursed me whilst hurriedly leaving the court. Rumour had it later, that someone or something had frightened her so much, she'd taken up a decent job, leaving the streets altogether.

I'd lain awake in my bed that night tickled pink that I had finally spent my seed but was mystified about how it had happened. It had been so rapid, yet so satisfying. I thought again of my hands around Ethel's throat and her shocked expression which, to my utter delight, proceeded to harden my organ whilst I lay in bed. Without any further assistance, I had heartily spent again. Savouring the ebbing pleasure, it had slowly dawned upon me that I was somewhat different from other men. My manhood could only be aroused whilst I inflicted pain. But more crucially, what deed might I have to perform to sustain such an arousal?

Near the police station situated on the corner of Juniper Row, there had been an area of waste ground where nomadic gypsies would park their four-wheeled caravans when visiting our neighbourhood. Unlike the Jews, whose widespread presence was disliked throughout the East End, gypsies were tolerated because we all knew they would move on. Wherever they camped and whilst they hawked their trinkets and ornaments from door to door, their children and paltry livestock were left behind to freely roam around the caravans. One night, I nicked a plump hen from their camp, knocked it senseless, sliced open its throat and cut out its innards. During the pleasurable task, I had felt my organ faintly stir, but nothing more. Two nights later, I had nabbed a small piglet, but instead of knocking the animal senseless, I suffocated it with my hands, utterly mesmerised by its wriggling death throes. Throughout its furious struggle, my manhood had steadily grown rigid. I instantly threw the dead animal to the ground, drew my clasp knife, pounced upon it, pushed back its lifeless snout and slashed open its throat. Whilst watching its spurting blood, I had spent in my trousers. I was a man possessed. Slicing open its stomach, I ripped out its innards and to my utter surprise and delight, had spent once more.

Trembling with excitement, I had rushed home, scarcely able to comprehend what was happening to me. Yes, of course, I had enjoyed the wave of exhilaration that had swept my body as I butchered the hapless piglet, but what type of fiend had I now become that required such a horrid sacrifice to satisfy a bodily hunger. Aware that it would be utterly mad to continue in such a manner, I resolved to find an alternative solution that would safely allow me to pursue my mania. Although some whores were known to provide unusual services, I wasn't so foolish as to think that one of them might gladly submit to death and mutilation. Therefore something else, a lawful activity, had to be found.

Somewhat relieved that the first of our five meetings had finally reached a fruitful conclusion, I had paid him ten guineas, agreeing that I should once more meet him outside the Northumberland Arms at noon the next day. Conscious that he worked during the week, I had decided upon five meetings, the equivalent of two weekends and one day, because I did not want his admission to be a lengthy burdensome affair. I had also felt that five sizeable payments would concentrate his mind, thus impelling our meetings forward and bringing our association to a speedy end.

Bidding him good night, I had stepped from the warehouse, reeking of stale tobacco that had impregnated the very fabric of my clothes. The fog by then had entirely cleared. Walking through the nearby covered alleyway of the court, I had entered Flower and Dean Street, deeply inhaling the cold night air, which had made a pleasant change from the dank, gloomy building I had just left. Strolling into Commercial Street, which once more seemed eerily quiet, I had strolled towards Whitechapel High Street, hailing a Hansom cab as I had done the previous day. Again returning to my chambers at the Inner Temple, I had carefully read what I had written down thus far, pondering all that my benefactor had told me. I had to admit that I had no way of knowing if he had spoken the truth. It had been perfectly clear that either he had possessed a fertile imagination or had indeed been dominated by an inner demon, dwelling within the recesses of his disturbed mind. Had he been entirely mad or only partially? I must confess that either peculiarity would have been sufficient to lynch him. But I had favoured the latter to be true. There had existed a terrible dark sadness about him. Perhaps he should not have been born, but unfortunately had not been given the choice. Perhaps he had not wanted to live, but what had been the alternative? I firmly believed that he had typified the utter loneliness of evil. After giving the matter no further thought, I had placed the sheets of paper in a stiff brown leather binder, securely locking the binder in a desk drawer. Though the events of the day had disturbed me somewhat, I had nonetheless retired to bed and had slept soundly.

Stepping from a Hansom cab, which had halted at the corner of White's Row, I had been surprised to see that the inhabitants of Spitalfields had recovered both their zeal and vigour. Commercial Street had resumed its boisterous, vibrant life, undoubtedly due to the popular bustling Sunday markets of Brick Lane and Petticoat Lane. Even the patrolling police constables, generally of a stern disposition, had appeared cheerful. Perhaps they knew that Jack the Ripper had gone for good, never to expose their inadequacies again. I had crossed the road, walked along Fashion Street and had arrived outside the Northumberland Arms at exactly midday. Immediately emerging from the covered alleyway, my benefactor had approached me and, to my utter surprise and sheer delight, had recommended that we continue our meeting in the relative comfort of the public house. Forever cautious, he had not wanted to be seen entering the dilapidated warehouse in broad daylight, especially with me, a stranger.

Except for a dishevelled old man leaning against the bar and coughing hoarsely, the Northumberland Arms had been devoid of people, undoubtedly due to the fact that it had been partially hidden up a side street. Off the beaten track, so to speak. Sitting at the back of the tavern and wondering what had become of the

dying dog, I had produced a pencil and several blank sheets of
paper, ready to write down whatever my benefactor had to say.

My father had a mate, who ran the John of Jerusalem
pub in Rosaman Street, Clerkenwell. Nice old fellow. Dead
now. My father had instructed me to help him out, which I
did, mostly at the weekends. The pub was not far from Fleet
Street and the City of London proper, thus the office folks
weren't around at the weekend. They were at home with
their families, enjoying their Sunday roast beef dinner. So
there wasn't much for me to do. Bloody boring, in fact. My
long trek home took me through Cripplegate, Moorgate
and Bishopsgate, which led me straight into Leadenhall
Street and then onto Aldgate. It had been the disgusting
smell that first caught my attention. The sickly sweet smell of
a slaughterhouse. Leadenhall Market had some of the
busiest slaughterhouses in London and, more often than not,
offered employment at night. I remember being rooted to
the spot. Why hadn't I thought of this before? Here was a
normal job that would safely allow me to continue with my
unusual habit.

After finishing my helpful spell at the John of Jerusalem
and much to the irritation of my father, I obtained a nightly
job at a slaughterhouse in Lime Street. A large number of
these enterprises were often shoddy affairs, where animals
were butchered in cellars, back-yards and, as in the case of
Spitalfields, in the actual shops where the meat was sold.
The building I worked in was paved with flagged-stones,
thoroughly aired and had an ample supply of fresh water. It
consisted of two sets of doors. One set permitted animals to
enter the building from the main yard. The second, opposite
the first, led to a smaller yard, where calves, sheep and pigs
were slaughtered on benches and then gutted. Slipping a
leather collar around the necks of larger animals, such as
cows and oxen, enabled a mechanical windlass to jerk
them to the ground, before splitting their skulls apart with a
poleaxe. Raised and suspended by metal hooks, they were
swiftly disembowelled, their entire innards spilling out and
plopping to the ground. Nothing was wasted. My first job
was to gather the slippery mass of hearts, livers and lungs in
a wicker basket and then dump 'em on long benches,

where they were sorted and sometimes sliced into smaller pieces. I couldn't believe my good fortune. Lawful death was all around me and I was part of it. I took great pleasure in the smell of freshly slain animals and the abundance of bloodied organs that at times had caused me to silently spend my seed whilst I had handled them.

Sometime later, having persuaded my father that I could best lend a hand in the 'Ryde' at night, I got a job closer to home in a slaughterhouse off Cable Street. I had by now become a deft hand at butchery, which didn't require a lot of skill, merely constant practice and a strong stomach. I could do it with my eyes shut. Rapidly removing the head of an animal allows the blood to gush from the slaughterman's bench to the ground below, where it's sluiced away with buckets of water. With an extremely sharp pointed knife, and taking care not to cut too deep and puncture the animal's innards, the body is swiftly sliced open. Reaching inside and removing its entire guts with a mere flick or two of the knife, everything comes away in one quivering heap. Now this takes very little time. Under a minute at the most. The Jews, however, employ a somewhat different method. Whilst alive, the animal's throat is sliced open, then it's hung upside down, allowing the blood to slowly drain from its body before being gutted. With a man or woman, the procedure would have to vary slightly. The heart would have to be halted by first suffocating the person. After that, the head could then be removed, whereupon blood would flow freely, unlike a pulsating heart which would instantly spurt blood all over the place. Removal of the innards would be the same, man, woman or animal.

I had felt nauseated, not by the vivid depiction, but by his visible delight, nay glee, whilst he had brashly described evisceration. His boastful remark that he could perform his work with his eyes shut had explained how he had been able to butcher his victims in near to total darkness. It had not been necessary for him to see them, merely essential for him to feel them. Familiar with specific organs that he had consistently handled, he would have known what to remove from a body by touch alone. Dr. Bond's profile of the Whitechapel murderer had indeed been correct. Jack the Ripper had most definitely been a dangerous man, prone to bouts of homicidal urges and erotic mania. My benefactor had certainly been smitten by both abnormalities, but for now he had satisfied his mania, slaughtering animals and spending his seed at work. Therefore, what other obsession had driven him to commit murder?

Mary Jane Kelly! I would've done anything for her. Given her everything. But she treated others and me as fools.

His sudden outburst had caught me completely off guard. It had appeared as if he had read my mind and had reacted to my question. His unexpected bitterness rapidly subsided, giving way to a sorrowful expression, suggesting that any thought of Mary Jane Kelly, to a large extent, had remained painful. Although I believed she had been the reason for the murders, I did not, as yet, know why. Staring at me longingly, he had sadly sighed,

Never forget when I first saw her. Can still see her today. Ginger hair, light blue eyes and a broad smile as wide as old Father Thames. But it was her Irish accent that really floored me. It was musical, like. A joy to hear. Totally bowled me over. She was three years younger than me, twenty-two perhaps. Fresh to our neck of the woods but not the district, she began to use the 'Ryde', no doubt drawn by the free tots of gin that I slipped her. I knew she was a whore but, unlike all the other dregs, she was special. Never walked the streets. A cut above everyone else. A blessed angel.

She had originated from Limerick, Ireland. When she was young her folks moved to Wales, where her father worked at an ironworks in Carmarthenshire. At sixteen, she married a coalminer by the name of Davis who, not long after, was killed in a mine explosion, leaving her high and dry and destitute. About a year later, she took off to Cardiff, at which point her cousin introduced her to whoring. She must have been about seventeen at the time. Moving to Bristol, she worked in a brothel, but once again returned to Cardiff, pregnant and penniless. Not long after, she had a daughter, but the poor mite died at birth. Beset with grief, she had lingered in an infirmary for the next eight months before bidding Cardiff farewell and moving to London. Now aged about twenty-one, she worked in a Knightsbridge bordello run by a French lady, whom she would often accompany to

Paris, under the fictitious name of Marie Jeanette Kelly. Finding the French lady domineering, she fled the bordello and worked in a brothel run by Mrs. Buki at St. George's Street off the Ratcliff Highway. The following year, she left Mrs. Buki and moved in with a labourer named Morgan Stone, living close to the Stepney Commercial Gas Works. Not long after, she left him and worked in another brothel run by Mrs. Carthy at Breezer Hill, Pennington Street, which was just off Shadwell High Street. That's where she was lodging when I met her.

Undoubtedly regaled to him by Mary Kelly, most of her early life had sounded quite ludicrous to me. At sixteen, her only husband had been dramatically killed in a mine explosion. At seventeen, she had been seduced into whoring by her cousin. At eighteen, she had given birth to a dead child. And finally, aged nineteen and stricken with grief, she had languished in an infirmary for the lengthy period of eight months. She had clearly fabricated these incidents to gain sympathy from whomever might listen to her, or more to the point, whomever she thought could be used to shield her from a wretched existence. A reasonable enough precaution but devious and utterly selfish. If the truth had been known, she most probably came straight to London from Ireland, entering the Knightsbridge bordello, which catered for a wealthy clientele here and on the continent. It was not uncommon for young women, especially someone as unsullied as her, to be regularly escorted across the English Channel to service Parisian gentlemen. Hence, the dominant French Madame and the use of the name Marie Jeanette Kelly. Almost certainly unskilled in the ways of the gentry and most likely inept at retaining a gracious demeanour, she had fled the bordello, retreating to the manageable customers of her own class in a common brothel.

The veil that had shrouded the motive behind the Whitechapel murders had now begun to lift, revealing the volatile combination that would ignite a hideous explosion of unprecedented terror. An impetuous, selfish woman, utterly enamoured by my benefactor, would fuel, provoke and unleash his fury that would finally and literally expunge her from the face of the earth. Mary Jane Kelly had indeed been very special. Unlike the other dregs whom he would eventually slaughter in the streets, he would ceremoniously dispose of her in the privacy of her own room.

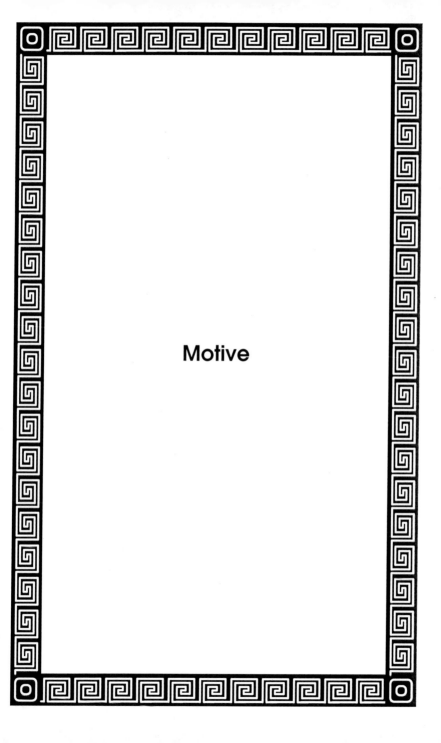

Motive

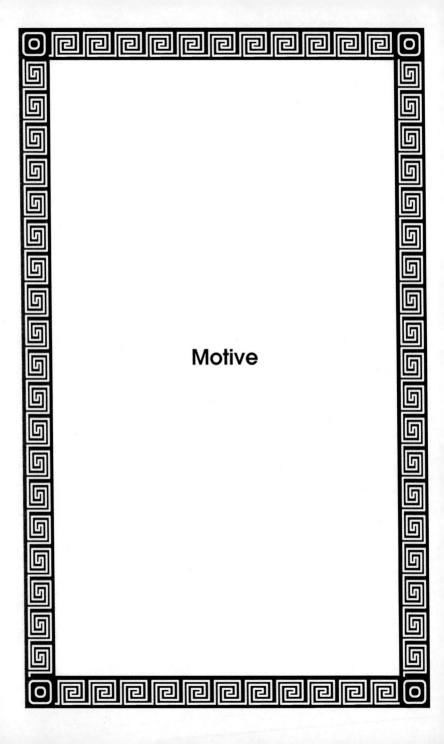

Motive

To avoid working the streets, Mary Kelly had repeatedly sought the relative safety of a common brothel or, when the chance had presented itself, the company of any man gullible enough to offer her shelter and give her money. These affairs had tended to be short-lived due largely to her fiery temperament and her vehement opposition to any kind of permanent union. When drunk, she had been quarrelsome, abusive and destructive but when sober, utterly beguiling.

I lay awake at nights thinking of her. Couldn't get her out of my mind. Wanted to know where she was, what she was doing. I ached for her. Never known such pain. Then or now. When she came into the pub, she only had to smile at me. Kept me dreaming for days. The slaughterhouse held no interest for me. Found it hard to spend my seed. Didn't matter. Thoughts about her were much more pleasurable. One night we went for a stroll. Shook like a bleedin' leaf, I had. She talked about her early life. I didn't say a word. Couldn't, I was tongue-tied. Just listened. Felt sorry for her and gave her a few coppers. She told me, I was kind, treated her with respect, like. Hadn't been shown that before. Looked upon me as someone special, she said.

A miracle had occurred. I'd been cured. Continuous thoughts of her had arrested my mania. I might yet pine to spend my seed but not whilst I felt like this. I was as normal men. I threw my job in at the slaughterhouse and returned to the 'Ryde'. Whenever she came into the pub, I was always there, didn't want to miss her. And then my father died. Passed-out and passed-on whilst working in the cellar.

His funeral was a sedate affair. One hearse, one coach, not many flowers. His burial made the news, though. A single line announcement in the obituary column of the East London Observer. My days at the 'Ryde' were over. The bleedin' brewery brought in a new landlord and I was out. Unbeknown to me, Mary Kelly had already upped and left Breezer Hill, moving to Bethnal Green Road. Only found out much later that she'd actually moved in with another man, a mason's plasterer named Joseph Fleming. At the time, however, I just wanted to know she was safe, to be near her. Thus I moved into where I now lodge, getting a job as a barman in the Ten Bells public house.

Aware that I had yet to make the tedious journey back to the boarding school, I had requested that we adjourn for the day. Nodding in agreement, he had suggested that we meet again five days later, on the Friday, at six o'clock in the evening and once more outside the Northumberland Arms. Giving him ten guineas, I had bade him good night, hurried to the Inner Temple, retrieved the stiff brown leather binder and, catching an express train, had arrived back at the school some hours later. The following morning, even though I had not been obliged to do so, I had toured the assembled classrooms, prudently meeting the teaching staff and pupils at the start of the new week. In the course of my short tour, I had become aware of an unusual hushed reaction from all and sundry once my presence was observed. My thirteen-year-old boy had been totally noticeable by his absence, and Mrs. S. had quite definitely smirked as I had strolled past her in the corridor. Utterly oblivious to the gravity of the situation, it had never once entered my head that the strange conduct of the entire school had been due to a circulating rumour that I would soon be dismissed from my post for having committed a mysterious unknown misdemeanour.

Later that evening, and the subsequent evening, whilst the boys had slept in their dormitories, I had carefully copied, using black ink, my benefactor's second deposition, which I had written in pencil whilst in the Northumberland Arms. I had painstakingly done this in order to preserve the deposition for posterity. Pencil graphite would undoubtedly fade with time. Iron-gall ink, less so. Slipping the re-written sheets of paper into the leather binder, I had wondered why my benefactor had decided to tell me everything. Yes, fifty guineas had indeed been an incentive, but something else had told me there had to be another reason. But what?

Except for the unusual silence that I had encountered at the boarding school, the rest of the dreary week had otherwise been uneventful. A bitterly cold Friday evening had once more found me standing outside the Northumberland Arms, stomping my feet and blowing into cupped hands in a futile attempt to keep warm. Emerging from the gloomy court, my benefactor had appeared silently and had hurriedly beckoned me with his hand. In no time at all, I had again been seated opposite him at the wooden table lit by the glow of the lantern, and plagued by that awful stench of stale tobacco that lingered through the warehouse. Sliding paper, pen and a pot of ink towards me, he had solemnly remarked, "He's gone, you know?" I had looked at him, somewhat bemused, "I beg your pardon. Who has gone?" He had then pointed to the darkened corner, "Died two days ago. Sold to the meat shop yesterday. Someone's meal today." He had, of course, spoken of the pitiful dog whose soul had departed this world but whose dead body had remained to provide valuable sustenance for the living. Meat, in whatever form, had not been something to discard, especially where money was to be made. Poverty had its own rules and impoverished people, however callous they might seem, would always responded accordingly.

I couldn't sleep. Couldn't stop worrying about her. What had become of her? Was she dead? O'Lord, I prayed not. If I was special like she had said, why hadn't she told me where she was going? Why she was leaving? I had endlessly traipsed up and down the main roads, trudged down side streets, in and out of alleys and courts, foolishly hoping to find her, but never saw hide nor hair of her. I began to fear that I might never see her again.

About sixty-six and getting past it, the landlord of the Ten Bells was a brawny Irishman named John Waldron. He's since gone. Alf Grainger runs it now. Having seen enough of the whores who drank in the pub each and every night, John Waldron had left me to deal with the unruly evening trade whilst he dealt with the fewer, less boisterous daytime customers. Spitalfields whores were the same as Shadwell whores. No matter whence they came, they were always the same. Foul-mouthed, noisy and frequently drunk. Even though the area had many pubs and beer houses where these women might drink, they preferred the Ten Bells because it was opposite Spitalfields Market, full of hard earning porters eager to quench their thirst and dip their wicks. Forever watchful, these Jezebels would lay in wait, ready to pounce upon any man who entered the pub even though he might only have a ha'penny in his pocket. Drunk or sober, happy or fed-up, I gradually got to know most of them by name, where they lodged and where they'd take a man to relieve him. At the weekend, many of them would prey upon the music halls, especially the Pavilion Theatre in

Whitechapel Road, which held more than three thousand people. As a result, the Ten Bells was at its quietest on Friday and Saturday nights. Thus, these two days, including any Bank Holidays, became my time off.

One minute she wasn't there, the next second she was. Wearing a shawl wrapped around her shoulders, she had stood just inside the doors of the pub when I spotted her. Soaked to the skin, she looked more like a drowned rat than the cheerful Irish lass I had last seen in Shadwell. I remember standing behind the bar, staring at her. I couldn't believe my eyes. I thought I was dreaming, until she looked at me and wearily smiled. She looked like a helpless lost child. My heart went out to her. I would have killed anyone right then and there to protect her. I sat her down, got her a drink and some food. She wolfed down the food and swallowed the drink. Told me she had gone to live with a bloke called Joe Fleming in Bethnal Green Road, but he'd lost his job. Had left him and was now lodging at Cooley's in Thrawl Street. She didn't have anyone to turn to, until she heard that I worked in the Ten Bells. Told her not to fret, she'd be looked after. She said I was the only person in the world she could count upon. My heart had soared. No matter that she'd been foolish. She'd learnt the errors of her ways and had returned to me. Or so I'd thought. Told me she knew that I truly cared for her, unlike other men who just wanted to have a good time with her. Couldn't tell her that my abated mania was the only thing that would arouse me. Didn't want to tempt fate with any bodily activity. Didn't want to harm her. Just wanted to be with her, look after her.

Mary Kelly had finally plunged into the heart of Whitechapel. Parallel with Flower and Dean Street, Cooley's doss-house in Thrawl Street had been four streets away from the Ten Bells and just one street away from where my benefactor had lodged.

I gave her a job in the pub. Cleaning tables, collecting glasses, chores like that. Paid her out of my own pocket. Didn't matter. Anything to keep her off the streets. It was heaven having her around. Nigh on three weeks later she didn't come into the pub one evening. Disappeared again. I went to Cooley's, whereupon I was told she'd up and left the day before. They couldn't say where. Second time she'd done it to me. Why again? I began to roam the streets once more, searching for her. Started to feel like a fool but couldn't help myself. Thoughts of her bothered me daily. How might I show her I truly cared? Why did I despise her too? My thoughts became muddled, confused. One minute I ached for her, the next minute I loathed her. I didn't know why. It was all becoming too much. My head felt ready to explode. Then I heard the news. She'd gone and shacked up with an Irish fish porter, name of Joseph Barnett.

His brother, Daniel Barnett, lodged in the same place as me. So did Henry Turner, but a little more of him later. Dan told me about Mary and Joe, not knowing that I knew her. He still doesn't. Dan, Joe and two other brothers worked at Billingsgate Fish Market down by the Thames. Had done for some time. Family tradition, like. Two days after I'd last seen Mary and whilst I was earnestly scouring the streets trying to find her, Joe had met her on the Friday night in the Britannia pub. The following day, they met again and, choosing to stay together, moved into a doss-house in George Street.

As before and remaining true to character, Mary Kelly had leapt from one man to the next. Her move into George Street, however, had hardly been an audacious achievement. Running from Flower and Dean Street to Wentworth Street, George Street had cut straight through Thrawl Street, where she had lodged at Cooley's. She had, in fact, simply moved from one doss-house to another just around the corner.

How could she have jumped ship for an idiot who had a daft habit of repeating someone's last words when he talked to them? Like a bleedin' echo, he was. Even Dan thought his brother wasn't altogether there. A little soft in the head, like. Joe must have thought he'd teamed up with royalty when he moved in with Mary. Couldn't get the two of them out of my mind. Him pawing her. Her stroking him. She deserved better. A lot better. Began to think that I'd have to teach her a lesson. Do something that would knock some sense into her, that would frighten her, would make her sit up and take note. If she wouldn't respond to kindness then perhaps she'd respond to fear. The idea began to excite me but I had no idea what to do. I dreaded the prospect of seeing them together in Commercial Street so I'd cut through the back streets and alleyways going to and from the Ten Bells. Dan told me that the two of them had moved to another doss-house in Little Paternoster Row, but had been kicked out for drunken behaviour and rent arrears. They now lodged at another doss-house in Brick Lane. Not exactly a life of Old Reilly, was it? Instead of going up, she was fast coming down, sinking into the mire. Joe was the problem, he was earning. While that lasted, she'd drink her life away until it was too late. Could kill Joe, but rather she left him instead. That way I'd know she would have seen, learnt what she might have become. But how could I get her to leave him? Had to do something out of the ordinary, something that would put the fear of God in her. Something she would suspect I had done, but could never prove.

Here at last had been the simmering cause for the Whitechapel murders. Although a completely credible motive in itself, I had long suspected that Mary Kelly had been merely part, albeit an integral part, of the reason for the crimes. I had become utterly convinced, listening to my benefactor, that his unusual mania must have also contributed to the slayings. True, Mary Kelly had most definitely ignited the murders but the impelling force for the continuation of the mutilations had to have been his carnal lust.

Had got myself an extra job. Here! Where we are now. Tobacco firm went bust. Owners wanted someone to keep an eye on it whilst it was empty. Caretaker, like. No takers yet. Building's too old, roof leaks, but suited me down to the ground. No one to bother me. Like being on my own, could think here. It was near the end of February, this year, when I bumped into the two of 'em in Crispin Street. They had just fallen out the Horn of Plenty, drunk. She had sneered at me, telling me that she'd rather drink in a pub than clean in a pub. Known for her lashing tongue, Joe had remained quiet, simply grinning. Bleedin' idiot. I was beside myself. After trying to help her, she'd thrown it back in my face. But for Joe, I swear I might have killed her then and there. Burning with anger, I turned away into White's Row and then along a narrow alleyway to Butler Street. A woman came towards

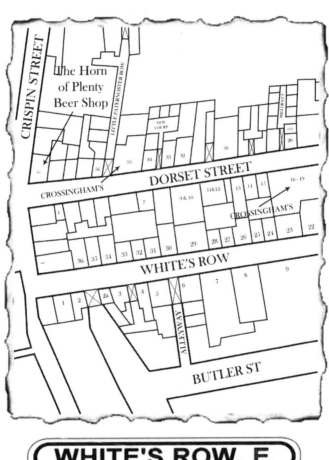

CRISPIN STREET

The Horn
of Plenty
Beer Shop

LITTLE PATERNOSTER ROW

NEW
COURT

MILLER'CT

44

26

5

96

85

84

33

82

30

CROSSINGHAM'S

DORSET STREET

9 & 10

11&12

13

14

15

16 - 19

7

CROSSINGHAM'S

1

36

35

34

33

32

31

30

29

28

27

26

25

24

23

22

WHITE'S ROW

1

2

2a

3

4

5

6

7

8

9

ALLEYWAY

BUTLER ST

WHITE'S ROW, E.

me, drunk I think. It was dark, she might have laughed, said something. Can't remember. I blew up. Took my clasp knife from my pocket, flicked open its blade, threw her to the ground, pulled up her dress and, whilst stabbing her in the stomach and legs, felt my organ stir. I was at sixes and sevens. I wiped my hands on her dress and then ran. Made my way down to Houndsditch. Had a pint of ale in the Cutler's Arms and calmed down. Heard later, her name was Annie Millwood. Died over a month later. Natural causes, they said. Believe that, you'll believe anything.

I returned to my lodgings, half expecting to feel the heavy hand of a copper upon my shoulder at any moment. I lay awake in my bed scarcely able to believe what I'd done. Though fearful of being seized by the police, I was also excited by what else had happened, that my organ had stirred whilst I had stabbed the woman. Less than two weeks later, Mary and Joe left the doss-house in Brick Lane and moved into 13 Miller's Court, Dorset Street. It tickled me pink to know that I had struck so near to where she now lived. The very next street, in fact. The police didn't collar anyone for the attack. They hadn't a clue who'd done it. But I stayed wary of them until I read that Annie had died. Unless she could return from the grave and point an accusing finger at me, I was almost in the clear. Then some unknown blessed idiot went and stabbed Ada Wilson in the throat. The police thought that both attacks were somehow related. Most likely committed by the same man. Ada had been stabbed on a Wednesday night in Maidman's Street, Mile End, whilst I had been working in the Ten Bells. Thus I had a cast-iron alibi for the time of her attack, which meant that, had the local police suspected me in the first place, I couldn't have attacked Annie Millwood.

Six days later, on Easter Monday, Emma Smith had been attacked at the corner of Brick Lane and Wentworth Street by three unknown men. The next day she died in hospital. Her death had made me sit up and take note. When I had stabbed Annie Millwood, I thought I'd done something out of the ordinary, but I hadn't. Down here, attacks on women were quite normal. If I was going to discipline Mary Kelly then I would have to do something different. Something truly outrageous and shocking. Something that would also give me a lot of pleasure.

If you suddenly stabbed someone at the wrong angle with a faulty clasp knife, its blade can quickly fold back, cutting into your own fingers. For what I had in mind, I'd decided I needed a razor sharp knife that would be both reliable and wouldn't cause me an injury. At the top end of Petticoat Lane, near Sandy's Row and in an ex-military shop, I'd found what I was looking for.

He had stood, turned away and then turned back, placing a pepper-and-salt jacket upon the table before me. Flicking open the left side of the jacket, he had revealed a worn leather sheath stitched to its inside. Taking a knife from the sheath, he had lain it in front of me for my scrutiny. The handle of the knife had a wooden pommel and had been wrapped in twine. It had no quillions and the pointed blade, six inches in length, had been leaf shaped and well sharpened at both edges. Something about the shape of the blade had struck me as being quite familiar. It had not been a customary blade, but a honed down spearhead. A Zulu assegai, to be precise.

During the Zulu War, the collection of souvenirs by the ordinary British soldier had been widespread. Rather than lose the chance to make a few shillings, soldiers had removed the heads of the spears and had brought them home in their packs, selling them to anyone who would purchase them. Some practical traders had fashioned the spearheads into knives but had cleverly retained the distinctive leaf shaped design. Created by the founder of the Zulu nation, Shaka, the assegai had been a short stabbing spear solely designed for fighting at close quarters and deliberately made for slashing and disembowelling any opponent. My benefactor had chosen well. It was without a doubt a most formidable weapon, capable of inflicting horrendous injuries upon a person in mere seconds. Solemnly picking up the knife, he had carefully slid it back into its sheath.

Now and then I would lay awake at night thinking how my organ had suddenly stirred whilst I'd stabbed Annie Millwood. My affection for Mary Kelly had once arrested my mania but my growing hatred for her had now begun to arouse it. I was anxious to taste bodily pleasure again and

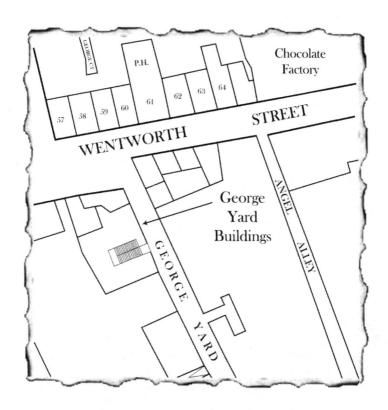

GEORGE YARD, E.

demonstrate what a terrible death awaited Mary Kelly if she flouted my warning. The prospect was, to say the very least, mouth-watering. Dan told me Joe had lost his job. Silly idiot had got caught stealing something. Dunno what he nicked, didn't much care. Now Mary would have to provide for them both, ply her trade in the streets. It's what I had feared most. I couldn't get to Mary with Joe still around so it was vital that I make her see sense, why she must leave him, why she must return to me.

Henry Turner had been a carpenter. I've mentioned him before. Nice fellow, older than me. He'd lived with Martha Tabram, putting up with her drinking for about nine years. Each time he gave her money she spent it on drink. It was always drink. Didn't I know that? She'd often come into the Ten Bells blind drunk and crash to the floor before I'd even had time to serve her a tot of gin. A bleedin' liability, she was. A millstone around Henry's neck. Three weeks before I killed her, Henry had left her, moving into where I lodge, whilst Martha had moved into a doss-house in George Street. Four things had earmarked her for death. One. The police would first suspect the obvious, Henry. Two. Martha bore the same first initial as Mary. Three. She lived in George Street where Mary had first lived with Joe. Four. Her being a whore and gin-sodden most of the time would make it easier for me to approach her and kill her. Three days after Henry last saw Martha in Leadenhall Street and gave her one-and-six, I had offered up her dead body to Mary as a foretaste of worse things yet to come if she didn't heed my warning.

It had been August Bank Holiday Monday. Out of sight, out of mind, as they say, I had followed Martha, her friend Pearly Poll Connolly and two guardsmen, for at least two hours whilst they'd waltzed in and out of pubs, ending up at the White Hart pub on the corner of George Yard and Whitechapel High Street. Shortly before midnight, all four had fallen out of the pub, Martha taking one guardsman up George Yard and Connolly leading the other towards the Angel pub on the corner of Angel Alley. Quietly tagging along behind Martha and the guardsman, both of whom were the worse for drink, I had worn the jacket you've just seen, a peaked cap and scarf. I'd needed different clothes. When finished with her, I could change back into my other clothes, which wouldn't have a smear of blood on 'em. Martha had stumbled, lost her balance and, pulling the guardsman with her, had fallen to the ground. It was a right bleedin' spectacle. Both of 'em sprawled on the ground, giggling and burping. I walked past them, stopping almost opposite George Yard Buildings near the top left-hand side of the street.

At about 1. 25 a. m. and undoubtedly looking for Martha, Mary Ann Connelly, alias Pearly Polly, and her guardsman companion had returned to the corner of George Yard and Whitechapel High Street, where they had quickly parted company. The guardsman had gone off towards Aldgate and she in the opposite direction towards Osborn Street, Whitechapel.

I watched the pair pick themselves up and shakily walk towards me. Making a meal of each other, they frequently paused, slobbering over one another. A few minutes later, a young couple arrived and entered George Yard Buildings, neither of 'em noticing Martha, the guardsman, nor me waiting in the shadows.

The couple had been Mr. and Mrs. Joseph and Elizabeth Mahoney, who had returned home after the relaxing respite of the Bank Holiday Monday. Within minutes, Elizabeth had once more popped out into the street to hurriedly purchase a late meal from a nearby chandler's shop in Thrawl Street.

Finally getting down to business, Martha had dragged the guardsman into the shadows beside George Yard Buildings barely moments before the young woman left the building and went into Wentworth Street. About ten minutes later, carrying something wrapped in paper, the woman returned and again entered the building. The guardsman emerged from the shadows and, sheepishly looking up and down the street, lurched past me and, like the young woman before him, entered Wentworth Street. Martha had next appeared and, tottering to the arched entrance of George Yard Buildings, had leant against its grimy brickwork for support. Like an ordinary fellow, I had causally walked towards her.

Unable to recognise me, or anything else through her drunken haze, she had hailed me, offering herself to me. Gawd, she'd smelt awful. Like a rotten kipper. We settled upon a tanner and she led me into the murky building, up a flight of stone steps to a first-floor landing.

I had seized her throat with my left hand, clamping my right over her mouth and nose. To my delight, my organ began to stiffen. She went limp. I laid her straight out on the ground, throwing up her dress. My organ throbbed eagerly. I felt my seed flow. Too quickly, far too quickly. I became angry. Furious, in fact. I wanted it to last. At least for a while. Inexplicably forgetting my new knife, I drew my clasp knife and wildly stabbed her in the chest over and over again. The pleasure I felt was enormous, beyond description. I spent once, twice and, stabbing her deep in the stomach, thrice. Feeling reborn and calming, I had then felt my new knife inside my jacket. Instantly sliding it from its sheath, I had plunged its blade straight through her chest-bone. Quickly wiping the knives and my hands on her dress, I crept down the stairs and slipped out into the street. Leaving George Yard and crossing Wentworth Street, I walked along George Street, crossed over Flower and Dean Street and was back here in just under five minutes.

At about 2 a. m. and whilst my benefactor had approached Martha prior to murdering her, Police Constable Thomas Barrett had briefly challenged a loitering guardsman in Wentworth Street, close to George Yard. The guardsman had told Barrett that he was waiting for his chum, who had gone off with a girl. Might this have been the same guardsman who had left Martha and was now searching for his pal who had gone off with Mary Ann Connelly? Whatever the case, this fleeting encounter had clearly revealed that, contrary to popular belief, the Whitechapel streets had not been completely deserted at the time of the murders. Similar to George Yard, my benefactor had, in fact, narrowly avoided other nearby patrolling police constables when he had murdered Mary Ann Nichols in Buck's Row and Catharine Eddowes in Mitre Square.

Giving my benefactor his ten guineas, we had adjourned, agreeing to reconvene the next day. Returning to my chambers at the Inner Temple that night, I had reflected upon his confession, satisfied that I had truly heard the motive for the murders. All that remained for me to do now was to methodically write down his account of the following murders which, I had reasoned, would not include the murder of Elizabeth Stride at all. It had been at this point of my deliberation that a question had come to mind. After retrieving the deposited letter from my cousin, what should I do with my benefactor's forthright confession? I could hardly squirrel the deposition away, perchance it might be found among my papers once I had retired to the hereafter. Nay, such a valuable document should be seen, read now, or the horrid truth might never be known. A document, if imprudently concealed, might encourage successive armchair sleuths to put forward improbable theories, alleging them to be the actual truth.

My penultimate meeting with my benefactor had again taken place in the odious warehouse. Sitting opposite him, I had been fortified by the heavenly knowledge that the following day would be the last time I would have to breathe its foul air. As was his candid manner, my benefactor had not wasted precious time with insincere pleasantries, but had continued his admission from where he had ceased the previous evening.

The newspapers had said that the person who murdered Martha Tabram might have also attacked Annie Millwood, Ada Wilson and Emma Smith. A lot they knew. The police clambered all over Henry Turner, but weren't able to find anything amiss. He went to the inquest, gave 'em what little he knew about Martha and was glad when the jury finally gave its verdict, wilful murder against some persons or persons unknown. That had suited me just fine. What I'd done was the talk of the neighbourhood, mostly among the whores in the Ten Bells. Many of 'em were frightened, each thought she might be the next one. I'd waited to see how Mary would react, see if she'd got the message. I began to hope she hadn't, give me a reason to do it again. The enormous pleasure I'd felt whilst stabbing Martha was something I'd not felt before. I needed to feel it again. I wanted to slice open the belly of the next one, feel her innards.

After I'd murdered Martha, the streets had stayed quiet for a few nights, but by the end of the month everything had returned to normal. Emerging from every nook and cranny, hundreds of whores began to openly ply their trade again. Dan told me that Joe was still without work and Mary had finally resorted to the streets, servicing men from the local pubs. Joe had since taken it upon himself to become her watchdog. He'd trail after her, making sure she didn't come to any harm. Can you imagine it? Mary up an alley with a man and Joe waiting across the street whilst she did her business. Dan had been right about his brother. Joe hadn't just got a slate missing; his entire roof had gone. It was time to give Mary a further warning. Time for me to take pleasure again.

Mary Ann Nichols had often used the Ten Bells but her favourite pub was the Frying Pan, corner of Brick Lane and Thrawl Street, where she lodged at number eighteen. She had been an ideal second victim. Bore the same name as Mary and had lived in the same street where Mary had first lodged at Cooley's upon her arrival in the area. Known as 'Polly' to her kind, Mary Nichols had been a frail, smallish woman who had solemnly revealed her forty-third birthday to me in the Ten Bells five days earlier. It had, in fact, been her glumness that particular night which had determined her fate. I thought her death would make a suitable belated birthday present. Put her out of her misery, like.

It had been a Thursday night. Earlier that day, two huge fires had broken out in the London docks, turning the night sky red. Like a bleedin' Indian summer, it was. The glow from the fires stretched right across the East End. It was beautiful, like. Polly had drunkenly fallen out of the Frying Pan well after twelve-thirty that night. I had watched her lurch along Thrawl Street and enter her lodging house. Patiently biding my time, I knew she had spent her bed money and would soon be back out on the streets looking for a fourpenny handout. I had been right. About an hour later, she had staggered out of the doss-house, turned right into Osborn Street and then bumped into another woman at the corner of Whitechapel Road. Polly seemed to know the other woman, who had tried to persuade her to go home with her, but Polly was having none of it. As St. Mary's Church had struck two-thirty across the road, Polly had separated

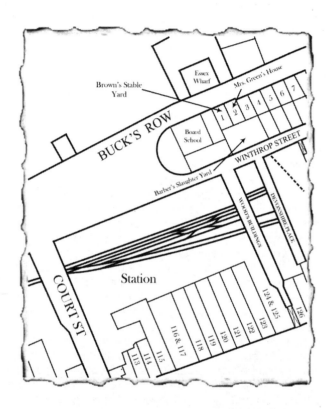

Essex Wharf

Brown's Stable Yard

Mrs. Green's House

1 2 3 4 5 6 7

BUCK'S ROW

Board School

WINTHROP STREET

Barber's Slaughter Yard

WOOD'S BUILDINGS

DEVONSHIRE PLACE

Station

COURT ST

113 114 115 116 & 117 118 119 120 121 122 123 124 & 125 126

BUCK'S ROW, E.

from the woman and tottered off eastwards along the Whitechapel Road. I had allowed her to stay just ahead of me, pausing only when she had beggarly tried to waylay a couple of men who'd instantly shoved her aside in disgust.

When she had got as far as the Duke's Head public house, I stopped her, offering her the price of a bed if she'd come around the corner into Baker's Row with me. Didn't have much choice, did she? Grinning and straightening her bonnet, which looked fairly new to me, she had followed me like a lamb to the slaughter. Caring not where she went, I led her across Baker's Row and into White's Row. I could have killed her then and there, but I had a precise spot in mind. A spot close to a particular place that would instantly attract the attention of the police after I had murdered her. Barber's Slaughter Yard in Winthrop Street.

I led her into Buck's Row just past the school. Slipping on the pavement, Polly had fallen against the stable gates. As I had done with Martha, I had seized her throat with my left hand, clamping my right over her mouth and nose. My organ had instantly hardened. I savoured the moment and then let her slide to the ground. I straightened her, drew my knife from its sheath and sliced through her throat. I spent my seed and, to prolong the sensation, cut her throat again. Throwing up her frock, I slashed open her front, exposing her innards. Oh, the pleasure, it was beyond belief. I had spent again and then had heard footsteps coming towards me from Brady Street. Wiping my blade across her worn Ulster and my hands on her frock, I had rushed past the school, slipped into Court Street, which led me straight back into Whitechapel Road. Read later that Charlie Cross had been the first to stumble upon her body. Must have been him I'd heard.

Charles Cross had indeed been the first to discover the body, followed by Robert Paul and then Police Constable John Neil. My benefactor did not have everything his own way that morning. In fact, he had come very close to being seen whilst hunched over his victim. The woman he had seen earlier at the corner of Osborn Street and Whitechapel Road had been Mrs. Ellen Holland, who had desperately tried to persuade a drunken Mary Ann Nichols to return home with her. Had Mary accepted Ellen's kind offer, she undoubtedly would have been alive today. Her bonnet, found beside her body, had indeed been a newly acquired item. Turned out of 18 Thrawl Street shortly before her death, Mary Ann Nichols had laughingly boasted to the deputy of the doss-house, "I'll soon get my doss money. See what a jolly bonnet I've got now." The escape route that my benefactor had taken from Buck's Row to Court Street had been entirely sensible. Thus he had avoided Wood's Buildings which, had he used, would have first required him to enter Winthrop Street, where three slaughtermen were hard at work in Barber's Slaughter Yard. Although his carnal satisfaction had been somewhat curtailed by the sudden arrival of Charles Cross, my benefactor had achieved another aim besides sending a gruesome warning to Mary Kelly. By choosing a specific victim and, as in this case, an exact location, he had purposely directed police attention towards cetain other people living or working near the murder site who could be suspected of committing the crime. In the case of Martha Tabram, Henry Turner. And in the case of Mary Ann Nichols, slaughtermen Henry Tomkins, James Mumford and Charles Britton.

The police gave the three of 'em a hard time. Fell on 'em like a plague of locusts. Desperate to catch me, they were. But the police were flogging a dead horse, weren't they? Anyhow, they finally let 'em go. Then they said I might be 'Leather Apron'. A Jew! A Yid! That gave me real fits. Vermin just like whores, weren't they? Gave me an idea, though. Dan said Joe and Mary had begun to argue. Mary was fed up with Joe following her about. Said he ought to be out looking for work, but whilst he tagged along behind her, he wouldn't. Because of the last murder, she had felt uneasy about working the streets at night. Had she finally sat up and taken note? I didn't know. Had to make sure. Decided to do another one. Do it right this time. Good and proper, like.

Dark Annie. Real name Annie Chapman. She was near to fifty, short, plump and had two bottom teeth missing. Could see the gaps when she grinned. She had blue eyes like Mary and lodged very close to her in Crossingham's doss-house, corner of Little Paternoster Row and Dorset Street. Chapman had been a perfect choice. Lived right on Mary's doorstep. Had to give some thought to her first initial, though. Hadn't wanted Mary to forget who M was.

Annie Chapman had indeed lodged close to Mary Kelly. Merely three courts away from Miller's Court and on the same side of the street. The significance of the initial M, although I had known of it before I had met my benefactor, had been nonetheless chilling. Also revealing was how he had rescued the scrawny dog from the savage jaws of a pit terrier a mere day before he had killed Annie Chapman. A sympathetic act which I had found quite remarkable for such a heartless murderer.

As a rule, I didn't work Friday evenings, but because one of the barmen wanted the night off, I had stood in for him. Chapman had come into the pub twice that evening. First time, about eleven, I think. Nursing a black eye she'd got from another whore the week before, she had drunk herself full and left shortly after midnight, saying she felt poorly and was going back to her doss-house. Just after two, she was back again, whining that she hadn't had the price of a bed and had been turned out of her lodgings. Desperate, like, she had quickly wrenched three brass rings from her fingers, slamming them down on the counter in exchange for a few tots of brandy. Gave her what she wanted, and more. Knew she was fond of using the back yards in Hanbury Street to service men. Number 29 in particular. Told her to meet me there and I'd give her the price of a bed. Sweeping up a piece of envelope from the pub floor and scrawling M on it, I had slipped it into my pocket, impatient to feel her innards. Two hours later, I shut the pub and went after her. She was waiting outside the house, worse for drink. Led me through its front door, along a passageway and through another door into its backyard.

I had suffocated her. Left hand around her throat and right hand over her mouth and nose. She had dropped to the ground awkwardly. Had to straighten her, lay her out neat, like. My organ had begun to stiffen. I yanked down the handkerchief around her neck and sliced through her throat. I cut deeply. Tried to remove her head but couldn't. Spent my seed. Oh, sheer delight. Slashed her throat again. Threw up her black skirt and tore open its pocket, taking out some things and putting 'em on the ground by the fence.

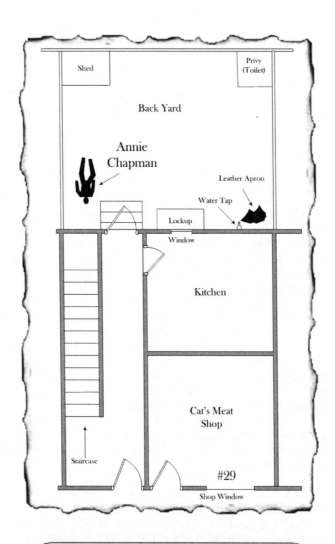

Flung back her two petticoats and sliced open her front. Thrust my left hand inside her. She was warm. I had returned to the slaughterhouse. I had spent again. The pleasure was immense. I'd cut away at her innards and, pulling 'em out, had thrown 'em over her right shoulder. Over the other shoulder, I'd thrown part of her stomach. Couldn't believe what I was doing. Didn't care. Spent once more. Drew the blade of my knife across her skirt, wiping it clean. Did the same with my hands. Took parts of her and wrapped 'em in a sheet of grease-paper, shoving the package into my pocket. Slipped the piece of envelope under her head and scarpered. Took me about five minutes to get back to my newfound friend and feed him. He ate most of her. What he didn't, I threw to the pigs in the court.

Since the murder of Annie Chapman, speculation about her missing organs had been rife. Had the murderer taken away parts of her uterus, vagina and bladder as obscene trophies to gloat over? Had the parts been procured for anatomical research? Nay, the simple reason for their removal, however preposterous it had sounded, could never have been guessed. My benefactor had butchered Annie Chapman as he might an animal, merely taking away parts of her organs as sustenance for the living. In this case, food for an injured, hungry dog. Along with everyone else, I had, of course, been utterly wrong in my hypothesis that the murderer had robbed Annie Chapman of her three brass rings. An apparently credible assumption which, I had to admit, had been blown asunder by the fact that Annie Chapman had actually removed the rings herself. As he had done before, my benefactor had knowingly chosen another ideal location to commit murder. At the time, 29 Hanbury Street had housed seventeen lodgers, which subsequently burdened an already beleaguered police force with additional people to investigate and eliminate from the case.

So help me God, I had felt bleedin' good. I'd really done her proper. All the East End was talking about it. The police were in a quandary, chasing their tails. Then Georgie Lusk stuck his nose in, didn't he? Him and his Jewish mates formed the Mile End Vigilance Committee, telling everyone they were going to nab me. As if they had any idea who I was in the first place. They weren't interested in protecting the likes of you and me, only wanted to safeguard their livelihoods, businesses, like. That's the problem with the Jews, like to keep everything in the family. Don't want to share anything, just take. Can't understand why we bother with 'em. Chose to write the police a note. Give myself a name. Didn't want Lusk having all the glory. Akin to villains before me, thought I'd use the name Jack. Liked the word Ripper, 'cos that's what I'd done to 'em. Sent the note to Abberline about nine days after I'd killed Chapman. Never heard back from him, though.

Signing himself Jack the Ripper, had my benefactor indeed sent a note to Inspector Frederick George Abberline at Scotland Yard? I had to confess that I had no means at hand by which I might substantiate his claim. However, if he had really penned such a message, then he would have dispatched the note to Inspector Abberline on or about the 17th September. A mere nine days after Annie Chapman had been murdered and ten days before the Central News Agency had received the 25th September letter, purporting to have come from Jack the Ripper, but which had undoubtedly been penned by someone other than the murderer. In a nutshell, a blatant hoax. If my benefactor had indeed spoken the truth and had dispatched a note to the police, had it been possible for both him and another person to have conceived the name of Jack the Ripper independently of each other? Extremely unlikely, I had thought. Therefore, one person must have copied the other. If the 17th September note had truly existed, then the 25th September letter had to be the copy, derived from the former. Meaning that someone had certainly had some kind of privileged access to confidential police files. Again, if the 17th September note had existed, might Inspector Abberline have deliberately withheld the note from the public's gaze, arming the police with a credible piece of evidence that only they and the murderer knew about? A piece of evidence that could be used to distinguish the murderer's confession from possible false confessions, perhaps?

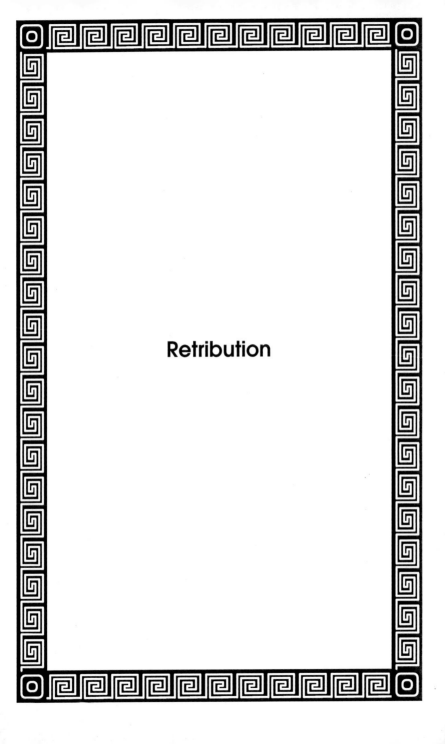

Retribution

Retribution

Missed Romford, though. About thirteen miles from here. Market town. There you can get anything. Fruit, vegetables, pigs, sheep and cattle. River Rom runs straight through it. Has a nasty habit of overflowing and flooding the place. It happened again, ten weeks ago. Swept through the town, striking the brewery and taking nigh on twenty-five thousand casks of ale with it. Scores of souls perished, poor blighters. Plenty of work down there, cleaning up the mess. Couldn't go, though. Had my little friend to look after, didn't I?

Kate Eddowes had lodged at Cooney's doss-house in Flower and Dean Street. Near to where we are now. Unlike the other dregs, she'd had a brain. A crafty one, she was. Too crafty for her own good, like. Spent most of her time with a bloke named John Kelly. Dunno why, but sometimes called herself Mary Ann Kelly. Remind you of someone, does it? The pair of 'em liked to go hop picking in Kent. Did it every autumn. Got 'em out of Spitalfields, she'd said. Gave 'em some air. Came into the pub on the Thursday night, flat broke. Slipped her a tot of rum. Told me that she'd returned to earn the reward offered for the capture of the murderer. Thought she knew him, she'd said. Might share the reward with me if I'd help her. Late Saturday afternoon, I met her in Houndsditch. She was still broke. I gave her half a crown and we agreed to meet outside the Sir John Foster pub after midnight, whereupon she would tell me the name of the murderer.

She came late. After one, I think. She said the police had thrown her into a cell for being drunk. Smelt like a bleedin' brewery, she had. We strolled along Duke Street, past the Great Synagogue, and stopped at Church Passage which led into Mitre Square. Told me that she knew of Joe Barnett, who had a strange habit of following his woman around the streets at night. The murders had begun not long after he'd lost his job. Perhaps he'd killed those women to scare his woman off the streets and back into the home, she said. Of course I had known differently, but Kate had struck a nerve. Her reasoning had been too close for comfort, like. Asked me if I might lend a hand and get proof, collect the reward and share it with her. Said I would. She instantly became cheerful. Like we already had proof of Joe's guilt and were

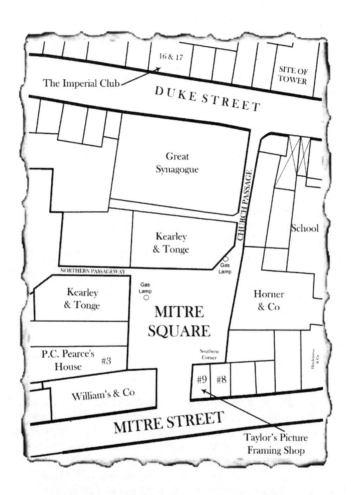

MITRE SQUARE, EC.

about to collect the reward the next day. Gaily, she offered herself to me. I had led her down Church Passage into the square and over to one of its darkened corners, whereupon I had immediately throttled her with my hands.

East London Observer Newspaper – 13 October 1888

THE WHITECHAPEL HORRORS
An Extraordinary Incident

A reporter gleaned some curious information from the Casual Ward Superintendent of Mile End, regarding Kate Eddowes, the Mitre-square victim. She was formerly well known in the casual wards there, but had disappeared for a considerable time until the Friday preceding her murder. Asking the woman where she had been in the interval, the Superintendent was met with the reply, that she had been in the country "hopping". "But," added the woman, "I have come back to earn the reward offered for the capture of the Whitechapel murderer. I think I know him." "Mind he doesn't murder you too" replied the Superintendent. "Oh, no fear of that," was the remark made by Kate Eddowes as she left. Within four-and-twenty hours afterwards she was a mutilated corpse.

She had dropped to the ground like a sack of potatoes. Straightening her, my organ had stiffened. I pulled down her neckerchief and sliced open her throat, cutting deeply and spending my seed. She had sought a reward, I was giving it to her. I cut away at her face, nicking her eyelids and slicing off the tip of her nose. I had then cut part of an M on both cheeks and sliced off an ear lobe. Upon hearing the sound of heavy footsteps, I had paused. A copper strolled down Church Passage, halted and peered into the square. He looked in my direction and then turned about and walked back up the passage. Didn't see me, too dark. I tore open the upper part of her dress, threw up her skirt and petticoat, slicing her open at the front. Thrusting my hand inside her, I had spent again. I wanted the sensation to last but I couldn't dally. I pulled out most of her innards, throwing 'em over her right shoulder. If I could have taken my time the pleasure would have been endless. I threw a bit of innards on the ground between her body and left arm. I sliced off a piece of her apron, wrapping a kidney and a portion of her womb in it. Shoving the meat into my pocket, I drew the blade of my knife across her skirt, wiping it clean. Did the same with my hands. I then darted across the square, along an alleyway into St. James Place and got back here in just under ten minutes. Sliced the kidney into two and gave one half to my little friend. He like that but not the womb. Threw that bit to the pigs the next day. Changed my clothes and went out again. Had to get rid of the piece of apron. Knew the police might be looking for it. I'd killed Kate near the Great Synagogue in Duke Street. Thought it was time to point the finger at Lusk and his mates. Ditched the piece of apron in a doorway and chalked a message to the police on the wall above it. Weren't too happy when I had read that Charlie Warren had it rubbed out, though.

At this point in my benefactor's admission, I had requested that he write down the word 'Jews'. He had steadfastly refused, sternly reminding me that although he had agreed to tell me everything, he had not consented to put pen to paper. Not to be deterred, however, I had then asked him to spell the word aloud which he had done.

J-u-w-e-s

Partially illiterate, he had misspelt the word but, in doing so, he had confirmed that he had indeed chalked the message on the wall above the piece of apron.

The Juwes are
The men That
Will not
be Blamed
for nothing.

Perhaps his reluctance to write down the word 'Jews' for me had been due to the fact that he knew he could not write or spell correctly. If that had been so, his necessity to avoid revealing his educational inadequacies had been entirely understandable.

I'd gone back to the square to mingle with the crowd which had come together after Eddowes' body had been found. That's when I'd heard that another whore had been murdered in Berner Street. Everyone had said I'd done her in. Two in one night? Believe that, you'll believe anything. Sure, I'd taken chances, but I hadn't been stupid. Had thought of the pros and cons, like. Two in one night would have increased the risk of getting caught. I'd be no good to Mary, dangling from the end of a rope, would I? Heard later that the Berner Street woman had been a Swede, name of Liz Stride. She had lodged for three years with a bruiser called Michael Kidney. Mean bugger, he was. Stride had left him only five days before she was killed. If anyone did it, he had. He even had the gall to turn up at Leman Street Police Station, drunkenly shouting at everyone that had he been the copper on duty when his poor Liz had been murdered, he'd shot himself. Bleedin' idiot! Mind you, did give me an idea, though.

Before her untimely death, Elizabeth Stride had briefly lodged at 32 Flower and Dean Street. On Wednesday, 26th September, the day after she had left Michael Kidney, the eminent philanthropist Dr. Thomas Barnardo, had called upon the same lodging house, unaware that he would shortly be compelled to write about its occupants, especially one particular person.

The Times Newspaper – 9 October 1888

THE CHILDREN OF THE COMMON LODGING-HOUSES
TO THE EDITOR OF THE TIMES.

Sir, - Stimulated by the recently revealed Whitechapel horrors many voices are daily heard suggesting as many different schemes to remedy degraded social conditions, all of which doubtless contain some practical elements. I trust you will allow one other voice to be raised on behalf of the children. For the saddest feature of the common lodging houses in Whitechapel and other parts of London is that so many of their inmates are children. Indeed, it is impossible to describe the state in which myriads of young people live who were brought up in these abodes of poverty and of crime.

Only four days before the recent murders I visited No. 32, Flower and Dean-street, the house in which the unhappy woman Stride occasionally lodged. I had been examining many of the common lodging houses in Bethnal-green that night, endeavouring to elicit from the inmates their opinions upon a certain aspect of the subject. In the kitchen of No. 32 there were many persons, some of them being girls and women of the same unhappy class as that to which poor Elizabeth Stride belonged. The company soon recognised me, and the conversation turned to the previous murders. The female inmates seemed thoroughly frightened at the dangers to which they were exposed. In an explanatory fashion I put before them the scheme which had suggested itself to my mind, by which children at all events could be saved from the contamination of the common lodging houses and the streets, and so to some extent the supply cut off which feeds the vast ocean of misery in this great city.

The pathetic part of my story is that my remarks were manifestly followed with deep interest by all the women. Not a single scoffing voice was raised in ridicule or opposition. One poor creature, who had evidently been drinking, exclaimed somewhat bitterly to the following effect:- "We're all up to no good, and no one cares what becomes of us. Perhaps some of us will be killed next!" And then she added, "If anybody had helped the likes of us long ago we would never have come to this!"

Impressed by the unusual manner of the people, I could not help noticing their appearance somewhat closely, and I saw how evidently some of them were moved. I have since visited the mortuary in which were lying the remains of the poor woman Stride, and I at once recognised her as one of those who stood around me in the kitchen of the common lodging house on the occasion of my visit last Wednesday week.

In all the wretched dens where such unhappy creatures live are to be found hundreds, if not thousands, of poor children who breathe from their very birth an atmosphere fatal to all goodness. They are so heavily handicapped at the start in the race of life that the future is to most of them absolutely hopeless. They are continually surrounded by influences so vile that decency is outraged and virtue becomes impossible

Surely the awful revelations consequent upon the recent tragedies should stir the whole community up to action and to resolve to deliver the children of to-day who will be the men and women of to-morrow from so evil an environment.

I am, Sir, your obedient servant,
THOS. J. BARNARDO
18 to 26, Stepney-causeway, E., Oct. 6.

The Times Newspaper – 2 October 1888

THE MURDERS AT THE EAST-END

At a late hour last night it was decided by the City Police to offer a reward for the discovery and conviction of the criminal, and the following notice was forwarded to us:-

"Murder - £500 Reward.

"Whereas, at 1:45 a. m. on Sunday, the 30th of September last, a woman, name unknown, was found brutally murdered in Mitre-square, Aldgate, in this City, a reward of £500 will be paid by the Commissioner of Police of the City of London to any person (other than a person belonging to a police force in the United Kingdom), who shall give such information as shall lead to the discovery and conviction of the murderer or murderers.

"Information to be given to the Inspector of the Detective Department, 26, Old Jewry, or at any police-station.

"JAMES FRASER. Colonel, Commissioner.
"City of London Police Office, 26, Old Jewry
October 1, 1888

I had found the reason for the murder of Catharine Eddowes quite ironic. Unbeknown to her, she had tried to enlist the help of the very man she should have avoided. She had sought financial gain only to find death and a subsequent reward offered for the capture of her killer. Stranger still, and merely twelve hours before she had died, her companion, John Kelly, had fearfully reminded her of the murderer, only to hear her flippantly reply,

Don't you fear for me. I'll take care of myself and I shan't fall into his hands.

After the two murders, one of which I didn't do, I had decided to lay low for a while. Didn't want to give anyone the chance of collecting the reward. The neighbourhood was swarming with police. Never seen anything like it. They were everywhere. For a whole week they went from house to house, searching rooms, peering under beds, rummaging through cupboards, inspecting knives and, on the whole, upsetting landlords and lodgers alike.

Star Newspaper – 17 October 1888

WHITECHAPEL
A House to House Search Among the Jews.

Mrs. Andleman, of 7, Spelman-street, Whitechapel, was interviewed by a Star reporter. She said: I came home from work yesterday, and as soon as I opened the street door, two men came up and said, "Do you live in this front room?" "Yes," I said. "We want to have a look at it." "Who are you, and what do you want?" "We are police officers, and we come to look for the murderer." Do you think I keep the murderer here, or do you suggest that I associate with him?" I replied. They answered that it was their duty to inspect the rooms. I showed them into my room. They looked under the bed, and asked me to open the cupboards. I opened a small cupboard, where I keep plates and things. It is not more than two feet wide and about one in depth. They made an inspection of that also. "Do you think," I said, "that it is possible for a man, or even a child, to be hidden in that small place?" They made no answer, and walked out. Then they went next door and inspected those premises.

Broadly publicised, the intensive house to house search had begun on Saturday, 13th October and had concluded six days later on Thursday, 18th October. Encompassing the Ten Bells and my benefactor's lodging house, the entire search had covered an area of just under half a square mile. Although the police search had ultimately failed to unearth the murderer, it had, however demonstrated to the public that the police were convinced that Jack the Ripper resided in the search area. In this belief the police had been entirely accurate. But they had known little or nothing of the man they had sought. Thus, had they routinely questioned him during the search without suspecting him in the least?

The police had questioned hundreds of blokes, including me. We'd all given the same answer, "Yes, sir. No, sir. Three bags full, sir." If you had an alibi for the time of the Stride murder then you couldn't have killed Kate, right? The police had misled themselves, lumping the two murders together. They had handcuffed themselves. Rather them than me, I'd thought. Dan had told me that Mary was at her wits end. Frightened to work the streets at night, she and Joe had got behind with the rent. At least she'd taken note. I wondered how long I'd have to wait before she tossed him aside. Hadn't forgotten Lusk and his mates, though. Sent him the remainder of the kidney I'd taken from Eddowes. Tucked a note inside the small cardboard box to remind him I was still about. Caused a bleedin' stir, it did. A doctor at the local hospital said the part had come from Kate whilst another in the City said it hadn't. The police, on the other hand, were of two minds. Me? I hadn't much cared either way, thinking only of her, Mary.

His eyes had glazed over. The tone of his voice had suddenly diminished, becoming vague and scarcely audible. An inner grief, nay, an expression of remorse had existed. Seizing upon his forlorn disposition, I had prudently brought the session to a close and, as before, had paid him ten guineas. Agreeing once more to meet him outside the Northumberland Arms at noon the following day, I had departed the abominable warehouse, longing for food and light refreshments. Courteously served a delicious meal of boiled beef and carrots at the Three Tuns public house in Jewry Street, I had again pondered what should become of my benefactor's final confession, or more appropriately, where and with whom it should be deposited. I had been entirely aware that my recent association with Jack the Ripper might be interpreted by some individuals that I had been a passive accomplice, which to my eternal shame, I had. In my obsessive desire to see Mary Jane Kelly dead, I had condoned the hideous slaughter of six defenceless women to satisfy my vile wish. Had I not revered Jack the Ripper, warmly referring to him as my benefactor? Had not my murderous thoughts been tantamount to his barbaric acts? Yes, it had been as if I had murdered the six unfortunate women myself. Jack the Ripper and I were both guilty. Guilty of crimes committed against the known civilised world. His confession, almost concluded, would ultimately be my confession, too.

That night, I had tossed and turned in bed, plagued by thoughts of my past wickedness. My entire existence had been one of utter selfishness. A life spent in total disrespect for my fellowmen, except for what I might gain. I had not possessed one grain of common decency, concerned only with bodily pleasures, devoid of spiritual compassion. Initially blind to the repellent motive for his crimes, I had heartily sought out Jack the Ripper, eager to learn the truth from his own lips. But now that I had heard most of his admission, my own morbid curiosity and lack of sensibility had profoundly disturbed me. True, I had attentively sat and listened to him, but what I had not expected to see reflected in him had been a part of me. Since birth he had undoubtedly been cursed and, absurd as it seemed, so had I. We were not separate entities but, in fact, had been two reprehensible sides of the same coin.

It had been a cold blustery Sunday morning. The relentless rain had lashed my face whilst I had walked along Fashion Street towards the Northumberland Arms for my final meeting with him. I had been in a sombre mood, beset by the ultimate recognition of my dishonourable life. Heavy hearted, I had arrived outside the public house, longing to conclude my association with him. As before, he had punctually emerged from the court, beckoning me with his hand and, as before, I had followed him through the rain swept court into the warehouse. An ordinary, innocuous act that he had not permitted the previous Sunday. Perhaps he had since realised that his prior precaution, though justified, had not been necessary. We had again sat opposite each other; he staring at me and I poised with pen, anxious to commit his words to paper. Evidently troubled by some inner thought, he had hesitated, but in the end he had coughed, clearing his throat.

Dan had told me that Joe and Mary had begun to fight. Her throwing things at him and breaking windows, like. Had a fiery temper, she did. Heard that Joe had griped about her taking whores back to stay for the night. Made her feel safe, she had said. Didn't matter, he hadn't liked it. By the end of the month it'd all come to a head between 'em. He'd left her. Believe that, you'll believe anything. Knowing her, she most likely threw him out. I couldn't believe it'd happened. The last murder had clearly done the trick. She'd finally sat up and taken note. With Joe gone, I'd been convinced she'd want me again. Need my help, like. I was ready to move heaven and earth for her. Give her anything. Clear her rent arrears, get her out of that hovel and give her a fresh start in life. Didn't matter that she'd strayed. She'd been my blessed angel, hadn't she? Forgave her. Couldn't help myself. Joe had gone and lost her. Now it was my turn to take her back. And then misfortune struck. I'd lost my job.

Happened just over three weeks ago. The brewery had tossed aside old man Waldron, bringing in Alf Grainger as the landlord of the Ten Bells. A new broom sweeps clean, as they say, and Alf Grainger was no exception to the rule. First day he'd entered the pub, I'd fallen out with him. Without as much as a blink of the eye, he'd booted me straight out the pub into the street. If Mary had thought about looking me up at the Ten Bells, she wouldn't have had much luck, which meant I had been forced to look her up. Trouble was that although Joe had left Mary, he returned every day to visit her in her room. Didn't stay too long but you never knew when he would arrive. He was irregular, like. Knew that because I had stood in the shadows of Miller's Court at night and watched her room. Noticed she had a habit of putting her hand through a broken window to unlock the door. Must have lost her key. When Joe wasn't visiting her, other whores were constantly in and out of the room, which had made it nigh on impossible for me to see her alone.

During the day it had been the same story. Forever in the company of her own kind. Never once noticed me, but it had felt good to see her. After a week of keeping an eye on her, I had begun to despair of ever finding her on her own. Wanted to talk to her, explain how I felt about her. But she always had someone with her. Sometimes it had been men. Several men! Different times. That had angered me. Why them and not me? It had been a Thursday. The day before I'd wiped her from the face of the earth. Dan told me that he'd fixed to meet Mary in the Horn of Plenty pub that night. Wanted to mend things between her and Joe, so he said. Had a hunch Dan wasn't being straight about himself and Mary. Why should Dan want to mend things between Joe and Mary when Joe was still calling on Mary anyway? I'd begun to smell a rat. Something weren't right, like. Anyhow, Joe had gone into Miller's Court just after seven-thirty that evening. Saw a woman leave after he'd arrived. Read later that it'd been Maria Harvey. Joe had stayed for about fifteen minutes then he'd left. Strolling right past the Horn of Plenty, he had turned left, no doubt dropping down into Raven Row, working his way back to his lodging house in Bishopsgate. After a few minutes, Mary had rushed out of the court and hurriedly gone into the pub.

Maurice Lewis, a tailor, had later testified that he had been in the Horn of Plenty at about 8 p. m. that evening and had seen Mary Jane Kelly drinking with a market porter known as 'Dan'. Lewis had also curiously suggested that the man might have been Joseph Barnett, stating,

Dan, a man selling oranges in Billingsgate and Spitalfields market, with whom she lived with up to as recently as a fortnight ago.

Joseph Barnett had not been known as Dan at all. A man selling oranges in Billingsgate and Spitalfields? Joseph had not worked for the past three months. Since July, in fact. Unlike his brother, Daniel Barnett had still possessed work and could afford to ply Mary with drinks. Something Joseph most certainly could not have done.

Mary had stayed in the Horn of Plenty for nigh on two hours. At around ten o'clock, her and Dan had fallen out of the pub, walking to the entrance of Miller's Court. She'd tugged him by the arm, trying to lead him into the court. That's when it had hit me, when I'd woken up, like. She'd just thrown aside one brother and was now after the other. I could've gone across the street and killed her then and there. Dan had obviously thought twice about her offer because he'd pulled back, walking away from her. Going after him, she'd caught up with him outside the Britannia pub. They'd talked for a while and then he'd left her, going off along Commercial Street.

She seemed to be at sixes and sevens. Didn't know what to do next. Then she'd gone into the pub. Choosing to give her one last chance, I'd followed her in. She'd turned a blind eye to me, until I'd bought her a drink. Wouldn't listen to me. Bleedin' drunk, she was. Made me feel foolish, like.

212

Only wanted a good time, she'd said. Then she'd upped and left me, edging closer to another fellow buying a drink at the bar.

The Daily News Newspaper – 10th November 1888

THE MURDER IN WHITECHAPEL

According to an account on which reliance has been placed, Kelly was seen at eleven o'clock last night in the Britannia public house, at the corner of Commercial Street, with a young man with a dark moustache. She was then intoxicated. The young man appeared to be respectable and well dressed.

I'd left the Britannia, riled. I'd murdered five other whores because I'd thought Mary had been different, but she'd been the same as 'em. Worse, in fact. She'd flitted from one bloke to another and when they could no longer provide for her, she'd tossed 'em aside, me included. I'd vowed then and there to kill her. She hadn't known it, but that Thursday night had been the last of her life. Mary never saw morning light again. She'd fallen out of the pub about eleven-thirty. How did I know? I'd heard the clock of Spitalfields Church chime the half-hour. She'd a bloke in tow. Older than me and carrying a pail of ale. An old biddy had followed the two of 'em into Miller's Court. Read later that it'd been Mrs. Cox, who was to scuttle back and forth to the court for the next three hours. Mary had started to sing loudly. Could hear her across the street. After a while, I'd felt taunted by her merriment. A slap in the face, so to speak. Wanted to kill her right then and there. Stop her mocking me, like. But I'd held my nerve. Knew my moment would come. Liz Prater had appeared. Often drank at the Ten Bells, she did. Hung around the entrance to the court for about thirty minutes and then went to her room. Half an hour later, Mary had blessedly stopped singing. At this point, it'd started to rain again. Cats and dogs, like. Hadn't mattered, though. I'd worn another jacket over my first. Been determined to see the night through. Knew the man with Mary would have to leave her before daybreak. Had to go to work, didn't he?

Sarah Lewis! Never heard of her until I saw her name in

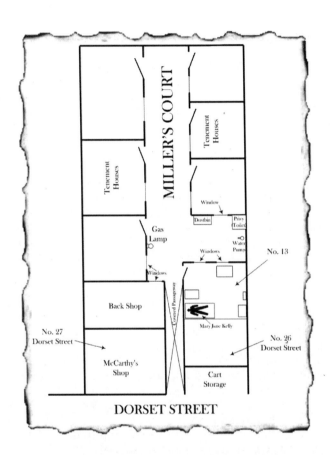

MILLER'S COURT, E.

the newspaper. Well, she'd gone into Miller's Court just after two-thirty. Hadn't been aware that she'd seen me, though. Might have stopped me from killing Mary that morning if I'd known. Somewhere around three o'clock, Mrs. Cox had returned to the court. This time she'd stayed put, like. Hadn't come out again. Started to think the man with Mary would never leave. Knew he'd be a good suspect for the murder if he did. About thirty minutes later, my patience had been rewarded. He'd emerged from the court, carrying his pail. Feeling the moment was nigh upon me, I'd held my breath. He'd turned up the collar of his overcoat and, with head bowed against the rain, had hurried away from the court towards Commercial Street. Lest he might return, I'd waited for a few minutes and then crossed the street, going into the court.

From the outside, I'd reached through the broken pane of glass and slipped the door bolt. Quietly entering the room, which was bleedin' dark, I'd caught sight of a candle on a table by the far window. I'd lit it. Mary lay alone in bed, asleep. I'd stood over her, staring down at her face. She'd looked so lovely, so innocent like. For a moment, I'd been spellbound. Felt no desire to harm her. She'd opened her eyes, blinked, recognised me. Her disdainful sneer broke the spell. I drew my knife. Her expression changed, begging forgiveness. I'd shook my head, denying her. She'd instantly raised her right hand to her face and screamed, "Murder!" Grasping her hand, I'd cut open her throat, slicing through her flesh to the spinal cord. Strange, like. Hadn't felt the cold until her blood had spurted. After hanging an overcoat in front of the broken window to stop the draught, I'd thrown some clothes into the grate and made a fire. Taking off my top jacket, which was sopping wet, I'd hung it over a chair to dry. I'd then dragged back the bedclothes, exposing her body. Apart from a chemise, she'd been naked. That's when I'd realised something odd had happened. My organ hadn't stirred.

Enraged by the thought that her death had somehow inhibited my bodily pleasure, I'd hacked at her face, slicing off her ears, nose, bits of eyebrows, cheeks, lips, chin. I'd then cut off both breasts, tossing one by her head, the other

215

by her foot. Had opened up her front and cut out all her innards, chucking bits by her head, either side of her body and between her feet. Bent her left arm and shoved her hand into her empty abdomen. Stripped the skin from her thighs and legs, slicing away lumps of flesh and putting 'em on a table. Held back her heart, though. Had wrapped it up in a petticoat I'd found in the room. Cut the organ up later and fed the pieces to my little friend. When I'd finished with her, I'd wiped my knife and hands on the bedclothes. More blood hadn't much mattered 'cos it'd gone everywhere. All over the bed and on the floor, like. Putting on my top jacket, which still felt damp, I'd blown out the candle and left the room, pulling the door shut behind me. Must have just gone five in the morning when I'd walked out of the court into the street. Hadn't been a soul around. Bleedin' deserted! Got back here in just under five minutes. Hadn't rushed. Took my time. Hadn't wanted to attract undue attention, like.

Although Caroline Maxwell had sworn that she had seen and spoken to Mary Kelly at 8. 30 a. m. on the morning of her murder, a statement which I had found completely at odds with the facts, I had now been left in no doubt that her conversation with Mary Kelly had taken place, not on the morning of the murder, but on another day entirely. Mary Kelly had been murdered shortly before 4 a. m. and therefore could not have been seen, or spoken to, by Caroline Maxwell at 8. 30 a. m. I, of course, had also erred, thinking that Mrs. Cox had heard the heavy footsteps of Jack the Ripper leaving Miller's Court at 5. 45 a. m. He had, in fact, departed some forty odd minutes earlier. A minute or two after 5 a. m.

What a bleedin hue and cry it'd turned out to be. I'd never seen or heard anything like it! Charlie Warren had tossed in the towel. Government had pledged a pardon. Fat lot of good that'd done anyone, though. Everyone had known I'd been a solitary killer. No accomplices, like. Even the Queen had got off her high horse and griped to ole man Salisbury about the murder. Wherever you went, it'd been on everyone's lips. Talked about nothing else, they had, especially the bleedin' womenfolk. Began to bother me, though. Didn't want to be reminded that I'd killed her. I'd lived the past three years, thinking solely of her. She'd given me a purpose in life. Something to hang onto, like.

Now she'd gone, I'd begun to feel life was pointless. Had no job, nothing! Totally adrift, I was. No anchorage, like. Mind you, got myself together three days later, though. Read that Sarah Lewis had seen me standing outside Miller's Court that morning. Stupid woman! She'd given a bleedin' statement at Mary's inquest and, in part, had described me.

I saw a man with a wideawake hat. There was no one talking to him. He was a stout-looking man, and not very tall. The hat was black. I did not take any notice of his clothes. The man was looking up the court; he seemed to be waiting or looking for someone. Further on there was a man and woman – the latter being drunk. There was nobody in the court.

Had decided to take a leaf out of Michael Kidney's book, like. Taking the bull by the horns, I'd strolled into the local nick and gave a statement, saying I'd seen Mary with a suspicious man shortly after two o'clock on the morning she'd been murdered. Said I'd seen 'em go into the court together and I'd remained outside 'cos I'd been worried about her safety. That's why Sarah Lewis had seen me. It'd been a right cock and bull story. A load of codswallop. But the local police had swallowed it, hook, line and sinker. They'd brought in Inspector Abberline from Scotland Yard to talk to me. Gave him a full description of the man I'd seen with Mary. Sent me out with a couple of his men to search for him. Traipsed the streets for nigh on two days, we did. Never found him. How could we? He'd never existed. Anyhow, that part had been fairly straight forward. It was the other part that I'd found much more difficult.

Took me to see Mary's body, couldn't get out of it. She'd lain upon a table. Well, what remained of her had. Couldn't believe I'd done it. Felt sick, but tried to stay calm. Didn't want to give the game away, did I? Then a copper let it slip that he'd heard Mary had been twelve weeks pregnant when she'd died. I'd felt horrible. There'd been another life in those innards I'd torn out of her. I'd killed that, too. Don't know what happened next, but I'd thrown up. Collapsed to the floor, weeping like a baby, they'd said. Police surgeon gave me a tonic, saying it was probably the shock of seeing the mutilated body that'd affected me but I knew different, didn't I? Knew I had to get away from Spitalfields. But how? Had no brass, like. Then you came along. Something else, though. You've given me the chance to get it off my chest. Not saying it has helped, but it might. Know what I mean?

I have to confess that I had been rather moved by his sense of remorse. An emotional quality that I had recently felt about my own life. We were truly alike, each of us now confronting an inner fiend that we had utterly ignored in our shameful pursuit of bodily pleasure. However, I had been dealt an extra card, so to speak. I had encountered two inner demons, his and mine. An enlightening experience I was determined to embrace and use to correct my own dishonourable life. He, on the other hand, had not been dealt an additional card. Thus, he had not experienced any reflective guidance, cursed solely with a deep sense of remorse that might one day devour him. In an act of sympathy, I had then asked him what he thought I should do with his confession.

Give me a few days to get away from here and then give it to 'em straight, like. Know what I mean? Folks should know why I did it, why I'm damned. I might end up lynched. Who cares? Good riddance, some will say. Probably right. Just let 'em know I played fair with you. Did what any man should do. I'd owned up, like.

As had happened before, his eyes had once more glazed over, vaguely staring into emptiness. A tear had slowly trickled down his cheek, ultimately to be absorbed by his moustache. I had quietly risen from my chair, knowing that, similar to his friendless existence, he had yet again wished to be alone. Placing ten guineas on the table before him, I had gathered my papers together and left the room. Upon reaching the bottom of the sodden wooden steps, I had paused, hearing the unmistakable melancholy sounds of a person sobbing high above me in the warehouse. Jack the Ripper had indeed been my benefactor. Because of his ceaseless love for Mary Jane Kelly, he had inadvertently shown me how I might cast aside the selfish cloak of arrogance and attain the virtuous mantle of humility.

In gratitude for his role in my spiritual salvation, I had hurried straight to my cousin's surgery in the Minories, retrieving the sealed envelope addressed to Inspector Abberline and destroying it.

Once more taking a late train, I had returned to the boarding school that night, guardedly clutching the confession in its leather binder as one might a precious jewel. It had been during the return train journey that I had again given considerable thought to whom I should dispatch the document. The Metropolitan Police, plagued by incompetence and having been deceived by hundreds of letters supposedly written by Jack the Ripper, had not seemed an ideal choice. But a higher authority to which the police were accountable definitely did. I had to be certain that whomsoever received the confession would prudently recognise its authenticity and act in a judicious manner. After careful consideration, I had therefore decided that the document should be sent anonymously to the Home Office, marked specifically for the attention of the Home Secretary, Mr. Henry Matthews. However, one nauseating feature of the confession had troubled me greatly. The appalling truth about my own degenerate life. Should I remove all reference to it, or should I, like Jack the Ripper, own up, leaving it as written?

I had awakened early the next morning, spiritually invigorated and utterly resolved to adopt a benevolent stance towards my fellowmen. An honourable trait, which would undoubtedly require a certain degree of tolerance on my behalf, but nonetheless a noble characteristic that I had decided should be upheld. Alas, my past immoral activities, easily swept aside by me, would not be lightly dismissed by other people, especially Mr. V. Summoned to his office, he had solemnly shown me the letter that I had formerly written to my thirteen-year-old boy, feigning eternal love. Having earlier spied him furtively departing my room, Mrs. S. had instantly challenged him, ultimately coercing him into divulging the facts of our indiscretion. In a treacherous attempt to secure clemency for himself, and to lay the entire blame at my door, he had also given Mrs. S. the incriminating letter, which she had then triumphantly presented to Mr. V. In due recognition for his Judas participation in the affair, the boy had received a just reward: instant expulsion from the school.

Quick in coming, my own sentence had been just as rapid. Immediate dismissal from the school, no appeal for leniency, and unpaid salary to be collected four days later, on the Friday. Solely due to my own appalling disregard for human morality, my career

219

as house teacher, barrister, nay my entire life, had now neared its ignominious end. I had recoiled from the hideous thought that I may have prompted an inevitable scandal. Would the detestable Mrs. S. take the matter further, sanctimoniously informing all and sundry of the shameful incident? An unpardonable sin for which I had no defence, nor the mental strength to combat. Would the parents of the boy learn the truth about me and then demand my head upon a silver platter for his premature dismissal? If so, my reputation would sooner or later be reduced to shreds. Life would be insufferable, tantamount to a lingering incurable illness. A quick and simple death, by my own hand, would be preferable to such an ignoble end. Better I should take a pistol to my head as if I had never existed.

Although I had utterly betrayed his trust in me, Mr. V. had extended me the courtesy of allowing me to quietly depart the school at night with my belongings. Hence, I had been spared the humiliation of seeing the condemnatory faces of colleagues I had, worked with for the past eight years. Gloomily retreating to my chambers at the Inner Temple, I had spent a melancholy night, beset by ghastly thoughts of a fruitless future, which had prevented me from sleeping. The next day, tired, hungry and unwashed, I had roamed aimlessly through the streets of our great capital, entirely overwhelmed by my rapid fall from grace. Would I be able to survive the social and family scorn? Or would I merely descend into a living hell? Amid these harrowing thoughts, a glimmer of hope had fleetingly presented itself. I would heed the advice previously suggested to me by my cousin, and emigrate to Australia with him. Begin a new life in a warmer country, start a new law practice. However, no sooner had I embraced the idea than I had banished the thought from my mind. How would I explain to my cousin my sudden change of heart? I could hardly tell him the shameful truth nor, on the other hand, could I lie to him. My new found sense of humility had precluded me from doing so.

Stirred by an inexplicable desire to see my mother, I had found myself drawn towards the East London asylum where she had been incarcerated four months earlier. Due to my dishevelled appearance, admittance to the asylum had not been easy but, with dogged determination, I had eventually gained entry, albeit in the continuous company of an elderly female warden. Confined to a spartan room, in reality a cell, my mother had appeared quite docile, due to a regular diet of medication, no doubt. Her skeletal face, cold eyes, so dead, had disturbed me at first but I knew I was looking upon the mere shell of a person. My mother had spiritually left this world a long time ago. Before I was born, perhaps? As a child, I had sought her affection but she had rejected me, or so I had thought at the time. I had, of course, been unaware that she was utterly incapable of such a sin, but due to my selfish, childish immaturity I had actually thought different and, in doing so, had committed the sin myself. I had, in actual fact, rejected her, my own mother. Kneeling before her and holding her frail hand, I had wept uncontrollably, grieving for a union that had never been. During my sorrowful outburst, my mother had remained entirely impassive. But then why not? Was she not mad? Nay, she was not. She had successfully discarded, as I also wished to do, the arduous yoke of a troublesome existence and had escaped to a tranquil haven somewhere beyond the reach of our world. Though I had not conversed with her in the asylum, I had however experienced a strong feeling that she had indeed spoken to me. Advising me upon my immediate crisis, she had suggested a grim solution to end the torturous ordeal.

Calmed by my mother's spiritual serenity but equally disturbed by the finality of her recommendation, I had departed the asylum, beset by indecision. Throughout the next two days, I had brooded, trying to think of alternative ways to resolve my predicament but always returning to her suggestion each time. Miserably returning to the boarding school on Friday morning, I had been met by the gatekeeper who, upon barring me from entering the building, confirmed my dismissal by contemptuously handing me a sealed envelope containing two cheques. Further humiliated by the gatekeeper's disdainful behaviour, I had fled the boarding school, seeking solace at the graveside of my past love. Humbly kneeling before his headstone, I had instantly undergone a prevailing sense of tranquillity that had slowly permeated my mind, expelling all troublesome thoughts. The sensation had been enchanting, nay heavenly. Then I had experienced something else, remorse for my past sins. The feeling had been painful, virtually unbearable. Yes, I had wept. I had wept and prayed. I prayed for the dignity of man and for the abolition of his vices. I prayed for six murdered women, begging their forgiveness. I prayed for absolution. But above all else, I had prayed for common humility and the condemnation of intolerance. Then I had heard his voice, calling my name. Faint at *first, but nonetheless distinct and clear. He had not forsaken me after all. Appearing before me, he had extended a translucent hand, warmly beckoning me. In an instant he had gone. But in that fleeting moment and not unlike my mother's suggestion, he had shown me how I might start anew. That evening, whilst of sound mind, I had decided that I would end my life once I had written my elder brother an explanation, Mr. V. an apology, and mailed the unedited confession of Jack the Ripper to the Home Secretary. My earthly existence, like that of my benefactor, had been blighted because of my utter disregard for human life. Having finally judged myself guilty of such evil, I had been left with no other alternative but to yield to the ultimate penalty. And may God have mercy on my soul.*

It is a far, far better thing that I do, than I have ever done; it is a far, far better rest that I go to than I have ever known.

A Tale of Two Cities.
Charles Dickens
(1812 – 1870)

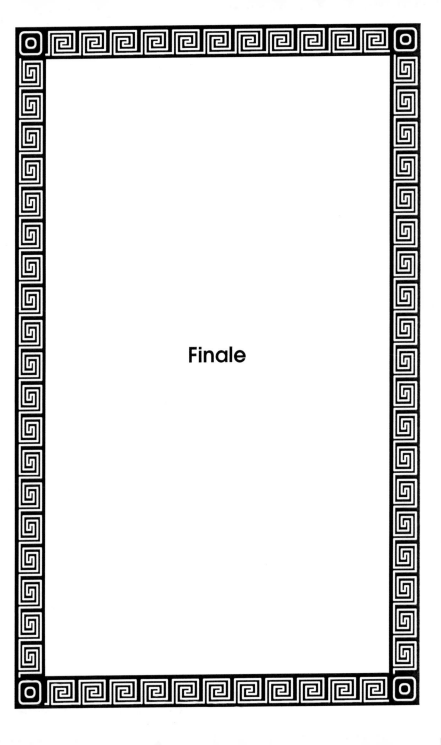

Finale

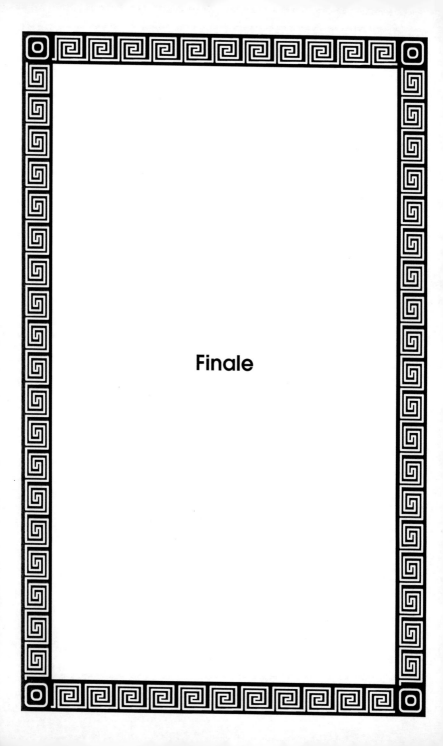

Finale

METROPOLITAN POLICE
Criminal Investigation Department
Scotland Yard

13th day of December 1888

SUBJECT Anonymous Confession
Surgery Location & Identity of Writer & Whitechapel Murderer

I beg to report that the surgery mentioned in the anonymous confession is located at 1 Sheppy Yard, Minories. The proprietor of the surgery is Dr. Lionel Druitt; his cousin being Mr. Montague John Druitt. In due course, Dr. L. Druitt confided in me that his cousin visited the surgery under the pretext to go 'slumming' throughout the district. It would appear that the Writer of the anonymous confession had done precisely the same. I was further informed by Dr. Druitt that his cousin had a peculiar fondness for young boys; something that the Druitt family had become increasingly alarmed about. The Writer of the anonymous confession also mentioned the same practice, including male sodomy, which itself is a crime in this country. Additional inquiries led the police to Bournemouth whereupon Mr William H. Druitt, elder brother of Montague J. Druitt, was interviewed. Mr. H. Druitt informed the police that his brother had been, until 30th November, a teacher at a private boy's school at 9 Eliot Place, Blackheath, but still retained his law chambers at 9 King's Bench Walk, Inner Temple Gardens.

It seems that Montague J. Druitt, initially a barrister-at-law, had fallen upon hard times and had taken to teaching to earn an income. Mr. W. Druitt further informed the police that his brother had got into serious trouble at the school and was dismissed from his post on Friday 30th November. Mr. W. Druitt did not elaborate on what the 'serious trouble' was about but added that his brother had since disappeared and that the entire family knew nothing of his whereabouts. The Writer of the anonymous confession clearly states the reason for the dismissal and that he intended to take his own life. In my opinion, it is probable that the Writer and Mr. M. J. Druitt are the same person. Further inquiries are now underway to discover his whereabouts.

There are other disclosures contained within the anonymous confession that might assist the police in identifying the unknown man who purports to be the Whitechapel murderer. One such disclosure pertains to the statement made to the police three days after the murder of Mary Jane Kelly, which was the same day that her inquest concluded on Monday 12th November. Another refers to the letter, dated 17th September 1888, which was anonymously sent to the police who have never divulged its existence. Other than the police, only the writer of the letter could have known of its existence. Most likely, the Whitechapel murderer. It is also plausible that the statement volunteered to the police on Monday 12th November at 6 p. m. could have been made by the murderer to evade arrest. I respectfully draw your attention to the attached.

1. 17th September 1888 letter signed Jack the Ripper.
2. 12th November 1888 C.I.D letter signed F.G. Abberline.
3. 12th November 1888 statement signed by George Hutchinson.

F.G. Abberline Inspr
T Arnold Supt

Jack the Ripper letter attached.

17th Sept. 1888

Dear Boss
                So now thay say I
am a Yid when will thay
lern Dear old Boss? You an
me know the truth don't we.
Lusk can look forever hell
never find me but I am rite
under his nose all the time.
I watch them looking for me
an it gives me fits ha ha. I
love my work an I shant stop
until I get buckled and even
then watch out for your old
pal Jacky.

Catch me if you Can

Jack the Ripper

Sorry about the blood still
messy from the last one. What
a pretty necklace I gave her.

C.I.D letter attached.

METROPOLITAN POLICE
Criminal Investigation Department
Scotland Yard
12th day of November 1888

SUBJECT Inquest of Mary Jane Kelly
& statement of George Hutchinson

I beg to report that an inquest was held this day at the Shoreditch Town Hall before Dr. Macdonald M. P. Coroner on the body of Marie Jeanette Kelly, found murdered at No. 13 Room, Miller's Court, Dorset Street, Spitalfields. A number of witnesses were called, including Mrs. Sarah Lewis, who gave a description of a man she had noticed waiting outside Miller's Court sometime before the murder occurred. The description given by Mrs. Lewis is scant in nature and cannot be corroborated by another witness. Mr. Joseph Barnett stated that he had lodged with the deceased and has since identified her. The Coroner remarked that in his opinion it was unnecessary to adjourn the inquiry and the jury accordingly returned a verdict of "Wilful murder against some person or persons unknown."

An important statement has been given to the police by a man named George Hutchinson which is attached herewith. I have questioned him this evening and I am of the opinion his statement is true. He informed me that he had known Mary Kelly for about three years and had occasionally given her a few shillings. On the night in question, he had been totally surprised to see her in the company of a man so well dressed that he had been compelled to watch them. He can identify the man, and arrangements were made at once for two officers to accompany him around the district with a view of finding the suspicious man.

Hutchinson is at present without regular employment and has promised to go with an officer tomorrow morning at 11. 30 a. m. to the Shoreditch mortuary to identify the deceased. Several arrests have been made on suspicion of being connected with the recent Whitechapel murders, but the various persons detained have been able to satisfactorily account for their movements and were released.

F. G. Abberline Inspr

George Hutchinson statement attached.

No. 6.
Special Report.

Commercial Street
Metropolitan Police
H Division

12th November 1888

Reference to ~~Papers~~
Re murder

At 6pm 12th George Hutchinson of the
Victoria Home Commercial Street came
to this station and made the following
statement.
About 2 am 9th I was coming by Thrawl
Street, Commercial Street, and just before I
got to Flower and Dean Street I saw the
murdered woman Kelly. and she said
to me Hutchinson will you lend me
sixpence. I said I cant I have spent
all my money going down to Romford.
she said good morning I must go and
find some money. She went away towards
Thrawl Street. a man coming in the opposite
direction to Kelly tapped her on the shoulder
and said something to her they both
burst out laughing. I heard her say
alright to him. and the man said you
will be alright for what I have told
you. he then placed his right hand around
her shoulders. He also had a kind of
a small parcel in his left hand. with a
kind of strap round it. I stood
against the lamp of the ~~Ten Bells~~ *Queens Head*
Public House and watched him. They both
then came past me and the man hid
down his head with his hat over his
eyes. I stooped down and looked
him in the face. He looked at me

George Hutchinson

Page 2/3

continued   stern. They both went into Dorset

Street I followed them. They both
stood at the corner of the court for
about 3 minutes. He said something
to her. she said alright my dear
come along you will be comfortable.
He then placed his arm on her shoulder
and gave her a kiss. She said she had
lost her handkerchief. he then pulled
his handkerchief a red one out and
gave it to her. They both then went up
the Court together. I then went to the
court to see if I could see them but
could not. I stood there for about
three quarters of an hour to see if they
came out they did not so I went away.

*Circulated
to a. s.*

Description age about 34 or 35. height 5ft6
Complexion pale, dark eyes and eye lashes
~~dark~~ slight moustache, curled up each
end, and hair dark, very surley looking
dress long dark coat, collar and cuffs
trimmed astracan, and a dark jacket
under. light waistcoat, dark trousers
dark felt hat turned down in the middle
button boots and gaiters with white
buttons. wore a very thick gold chain
white linen collar. black tie with horse
shoe pin. respectable appearance

George Hutchinson

Page 3/3

Re murder

walked very sharp. Jewish appearance.
Can be identified
George Hutchinson

E Badham Sergt

E Ellisdon Insp

Submitted FGAbberline Inspr   *T Arnold Supdt*

T Arnold Supt.

METROPOLITAN POLICE
Criminal Investigation Department
Scotland Yard

14th day of December 1888

SUBJECT George Hutchinson & M. J. Druitt.

I beg to report that George Hutchinson did attend the Shoreditch mortuary 13th November at 11. 30 a. m. but was unable to identify the deceased due to the extensive mutilations to her face. The sight of the deceased so unsettled him that he became distraught and was physically ill. This sudden outburst gave rise to some concern but after being attended by the Divisional Police Surgeon he regained his composure. His behaviour at the mortuary that morning has never been reported in any newspaper at any time. But the man purporting to be the Whitechapel murderer accurately described the incident in the anonymous confession, giving credence to the fact that George Hutchinson could be the Whitechapel murderer. However, it is also conceivable that the Whitechapel murderer knows of George Hutchinson & through the anonymous confession has attempted to incriminate him. But without knowing the true identity of the Writer of the anonymous confession, from whom the police would require a statement, George Hutchinson cannot be detained by the police on written hearsay alone.

A police search has been made of George Hutchinson's room at the Victoria Workingmen's Home, 39-41 Commercial Street, but no incriminating evidence was found. Dr. L. Druitt has since failed to recognise George Hutchinson as a casual patient who might have attended his surgery. George Hutchinson, in turn, has stated that he has never met Dr. L. Druitt before and has never visited or heard of the surgery at 1 Sheppy Yard. An extensive police investigation into the background of George Hutchinson is now underway. The police are also searching to locate the disused warehouse referred to by the Writer of the anonymous confession, but for the moment without success.

An extremely close watch is being kept on George Hutchinson whose movements & habits appear innocuous and normal. Mr. W. H. Druitt has informed the police that the whereabouts of his brother, Mr. M. J. Druitt, is still unknown & that the entire family have raised concerns for his life. The police are continuing with their investigations to locate Mr. M. J. Druitt.

F. G. Abberline Inspr
T. Arnold Supt

METROPOLITAN POLICE
Criminal Investigation Department
Scotland Yard
19th day of December 1888

SUBJECT George Hutchinson & M. J. Druitt
COM To Home Office
Re Pressing investigation.

I beg to report that the investigation conducted by Insp. Abberline to locate the dilapidated warehouse mentioned by the Writer of the anonymous confession has proved to be successful.

The warehouse was found to be located at 41-42 Flower & Dean St. & was initially leased by the present owners J. Marshall & Sons to Harris Bros. for the storage of tobacco products. Mainly due to a decline in trade & financial debts incurred by Harris Bros. the warehouse has remained unoccupied for the last five months.

The warehouse consists of 3 large storage floors & offices & is situated on the northern side of the street. The police made a comprehensive search of the building & on the 3rd floor in a back room found the innocent remnants of recent use.

The police did, however, find some discarded scraps of writing paper in a sink & immediately removed them from the room for closer scrutiny later. Having now dried out & pieced together the discarded scraps of paper, the police are of the opinion that the attached reconstituted single sheet of paper is identical to the paper used by the Writer of the anonymous confession.

Having been immersed in water, the ink had unfortunately ran on the discarded scraps of paper and except for a few words at the bottom of the reconstituted page the rest of the writing is illegible.

However, I can now confirm that after a careful study the few remaining comprehensible words written at the bottom of the page are of a sufficient clarity as to leave the police in no doubt that they were written by the Writer of the anonymous confession.

Insp. Abberline has therefore increased police efforts to find Mr. M. J. Druitt and has intensified the close watch on Mr. George

Hutchinson. Additional police investigations are now underway to determine whether or not Mr. George Hutchinson is employed by J. Marshall & Sons as a temporary caretaker.

I am
Sir,
Your most obedient Servant
J. Monro

The Under Secretary
of State
Home Office.

ATTACHED
Legible words at bottom of
reconstituted sheet of paper.

All is not necessary all, but might invariably be all.

The Times Newspaper – 21 December 1888

HAS THE WHITECHAPEL
MURDERER STRUCK AGAIN?

Yesterday morning the body of Rose Mylett was found in Clarke's Yard, Poplar. She had been an 'unfortunate' and had been strangled but not mutilated. Could the murderer have been disturbed as had happened in Dutfield's Yard, Berner Street? Two sailors are being questioned by the police and an inquest into the death of the poor woman will be held Friday.

METROPOLITAN POLICE
Criminal Investigation Department
Scotland Yard

27th day of December 1888

SUBJECT The Poplar Murder
COM The Home Office
Re Rose Mylett

I beg to report that the police are of the opinion that the death of Rose Mylett is not connected with the series of murders perpetrated by the Whitechapel murderer. The woman had been strangled with a length of cord similar to packing-string. The marks of strangulation were plainly visible on the throat and neck & there were no other signs of violence. Her throat had not been cut & mutilations to the body had not occurred. After making his examination the Divisional Surgeon stated that the poor woman had been throttled with a length of cord whilst in a drunken stupor & the ground upon which she had lain had not been disturbed by any struggle. The Criminal Investigation Dept. is doing all it can to detect the perpetrator of this mysterious crime.

I am
Sir,
Your most obedient Servant
J. Monroe

The Under Secretary
of State
Home Office.

5185/14   31 DEC. 88
Pressing A49301/191   WHITEHALL
                                              30 December 1888

Sir,
    With reference to previous correspondence. I am again directed by the Secretary of State to signify the utmost urgency in locating Mr. M. J. Druitt whom Mr. Secretary Matthews is of the opinion would be the principal witness for the Crown in procuring a possible conviction against Mr. George Hutchinson of being the Whitechapel murderer. I refer you to my previous correspondence 5 December 1888 in which I expressed Mr. Secretary Matthews' opinion that the Writer of the anonymous confession, a probable Mr. M. J. Druitt, had indeed spoken with the Whitechapel murderer, a probable Mr. George Hutchinson. Mr. Secretary Matthews is also of the opinion that the police should retain its close watch on Mr. George Hutchinson until Mr. M. J. Druitt is located.

I am
Sir,
Your obedient Servant
E. Ruggles-Brise

The Commissioner
of the Metropolitan Police.

Richmond & Twickenham Times Newspaper – 1 January 1889

FOUND DROWNED

Shortly after mid-day on Monday, a waterman named Winslade, of Chiswick, found the body of a well-dressed man floating in the Thames off Thorneycroft's Wharf. There were no marks of injury on the body, but it was rather decomposed. Winslade at once informed Police Constable George Moulson, 216T, and without delay the body was conveyed on an ambulance to the mortuary.

Southern Guardian Newspaper – 5 January 1889

SAD DEATH OF A LOCAL
BARRISTER

An inquest was held on Wednesday by Dr. Diplock, at Chiswick, respecting the death of Montague John Druitt, 31 years of age, who was found drowned in the Thames. P. C. Moulson, 216T, stated that when he had searched the body he had found four large stones in each pocket of the overcoat; £2 10s. in gold, 7s. in silver, 2d. in bronze, two cheques on the London and Provincial Bank, one for £50 and the other for £16, a first-class railway season pass from Blackheath to London – South-Western Railway – a second half return ticket, Hammersmith to Charing Cross, dated 1st December, a silver watch, gold chain with spade guinea attached, a pair of kid gloves, and a white handkerchief.

The deceased was identified by his brother, Mr. William Harvey Druitt, a solicitor living in Bournemouth, who stated that the deceased was a barrister-at-law, but had lately been an assistant at a school in Blackheath. Mr. W. H. Druitt further stated that when he had found that the deceased had got into serious trouble at the school and had been dismissed on the 30th of November last year he had gone and searched the residence of the deceased and found a note addressed to him. Mr. W. H. Druitt gave the Coroner the note which read in part, "Since Friday I felt I was going to be like mother, and the best thing was for me to die." The jury returned a verdict of "Suicide whilst of unsound mind."

The deceased was a prominent member of the Kingston Park Cricket Club, and as such was exceedingly well known in the county. The funeral took place yesterday afternoon at

Wimborne cemetery, and the coffin was followed to the grave by family relatives and a few friends, including Mr. W. H. Druitt, Mr. L. Druitt, Mr. Arthur Druitt, Rev. C. H. Druitt, Mr. J. Druitt, sen., Mr. J. Druitt, jun., Mr. Wyke-Smith and Mr. J . T. Homer. The funeral service was read by the vicar of the Minister, Wimborne, the Rev. F. J. Huyshe, assisted by the Rev. Plater.

METROPOLITAN POLICE
Criminal Investigation Department
Scotland Yard
8th day of January 1889

SUBJECT Suicide
COM The Home Office
Re Mr. M. J. Druitt

I beg to report the death of Mr. J. Druitt. His decomposed body was found in the Thames at Thorneycroft's Wharf by a waterman on 31st December 1888. The body had been immersed in the water for nearly a month, indicating that he had committed suicide whilst of unsound mind on or about the 1st December 1888 merely three weeks after Mary Jane Kelly was found murdered at No. 13 Miller's Court, Dorset Street & two days before the Home office received the anonymous confession which would suggest that it was posted on the day of his suicide. The amount of money found upon the deceased might lead people to wrongly believe that he intended to flee from something but then for whatever reason took his own life.

It will be seen that Mr. M. J. Druitt was undoubtedly the author of the anonymous confession and so much so that the police have been able to deduce certain facts from the confession to suggest the possible identity of the Whitechapel murderer.

1. The scraps of writing paper recovered from the sink in the warehouse at 41-42 Flower & Dean St. & later reconstituted by the police to form a single sheet of paper is of the same paper used by the Writer of the anonymous confession. The ten enigmatic words, "All is not necessary all, but might invariably be all." written at the bottom of the reconstituted single sheet of paper are identical to the handwriting of the Writer of the anonymous confession. The police have also studied the handwriting of the suicide note left by

Mr. M. J. Druitt to his brother Mr. W. H. Druitt and found it to be identical to both the hand writing of the anonymous confession and the ten written words on the reconstituted single sheet of paper.

2. Could Mr. George Hutchinson be the Whitechapel murderer? The incident that took place at the Shoreditch mortuary on the 13th November 1888 at 11. 30 a. m. & never publicly published at any time would indicate that Mr. George Hutchinson had indeed relayed the incident to Mr. M. J. Druitt who then committed it to paper. It is possible, but very unlikely, that Mr. George Hutchinson did not relay the incident to Mr. M. J. Druitt & that Mr. M. J. Druitt was given the information by a third party who was in attendance at the Shoreditch mortuary at the time of the incident. This is, of course, merely an assumption and cannot be proven. Recent police inquiries have also revealed that Mr. George Hutchinson was indeed employed as a temporary caretaker by J. Marshall & Sons to watch over the derelict warehouse at 41-42 Flower & Dean St. but inexplicably abandoned the job at about the time of the death of Mr. M. J. Druitt. The police are therefore of the opinion that Mr. George Hutchinson might be the Whitechapel murderer but without a testimony from Mr. M. J. Druitt the police are entirely hamstrung and could not consider charging George Hutchinson with the Whitechapel murders. Just before Christmas of last year Mr. George Hutchinson left Whitechapel for Romford, Essex. He still remains in Romford, continuing to seek gainful employment. The Essex County Constabulary were alerted to keep a close watch on him and are regularly reporting his every movement to Scotland Yard.

3. Was Mr. M. J. Druitt actually the Whitechapel murderer and confessed his crimes through a fictitious character he created in the anonymous confession? The confession written by Mr. Druitt is indeed full of damning evidence to suggest that this may have been the case. Most damning of all is the vivid description of his first meeting with the Irish woman Kelly who was brutally murdered in 13 Miller's Court on 9th November last year. This first meeting as experienced by Mr. Druitt strongly connects him to Kelly and offers a plausible motive for her murder. His suicide just three weeks after her death is extremely suspicious and should not be treated as mere coincidence. The police respectfully propose that interviews be conducted with members of the Druitt family after their period

of bereavement to shed further light on the character of Mr. M. J. Druitt.

I am
Sir,
Your most obedient Servant
J. Monro

The Under Secretary
of State
Home Office.

5185/14   11JAN. 89
Pressing A49301/191   WHITEHALL
                                                         10 January 1889
Sir,
        With reference to previous correspondence. I am directed by
the Secretary of State to inform you that the police will <u>refrain</u> from
conducting interviews with any member of the Druitt family. Mr.
Secretary Matthews is of the opinion that no useful purpose can be
served by badgering such a prominent Bournemouth family. If Mr.
M. J. Druitt were the Whitechapel murderer (could he have known
of the Shoreditch mortuary incident if he had indeed created a
fictitious character through which to confess?) then a higher court
now sits in judgement and the matter is out of the hands of the
police.
        Secretary Matthews still holds to the opinion that Mr. George
Hutchinson is probably the Whitechapel murderer and had Mr. M.
J. Druitt lived, he would, as a barrister-at-law, have testified so. It is
very important that the Essex County Constabulary maintain a
close watch on Mr. George Hutchinson so that the Metropolitan
Police can prevent these types of Whitechapel murders from
occurring again.

I am
Sir,
Your obedient Servant
E. Ruggles-Brise

The Commissioner
of the Metropolitan Police.

METROPOLITAN POLICE
Criminal Investigation Department
Scotland Yard

23rd day of January 1889

I beg to report that yesterday the Essex County Constabulary informed Scotland Yard that Mr. George Hutchinson is nowhere to be found. It would appear that he evaded the surveillance of the Essex police and got away during the weekend of the 20th & 21st inst. The detective branch of Scotland Yard has been instructed to work closely with the Essex County Constabulary to determine the whereabouts of Mr. George Hutchinson as quickly as possible. Detectives have been dispatched to major ports & H Division, Whitechapel, has been alerted.

F. G. Abberline Inspr
T. Arnold Supt.

METROPOLITAIN POLICE
Criminal Investigation Department
Scotland Yard

10th day of April 1889

SUBJECT George Hutchinson
Re Still at large.

I beg to report it is now just over 2 months since George Hutchinson evaded the close watch of the Essex Constabulary. Despite many sightings of him, which have all been misleading, the police are no closer to locating George Hutchinson than they were in January. It is the opinion of the police that he has either completely gone to ground, is dead or has left the United Kingdom for another country. If 2 & 3 are indeed correct then he is beyond the reach of our authority. If he has simply gone to ground then the police will vigorously pursue him should he raise his head.

I am
Sir,
Your most obedient Servant
J. Monro

The Under Secretary
of State
Home Office.

The Times Newspaper – 10 April 1889

Situation Vacant.

Eliot Place School – There will be a Vacancy next term for an Assistant Master to teach Mathematics and part of the English subjects. Salary £150 with board and rooms. Applications should be addressed to Geo. Valentine, 9 Eliot Place, Blackheath, ES.

The Times Newspaper – 18 July 1889

HAS THE WHITECHAPEL
FIEND RETURNED?

A state of near panic exists in Whitechapel today. In the early hours of yesterday, a woman of the 'unfortunate' class was found brutally murdered in Castle-alley, Whitechapel. The narrow dingy alleyway, off Whitechapel High-street, was obstructed by a few tradesmen's carts and barrows and it was not until Police Constable Walter Andrews was upon two of those carts that he saw the body of a woman lying between them. Her throat had been cut and blood flowed from the wound. Her skirts had been turned up, exposing her abdomen, which appeared to be mutilated. PC Andrews had no doubt that he had found yet another victim of the Whitechapel murderer. He bent down and touched the woman's face. It was still quite warm, which suggested that the attack had taken place very recently, quite possibly in the last minute or so. An inquest was held later in the day whereupon the deceased was identified as Alice McKenzie who had lodged at 52 Gun-street, Whitechapel.

The inquest further revealed that some hours before her death, Alice McKenzie had gone drinking with a blind boy named George Dixon. They had gone to a public house near the Cambridge Music Hall where the deceased had become acquainted with a stranger. Shortly afterwards Alice had taken George Dixon back to 52 Gun-street, left him there and had gone out again, perhaps to meet the stranger. Margaret Franklin and Catherine Hughes last saw Alice McKenzie alive, walking along Flower & Dean-street. The police are at the moment questioning William Brodie who confessed to the murder but is thought to be insane.

METROPOLITAN POLICE
Criminal Investigation Department
Scotland Yard
A493011/1

<u>Immediate</u>   17th July 1889

Sir,

I beg to report the ghastly murder of a woman in Castle-alley, Whitechapel, this morning.

As soon as I received a telegram announcing the commission of the crime I started about 3 a. m. for the scene, for the purpose of assisting with the inquiry.

I need not say that every effort will be made by the police to apprehend the murderer, who, I am inclined to believe is identical with the notorious "Jack the Ripper" of last year.

It will be seen that in spite of ample police precautions the assassin has once more succeeded in getting away with another murder, leaving no clue behind as to his identity.

I have the honour to be,

Sir,
Your obedient Servant
J. Monro.

The Under Secretary
of State
Home Office.
&c &c &c.

METROPOLITAN POLICE
Criminal Investigation Department
Scotland Yard

27th day of July 1889

I beg to report that William Wallace Brodie was this morning again brought up on remand before F. Lushington, Esq., at Thames Police Court.

I acquainted the learned Magistrate with Brodie's addiction to drink and that the police have no evidence to connect him with the murder of Alice McKenzie. Prisoner was ultimately discharged but re-arrested upon the warrant for fraud. He will be taken before Magistrate on Monday 29th.

To date, the police do not possess a single clue that might lead them to detain the perpetrator of the murder.

Henry Moore, Inspr
T. Arnold Supt.

The Times Newspaper – 14 February 1891

HORRIBLE MURDER
SWALLOW GARDENS

Early yesterday morning at 2. 15 a. m., Police Constable Ernest Thompson was patrolling along Chamber-street and was about to enter Swallow-gardens when he heard heavy footsteps hurriedly moving away from him, heading in the direction of Royal Mint-street. On the beat for the first time, PC Thompson thought nothing of this sound until he turned into Swallow-gardens and saw a woman, lying on her back, who had obviously been attacked.

Shining his lantern upon the prostrate woman, Thompson saw to his horror that her throat had been cut and blood still issued from the wound. Even worst perhaps was the fact that as he was about to produce his whistle to summon assistance one of the woman's eyelids eerily flicked open.

After the body was moved to the Whitechapel mortuary, the police made a careful search of the immediate area but nothing was found that could amount to evidence.

William Friday and the two Knapton brothers later swore that they had seen the woman and a man standing in a doorway in Royal Mint-street half-an-hour before her body was found. All three men are now providing the police with a description of the man.

The Times Newspaper – 16 February 1891

SWALLOW GARDENS
VICTIM IDENTIFIED

The woman found murdered in Swallow-gardens three days ago has now been identified as Frances Coles. The deceased was identified by her father, James William Coles of the Bermondsey Workhouse, Tanner-street. In life, Frances Coles, aged 25 and attractive, had been an 'unfortunate' since she was about eighteen. The similarity of Frances Coles and Mary Jane Kelly will undoubtedly not fail to escape our readership. Both women were of the same age, attractive and had their throats cut. But that is where the similarity most definitely ends. In death, Frances Coles retained some of her attractiveness, but the same could not be said of Mary Jane Kelly. Her face, her entire body was assailed with such ferocity as to suggest that an eruption of rage had been unleashed upon her, which in a moment of sheer horror nearly succeeded in obliterating her from the face of the earth.

A ship's fireman, James Thomas Sadler, who intimately knew Frances Coles and argued with her shortly before her death, has been taken into police custody for questioning.

METROPOLITAN POLICE
Criminal Investigation Department
Scotland Yard

3rd day of March 1891

Re Swallow Gardens Murder
James Thomas Sadler

With reference to the case of Frances Coles; who was found murdered at Swallow-gardens on 13th Ins.

I beg to report that since yesterday several statements have been taken from numerous witnesses but none can shed any light on the identity of the man who was last seen with Frances Coles just before her death.

The prisoner James Thomas Sadler was today again brought up at Thames Police Court, before F. Mead Esqr. Mr. Charles Matthews appeared for the Police Prosecutor; and Mr. Lawless appeared for the accused; and upon application of the former, prisoner was discharged. Sadler on his liberation was taken away in a cab by his solicitor Mr. Wallis and a representative of the "Star" Newspaper. As the cab left the court spontaneous cheers were raised by the crowd on behalf of Sadler.

No other persons have been detained in connection with this case.

Henry Moore, Inspr.
T. Arnold Supd.

Epilogue

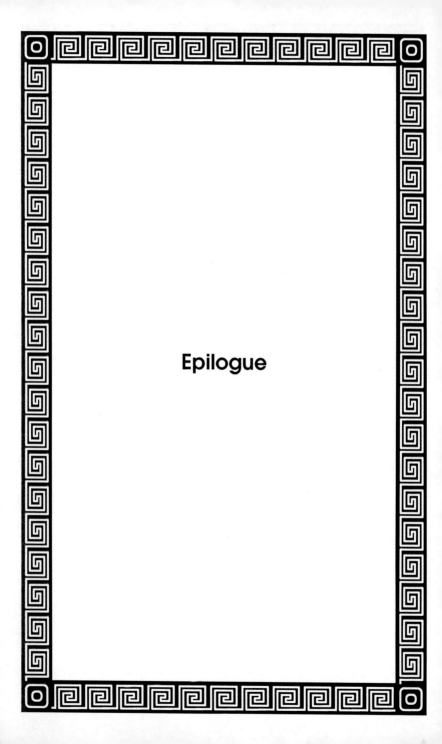

Epilogue

Cassell's Saturday Journal – 28 May 1892

RETIRED INSPECTOR FREDERICK G. ABBERLINE
RECALLS THE WHITECHAPEL MURDERS

"Theories!" exclaims the Inspector, when discussing the Whitechapel murders. "We were lost in theories; there were so many of them." Nonetheless, the Inspector thinks he has a new theory. From the evidence of his own eyesight, he strongly believes that the Miller's Court atrocity was the last of the real series. "With the death of Mary Jane Kelly" the Inspector explains, "the murderer reached the culminating point of his morbid mania. He had achieved his purpose. He had finished. He had nothing left do, nowhere to go. The subsequent murders were mere imitations of his."

METROPOLITAN POLICE
Criminal Investigation Department
Scotland Yard
23rd day of February1894

COM Chief Constable C.I.D
Confidential

A much more rational and workable theory is that Jack the Ripper's brain gave way altogether after his awful glut in Miller's Court, and that he immediately committed suicide, or, as a possible alternative, was found to be so hopelessly insane by his relatives, that they had him confined in some lunatic asylum.

No one ever saw the Whitechapel murderer: many homicidal maniacs were suspected, but no shadow of proof could be thrown on any one. I may mention the cases of 3 men against whom the police held reasonable suspicion. Personally, after much careful & deliberate consideration, I am inclined to exonerate the last 2, but I have always held strong opinions regarding No. 1, and the more I think the matter over, the stronger do these opinions become. The truth, however, will never be known, and did indeed, at one time, lie at the bottom of the Thames if my conjections be correct.

No. 1. Mr. M. J. Druitt a doctor of about 41 years of age & of a fairly good family, who disappeared at the time of the Miller's Court murder & whose body was found floating in the Thames on 31st Dec: i.e. 7 weeks after the said murder. The body was said to have been upwards of a month in the water, or more. From private information I have little doubt but that his own family suspected this man of being the Whitechapel murderer; it was alleged that he was sexually insane.

No. 2. Kosminski, a Polish Jew, & resident in Whitechapel. This man became insane owing to many years' indulgence in solitary vices. He had a great hatred of women, specially of the prostitute class, & had strong homicidal tendencies; he was removed to a lunatic asylum about March 1889. There were many police reports connected with this man, which made him a strong "suspect."

No. 3. Michael Ostrog, a Russian doctor, and a convict, who was subsequently detained in a lunatic asylum as a homicidal maniac. The man's background was of the worst possible kind, and his whereabouts at the time of the murders could never be ascertained. He is still alive.

M. L. Macnaghten
Assistant Chief Constable

Pall Mall Gazette – 24 March 1903

INSPECTOR ABBERLINE INTERVIEWED
THE IDENTITY OF THE WHITECHAPEL MURDERER
REPUDIATED

Our reporter drew Mr. Abberline's attention to a recent newspaper article, which reiterated the story that Jack the Ripper had been a young medical student who had been found drowned in the Thames shortly after the last murder.

"Yes," said Mr. Abberline, "I know all about that story. But what does it amount to? Simply this. After the last murder, the body of a young barrister was found in the Thames, but beyond the fact that he had taken his own life so soon after the last murder, indicated nothing suspicious to the police. At the request of the Home Office, the police did however investigate the subject and finally accepted documented evidence that the barrister could not have been Jack the Ripper."

"Knowing that similar murders began in America after the last murder here, strongly implied that the murderer might have emigrated. But further investigations into that matter were far from certain, leaving the police totally mystified as to what had become of the Whitechapel murderer."

Postscript

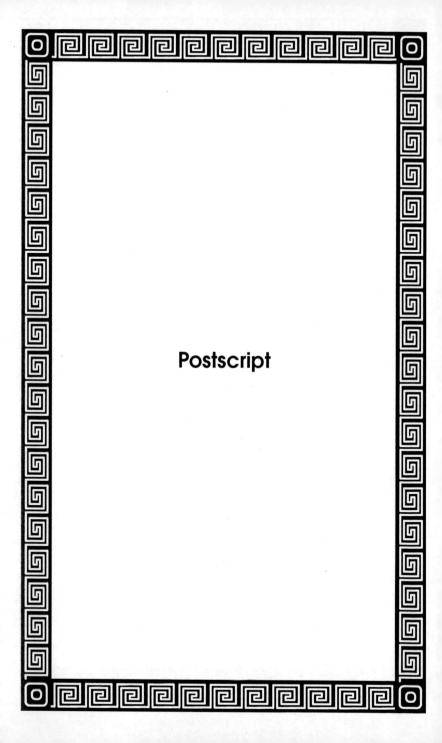

Postscript

Melville Macnaghten joined the Metropolitan Police as Assistant Chief Constable of the CID in June 1889, seven months after Mary Jane Kelly had been laid to rest in the Roman Catholic Cemetery at Leytonstone. Macnaghten's Confidential report, dated the 23rd day of February 1894, written some five years after Mary Jane Kelly had been hideously murdered, had contained two factual errors that should not be overlooked. Montague John Druitt had never been a doctor and had died aged 31, not 41. It had been a copy of Macnaghten's 1894 Confidential report, unearthed in 1959 by the journalist and television presenter Daniel Farson, that had first presented Montague John Druitt to the world as a candidate for being the Whitechapel murderer. Although historical evidence has since exonerated Macnaghten's prime suspect, Montague John Druitt nonetheless still remains a permanent favourite with some Ripperologists, continuously declaring that he had indeed been Jack the Ripper.

Whatever became of the enigmatic George Hutchinson? The simple answer is that no one knows and will probably never know. Although the records of the Victoria Home for Workingmen, Commercial Street, Spitalfields, clearly showed that Daniel Barnett, brother of Joseph Barnett, had still lodged there in 1891, the name of George Hutchinson is noticeable by its absence. Did George Hutchinson escape to America after the Whitechapel murders as mentioned by Inspector Frederick George Abberline or did he stealthily return to the East End of London in July 1889 and February 1891 to brutally murder Alice McKenzie and Frances Coles? The truth will probably never be known but what is known is that during the reign of Queen Victoria the characters of our story, good and evil, attractive and ugly, privileged and destitute, loved, quarrelled and died. Now they are all equal.

No one can believe now how terrified and unbalanced we all were by his murders. One can only dimly imagine what the terror must have been in those acres of narrow streets where the inhabitants knew the murderer to be lurking.

A London Girl of the Eighties
Molly V. Hughes
(1866 – 1956)

Bibliography

This is by no means an exhaustive list of publications and books on Jack the Ripper, but are all recommended reading for anyone interested in the Whitechapel murders.

Publications

Jack the Ripper Whitechapel 1888 '2005 Calendar', written by Geoff Cooper and Gordon Punter and published by ripperArt, 2004.

Jack the Ripper Whitechapel Map 1888, written by Geoff Cooper and Gordon Punter and published by ripperArt, 2003.

Jack the Ripper Whitechapel 'Map Booklet' 1888, written by Geoff Cooper and Gordon Punter and published by ripperArt, 2003.

Books

Jack the Ripper: The Definitive History, written by Paul Begg and published by Longman, 2003.

Jack the Ripper: An Encyclopaedia, written by John J. Eddleston and published by Metro Publishing Ltd, 2002.

The Ultimate Jack the Ripper Sourcebook, written by Stewart Evans and Keith Skinner and published by Robinson, 2000.

From Hell, written by Bob Hinton and published by Old Bakehouse Publications, 1998.

The Complete History of Jack the Ripper, written by Phillip Sugden and published by Robinson, 1994.

Index

A

Aarons, Mr. Joseph 83, 120
Abberline, Inspector Frederick George 2, 57, 69, 80, 120, 134, 136, 138, 154, 200, 217, 224, 225, 227, 229, 236, 241, 242, 243
Adams, Polly 169
Albert, Prince 23
Albrook, Lizzie 128
Alderney Road (Nos. 1-3) 83, 117, 120
Aldgate 28, 105, 106, 107, 110, 129, 154, 155, 175, 190, 207
Aldgate High Street (No. 28) 94
Aldgate High Street 28, 154
Alexander the Great 7
Alsop, Jane 169
America 242, 243
American Cloth 132
Anderson, Dr. Robert 146
Andleman, Mrs. 208
Andrews, PC Walter 237
Angel (public house) 189
Angel Alley 51, 53, 189
Angel, Miriam (referred to as a Jewess in police memo) 100
Anglo-Saxon 161
Anonymous confession, Writer of 1, 2, 223, 228, 229, 231, 233, 234
Apron, piece of (Catharine Eddowes) 92, 110, 111, 112, 155
Aristocrats 16
Arnold, Superintendent Thomas 71, 85, 111, 112, 138, 139, 153, 224, 227, 228, 229, 236, 238, 240
Ascot Races 37
Ashcroft, William 34
Athena 8, 9, 10
Australia 54, 220

B

Babylon 2, 7, 69, 108, 145, 155
Back Church Lane 93, 98, 99, 103
Back Lane 168
Badham, Sergeant Edward 76, 77, 227

Baker's Row 58, 68, 71, 195
Balaclava 16, 167
Balmoral Castle memo (initialled VR) 141, 144
Banner Street 115
Barber's Slaughter Yard, Winthrop Street 59, 64, 65, 195, 196
Barber's Yard, Hanbury Street 82
Barnaby & Burgho (English bloodhounds) 137, 138
Barnardo, Dr. Thomas (letter to the Times newspaper) 205
Barnardo, Dr. Thomas 205, 207
Barnes, PC 77, 78
Barnett, Daniel 183, 189, 193, 196, 209, 210, 211, 212, 243
Barnett, Joseph 128, 129, 144, 149, 150, 183, 184, 186, 189, 193, 196, 201, 209, 210, 211, 212, 225, 243
Barrett, PC Thomas 51, 53, 191
Barrister (sad death of a local barrister, Montague John Druitt) 232
Barrister 36, 54, 242
Battalion, 2nd, 24th Regiment of Foot 18
Batty Street 101
Batty's Gardens 103
Baxter, Wynne Edwin 57
Beck, Inspector Walter 136
Beehive Tavern 101
Bell Lane 155
Beresford, Lord Henry aka Marquis of Waterford 169
Bermondsey Workhouse, Tanner Street 239
Berner Street (No. 30) 97
Berner Street (No. 36) 97
Berner Street (No. 40) 94
Berner Street (No. 42) 94
Berner Street (No. 44) 96
Berner Street (No. 64) 96
Berner Street, St-George-in-the-East 91, 93, 94, 96, 97, 98, 99, 101, 103, 132, 205, 230
Berouw (Dutch gunship) 34